T0330139

Information Communication Technology and Economic Development

This material is based upon work supported by the National Science Foundation under Grant No. 0218126. Any opinions, findings, and conclusions or recommendations expressed in this material are those of the author(s) and do not necessarily reflect the views of the National Science Foundation.

Information Communication Technology and Economic Development

Learning from the Indian Experience

Edited by

Tojo Thatchenkery

George Mason University, USA

Roger R. Stough

George Mason University, USA

Edward Elgar

Cheltenham, UK • Northampton, MA, USA

Published by
Edward Elgar Publishing Limited
Glensanda House
Montpellier Parade
Cheltenham
Glos GL50 1UA
UK

Edward Elgar Publishing, Inc.
136 West Street
Suite 202
Northampton
Massachusetts 01060
USA

A catalogue record for this book
is available from the British Library

ISBN 1 84542 175 2

Printed and bound in Great Britain by MPG Books Ltd, Bodmin, Cornwall

Contents

Contributors

Suma Athreye is a Senior Lecturer in Economics at the Faculty of Social Sciences at the Open University, UK. Her research interests include public policy towards technological and industrial development, clustering and innovation, hi-tech entrepreneurship, development of the software industry and outsourcing. She has published extensively in all these areas.

Govindasamy Balatchandirane is a faculty member in the Department of East Asian Studies, University of Delhi, India. He is involved in several international research projects on information communication technology (ICT), higher education, and economic development of India and its potential transferability to East Asia. He has been a visiting faculty at Kanazawa University and Yokohama National University, Japan.

Nagarajan Dayasindhu is a Senior Research Associate, Software Engineering Technology Labs with Infosys Technologies Ltd, Bangalore, India. His research interests include information technology (IT) outsourcing strategies and competitiveness in the IT services industry. His papers have been published in leading journals and conferences.

Kingsley E. Haynes is Dean of the School of Public Policy and University Professor of Public Policy at George Mason University, Fairfax, Virginia. His research activity is in the area of infrastructure investment and economic development. He has had extensive experience in managing projects in energy, water resources, telecommunications and transportation in the USA, Canada, Brazil, Egypt, Jordan, Sudan and Malaysia.

Ron Hira is Assistant Professor of Public Policy at the Rochester Institute of Technology in Rochester, NY, where he specializes in technology policy and offshore outsourcing. He is the author of *Outsourcing America* published by the American Management Association, and is Vice-President of Career Activities for the Institute of Electrical and Electronics Engineers (USA). He is also a licensed professional engineer.

Mary Mathew is an Assistant Professor in the Department of Management Studies, Indian Institute of Science (IISc), Bangalore, India. She is also the Associate Faculty of the Intellectual Property Cell and Center for Product Design and Manufacturing, IISc and the resource executive for the Society for Innovation Development, IISc. Her various research projects on ICT-related issues have been sponsored by India's Ministry of Science and Technology, Ministry of Communications and IT and the European Commission, Brussels.

Stanley Nollen is Professor of International Business at the Georgetown University McDonough School of Business in Washington, DC. His research interests center on the performance of firms in the IT industry in India and the experiences of firms in the transition economies of central Europe. He was previously a Fulbright scholar in Delhi and a visiting professor at the London School of Economics and Antwerp University.

Rupa Ranganathan works with the Operations Evaluation Department at the World Bank. She holds a Bachelors in Political Science from Allegheny College and a Masters in Public Policy from George Mason University. She has been working on a number of issues dealing with economic development including the impact of ICT on development.

Kavil Ramachandran is a Professor of Entrepreneurship and Strategy at the Indian School of Business (ISB), Hyderabad, India. His research is centered on entrepreneurship, knowledge clusters and growth strategies of Indian firms. He is also the head of the ISB K-Hub, a semi-virtual business accelerator for supporting new ventures in India.

Sougata Ray is an Associate Professor of Strategy at the Indian Institute of Management, Calcutta, India. His research interests include strategic management, knowledge clusters, competitive strategies and strategic alliances of Indian firms. He is the recipient of several awards for research and teaching and consults with large Indian organizations on various aspects of corporate strategy.

Maria Elena Salazar is a Ph.D. candidate in the School of Public Policy at George Mason University, Fairfax, Virginia, USA. Her research interests focus on local economic development, specifically in Mexico and other developing countries.

Cherian Samuel works as a Monitoring and Evaluation specialist for the World Bank in Washington, DC and has been with the Bank Group for the past ten years. His research interests include ICT and economic development, structural change, corporate governance and investment climate issues.

Aparna Sawhney is an Assistant Professor in the Department of Economics and Social Sciences at the Indian Institute of Management, Bangalore and is a consultant for trade and environmental studies at the Indian Council for Research on International Economic Relations in New Delhi. Her teaching and research interests are in the areas of trade, environment, development and the World Trade Organization.

Vasanthi Srinivasan is an Assistant Professor in the area of Organizational Behavior and Human Resources Management at the Indian Institute of Management, Bangalore. Her research interests are in careers, international human resources management and team-based organizations. Her teaching, consulting and research have largely focused on the software industry in India.

Gita Surie is a Senior Fellow at the Wharton School of the University of Pennsylvania and Assistant Professor at Adelphi University, USA. Her current research focuses on innovation, entrepreneurship and multinational corporations.

Roger R. Stough holds the NOVA Endowed Chair and is a Professor of Public Policy at George Mason University, Fairfax, Virginia. He directs the Mason Enterprise Center and is Associate Dean for Research in the School of Public Policy. He has published 15 books and many journal articles in the fields of economic development and transport policy.

Tojo Thatchenkery is an Associate Professor at the School of Public Policy, George Mason University, Fairfax, Virginia, USA. His research interests include ICT and economic development of South Asian countries, social capital and economic advancement of ethnic groups, and organizational mobility of Asian Americans in US organizations.

Acknowledgements

We wish to acknowledge the generous support received from the United States National Science Foundation in organizing the international conference on ICT and Development in Bangalore, India, which laid the foundation for this book. Most of the chapters in this book are enhanced, revised, or adapted versions of the papers presented at the conference. We also wish to acknowledge George Mason University's School of Public Policy Dean Kingsley Haynes and Professor Don Kash, who provided invaluable intellectual support from the very beginning of this project. Professor K.B. Akhilesh of the Management Department at the Indian Institute of Science, Bangalore, our Indian partner for the conference, provided significant support including excellent conference facilities.

We are indebted to several talented individuals in the endeavor of putting the book together. M. G. Gopakumar of the Tata Management Training Center, Pune, India; Mucket Joshi, Independent Consultant, Gordon Shockley, Daisy Botros, and Donna Sherrard of the School of Public Policy helped in various aspects of editing and preparing the manuscripts.

We thank Alan Sturmer, Senior Acquisitions Editor of Edward Elgar Publishing for enthusiastically commissioning our book, Tara Gorvine for early support, Katy Wight, Promotions Manager for her publicity efforts, Caroline McLin, Managing Editor and Bob Pickens, Desk Editor for their excellent production support all through the project. Without their active assistance and commitment, this project would not have been possible.

Last, but not the least, we are indebted to our families – Tessy and daughter Sruthi, Barbara and children Jon and Brandon for their love and constant support.

Tojo Thatchenkery and **Roger R. Stough**

1. Introduction

Tojo Thatchenkery and Roger R. Stough

This book describes the technology-driven economic development of India. India's development pattern over the last ten and a half years is distinctive when compared to other developing nations as it has become a highly visible participant in the intellectual capital-driven information technology (IT) services industry. Since the 1990s India has been one of the fastest growing economies in the world. A report authored by Goldman Sachs in 2003 (O'Neill et al., 2003) stated that by the year 2050, India will become the third largest economy in the world, behind China and the USA. The report predicts that India's gross domestic product (GDP) will overtake that of Italy by 2015, France by 2020, Germany by 2025 and Japan by 2035.

The reason why India's development is different may stem from the nature of the information communication technology (ICT) industry and the freedom it has enjoyed from government regulation to develop this industry. ICT is the synthesis of computers, telecommunication/ communication technologies and databases enabled by digital electronics. This book examines how India developed its ICT capabilities and represents different perspectives on India's development. For example, one chapter examines how India established critical linkages with the US ICT industry in the 1990s. That relationship is thought to have played a significant role in the rapid development of India's ICT industry. Another chapter investigates India's strategy to develop ICT companies in a particular sub-national region of India, Bangalore in the state of Karnataka, and shows how it paid off by linking people in the state to the external world of information and knowledge through ICT diffusion.

This book also infuses new knowledge into a highly visible and often controversial debate going on in the USA currently regarding outsourcing jobs to India and other countries. They provide new knowledge regarding what has really happened to India's economic development as opposed to what one hears in the media. Finally, it reveals new insights regarding the complex process of globalization by showing how the generation and circulation of intellectual capital in the USA and India in ICT has led to greater productivity in the USA while facilitating the economic development of India.

ORGANIZATION OF THE BOOK

This book is organized around this Introduction and three major parts. Part I includes chapters that examine the ICT industry in India and its relationship to economic development. These contributions include a general examination of development theory and practice over the past 60–70 years and the ways in which India adopted or chose not to adopt aspects of this body of knowledge and practice. It also includes three specific analyses of India's ICT industry regarding the causes for its development and composition. Part II focuses specifically on the role of knowledge and innovation diffusion in the evolution of the ICT sector and its jump into the 21st century. Finally, Part III includes four chapters on specific topics in ICT development including ICT cluster development beyond its initial emergence in Bangalore, managerial know-how and diversification, intellectual property and offshore outsourcing.

This book treats the role of the ICT sector in India's development to date and speculates on its future including diversification and ICT spillover effects on other sectors. It provides a good introduction to the Indian development experience and the role ICT has and will likely play in the drive to sustained economic growth and development in India.

Part I   Information Communication Technology and Economic Development of India

The chapters in Part I provide background information and analyses on Indian development, the nature of the ICT industry there, and how it has contributed to economic growth and development. In this context, Chapter 2 by Roger Stough, Kingsley Haynes and Maria Salazar begins Part I by setting the stage for the other contributions in the book. It reviews the major theories and practices deployed in an attempt to create developed countries out of developing ones over the past 60 or 70 years and offers interpretive asides of how all of this influenced India's development path. It examines critically stage theory formulations like Rostow's stages of economic growth, growth pole concepts and export-oriented growth policies. Further, hard and soft infrastructure approaches are considered and issues regarding the contemporary development situation in India are identified.

Tojo Thatchenkery, Roger Stough, Govindasamy Balatchandirane and Rupa Ranganathan get directly to the core focus of the book in Chapter 3 in their examination of the role of ICT in the Indian development experience. This chapter provides detailed data on the growth of the Indian ICT industry, its scale and scope, the forces that contributed to its rapid growth and development and factor cost issues. Next they examine the role of ICT in India's economic and social development and not only advance the 'leapfrog hypothesis' in this context but also provide some reservations about this theory. The authors also examine the impact of ICT on such realms as education, health, gender, poverty and governance. The authors raise a variety of questions concerning the future of ICT in India and India's development including forward and backward linkage development of the ICT sector. Policies concerning positive and negative spillover effects are also examined.

Cherian Samuel in Chapter 4 examines the evolution of the service sector in India showing that much of the decrease in employment in the agricultural sector has been countered by growth of service sector jobs and thus that India, in this respect, is like many other countries in the late 20th and early 21st centuries. This is important for two reasons. First, India is unlike many other countries at its stage of development such as for example, China, in that it has mostly substituted service jobs rather than manufacturing jobs for a loss in agricultural employment. In short, development-led structural change in India did not follow the expected or so-called classic pattern. The dominant role of the ICT services is documented and explained in the context of this analysis. The chapter concludes that numerous infrastructural-related constraints (hard and soft) may prevent ICT sector development from underpinning a successful example of development leapfrogging.

In the final chapter of Part I Aparna Sawhney conducts a detailed examination of the factors responsible for ICT growth in India. Part of the focus of this analysis is on the export component of the ICT sector which historically was largely in low-end ICT services including lower-end software design, coding components, maintenance of legacy systems and various back-office operations. Earlier ICT service exports focused on 'body shopping' but today specialization is mostly focused on providing on-site services versus offshore services. Only about 5 percent of exports today are provided offshore. With regard to the factors responsible for the rise of the ICT sector in India, the author introduces a long list of factors including low-cost technical labor, early entrant advantage, government support, access to technology from foreign countries, organizational skills, adjustment to global market trends and entrepreneurial dynamism. Among all of these, however, development and maintenance of high-quality and reliable ICT services is viewed as centrally important. This is illustrated by the almost religious commitment to signaling or conveying quality certification on the part of Indian software companies and their belief that this is absolutely necessary to climb the service value ladder.

Part II   Knowledge Spillovers and Innovation in the ICT Sector

In Part II three chapters examine the way in which knowledge acquisition and innovation have evolved and manifested themselves in the Indian ICT experience. In Chapter 6 Mary Mathew assesses the development of innovation and diffusion patterns over the evolution of the Indian ICT industry. Initially the ramp-up of the ICT sector appropriated and adopted new technologies from abroad. The adoption of technology sequentially triggered a variety of innovations within the ICT and software sectors and later in other parts of the economy. Parallel to this expanding process of innovations was the growth of a knowledge base and skilled human capital. The author notes that patent data from India shows that there is now some indigenous innovation occurring but that insufficient evidence exists to conclude that there is significant domestic ICT product innovation. This may be due to the fact that much of the industry in India is services-oriented and related process innovations are more difficult to track as they rarely show up in the form of patents.

In Chapter 7 Gita Surie examines the effect that Indian company interaction with global firms has on performance and innovation. Evidence from the evolution of the Indian software industry and a leading global software firm is used to support a conclusion that interactions with global firms through the creation of cross-border communities of practice (COPs) catalyzed local development by initiating learning and replication through knowledge spillovers in the local environment. This, in turn, spurred competition and internationalization. In short, participating in communities of practice helped drive Indian software firms to adopt global best practices and to motivate innovative behavior.

Nagarajan Dayasindhu at the Infosys Software Engineering Technology Laboratories discusses in Chapter 8 the importance of tacit knowledge or more broadly inimitable network resources. Inimitable resources are those that are incapable of being imitated or copied and as such are a basis for sustained competitive advantage for organizations. While reasons for inimitable resources existence have been researched generally they have not been examined for network resources that exist within a network of organizations. Important network organizational resources include network membership, structure, tie modality and management. This chapter explains why such network resources become inimitable for an organization that is a part of a network of organizations in the context of the Indian ICT industry. The research reported classifies inimitability of network resources into path and knowledge dimensions. The path dimension, it is concluded, is important for the inimitability of all network resources but the knowledge dimension is important for tie modality and network management only.

In short, the path dimension of inimitability is more important than the knowledge dimension.

Part III   Industry Issues and Patterns

In Part III four chapters are presented that deal with specific ICT-related issues and their importance to the development process. The first of these, Chapter 9 by Kavil Ramachandran and Sougata Ray focuses on the formation of ICT-dominated industrial clusters and how they evolved. While the ICT industry has played a major role in India's development, as explained above, this success has not been evenly distributed across the country. Today notable clusters exist in Bangalore, Chennai, Hyderabad and Pune as well as in large urban agglomerations like Mumbai and Delhi but these are not so notable because they are embedded in the broad and deep industrial structure that exists there. It is noted that some of these centers like in Bangalore are naturally formed clusters but others are more driven by public policy and leadership like in Hyderabad where the government itself had to exhibit entrepreneurial properties to create a viable cluster. Much of the chapter is a comparison and contrast analysis of ICT cluster formation in Bangalore and Hyderabad. The chapter examines factors that contribute to the creation of ICT clusters in general and in particular where conditions are not ripe for natural cluster formation such as with late entrants like Hyderabad and Pune. A major conclusion reached by Ramachandran and Ray is that the entrepreneurial strength of the state and the pool of local entrepreneurs are equally important for rapid cluster formation.

Suma Athreye and Vasanthi Srinivasan in Chapter 10 examine practices adopted by Indian software services firms in the late 1990s and show that they developed considerable organizational capability in the management of large-scale labor resources and related processes crucial to the successful operations of offshore business models. The apparent similarity of the business models whereby most of the programming work was done in India with firms managing the development of software to offshore client specifications led to many software firms entering the sector. This model was progressively adopted over the mid to late 1990s resulting in nearly 60 percent of all revenues to Indian software firms today. The similarity of the model and managing relations with the offshore company contributed to increased market entry in the Indian software industry. In this context, the authors investigate the question of whether the managerial similarities between software and business process outsourcing (BPO) give diversifying firms a performance advantage in the expanding ICT sector. The focus of this research is on firms that diversified into BPO compared to other types of entrants into the ICT sector.

Intellectual property (IP) issues are of considerable importance in the global ICT industry in general and increasingly so in India. Stanley Nollen in Chapter 11 examines the emergence of IP issues in India in the ICT industry of the early 21st century. There is a wealth of specific information on IP in India in this chapter that ranges from input and output patterns to infringement and copyrighting practices. In sum, IP is an awakening element of the Indian ICT industry with notable increases in attempts to define value and protect it. Copyrighting and patents are at much higher levels than in the past, which bodes well for the broader integration of the Indian ICT industry into a global best practices framework.

Recently the most visible policy issue regarding Indian offshoring and back-office operations is in connection with the exportation of jobs from the developed countries to the developing ones. This is a particularly important issue for the ICT sector in India as both inshoring of workers from India and outsourcing of work to India has been a central element of India's competitiveness in this sector. Ron Hira in the concluding chapter of the book, Chapter 12, examines how offshore outsourcing may affect Indian ICT firms' labor mobility needs and the politics of liberalizing US labor mobility policies. The analysis shows that the vast majority of high-skilled temporary workers to the USA come from India and most of these work in the ICT sector. The chapter examines how demand for labor mobility may change due to offshoring and offshore outsourcing. In conclusion the chapter speculates on the US labor mobility context and what some of the policies' impact will be on the Indian ICT industry.

Overall, the chapters provide a balanced view of the link between ICT and economic development of India. What stands out from the various chapters is how unique India's development has been. A country whose GDP is still influenced mostly by the monsoons has quietly grown to have the largest trained workforce in the world and is likely to emerge as a world economic power. The recently released *National Intelligence Council Report* (Mapping the Global Future, December 2004) suggested that the world economy might be 80 percent larger in 2020 than it was in 2000. Though the USA may still be the world's dominant economic power in 2020, China and India will see their influence expand significantly. 'In the same way that commentators refer to the 1900s as the "American Century," the 21st century may be seen as a time when Asia, led by China and India, comes into its own', the council wrote in its report, which was produced as a synthesis of the views of all 15 of US intelligence agencies. According to the report, India is better positioned than most countries to make use of new technologies, which has helped it to leapfrog stages of development. With its well-entrenched democratic institutions, significant intellectual capital and world-class firms in hi-tech sectors, India certainly appears to be on track to become one of the top economies of the world in a decade or two.

REFERENCES

The National Intelligence Council (December 2004), *Mapping the Global Future: Report of the National Intelligence Council's 2020 Project*, Pittsburg, PA: Government Printing Office.
O'Neill, Jim, Roopa Purushothaman, and Dominic Wilson (2003), *Dreaming with BRICS: the Path to 2050*, New York: Goldman Sachs Economic Research.

PART I

Information communication technology and economic development of India

2. Economic development theory and practice: the Indian development experience

Roger R. Stough, Kingsley E. Haynes and Maria Elena Salazar

INTRODUCTION

There is a long and complex literature on the theories and practice of economic development at the national, provincial, regional and local levels. While the intent of this chapter is to review the mainstream of this literature in an effort to help set the stage for an examination of the Indian development experience, it is not possible to do full justice to the topic in a short study such as this. Consequently, we have necessarily focused on major theoretical concepts and planning applications dating from the middle part of the 20th century when India moved from colonial status to independence.

In the mid-20th Century, as today, staging was a central assumption of most approaches to development planning. For example, it was at this time that Rostow formulated the five-stage model of economic development (1960). At about the same time Perroux (1950) formulated growth pole theory later popularized in English by Higgins and Savoie (1988) and by Hirschman (1958) who ignited a debate that still continues in some quarters regarding balanced versus unbalanced approaches to growth. Later in the 1970s the export promotion model emerged as several small countries in Asia (Taiwan, Hong Kong, Singapore and Korea) successfully deployed this strategy originally developed by Japan in the 1960s. Throughout this time supply side or infrastructure efforts were ever present. This approach included social overhead investments such as in human capital (education and training) but the primary focus was on hard infrastructure. As these models were unfolding in concept and practice through different applications around the world, India set off on an independent course. It began with a strategy of autocracy and what appeared as the simultaneous development of all economic sectors. It did this by using its large internal market as the driver. In short, it adopted a balanced growth strategy focused on its large internal market. As such it was, in contemporary terms, a massive commitment to an endogenous model for its development strategy. In the 1950s this was exceptionally contrary to prevailing thought.

At the same time as these theories and their application were occurring neoclassical economic growth theory was mostly silent. It offered little beyond the notion that growth and development are largely functions of labor and capital factor price differentials, that is, comparative advantage among countries and/or regions. Yet, Tinbergen (1959) and later Solow (1956) around the mid-century showed that factor price differentials explained at best about half of the variance in economic growth. Further, Denison's (1967) empirical work on the impact of education and human capital on economic growth suggested that this was an underappreciated dimension but no linkage or conclusion was identified. These findings begged for further theoretical development. Solow argued that much of the residual variance was due to technological change. However, it was not until the mid-1980s that growth theory advanced much beyond the Solow interpretation. 'New growth theory', as it is now called, argued that the technology variable was indeed important but that technological change and the ability to innovate was increasingly dependent on human capital. But this ability is often local, that is, endogenous, and thus a phenomenon that varies with local conditions such as leadership, labor force characteristics, innovation patterns and institutional capacity. Most development plans today focus increasing attention on local, regional and national institutions, and thus endogenous growth concepts.

In this chapter the focus of the analysis begins with a description and assessment of Rostow's stage theory of economic growth. This is followed by an assessment of growth pole theory and export promotion concept. The final part of the chapter presents a short assessment of the current Indian development effort within which endogenous growth concepts are discussed. The supply side and new growth theory approaches are examined as embedded elements in the assessments of the various growth models.

This study is important because of the nature of the Indian development experience. First, in an overall sense India's approach to independence was, on a grand scale, endogenous in nature as India tried to develop on the basis of its internal market. Thus it adopted an approach that was contrary to the export promotion approach as well as many other models. Second, after some 40 years of five-year development plans built around a largely supply-side and import substitution approach, it developed a globally competitive information technology services industry that has continued to grow and remain competitive. From the perspective of a staged model of growth this is not an expected outcome. In short, developing a competitive higher-end services industry is not seen as a likely or even a possible outcome until a country develops export competitive industries in agriculture, low to higher-end manufacturing and services, and creates advanced infrastructure. While it is certainly the case that India has, since the early 1990s, adopted a stronger market- and export-promotion-oriented approach to development with some success, the rapid increase in information technology (IT) exports that began in the late 1980s cannot be attributed to the early 1990s' liberalization policies. So the question remains, what have been the building blocks leading to the 'leapfrog' activity leading to IT-oriented economic development?

STAGES OF GROWTH THEORY

Introduction

The economic development theories of the 1950s and early 1960s viewed the process of development as a series of successive stages of economic growth through which all countries must pass (Todaro, 1994, 68). These theories were based on the idea that having the right quantity and mixture of certain factors such as savings, investment and foreign aid was a sufficient condition for developing countries to proceed along the path followed by developed countries (Todaro, 1994, 68).

The theory of economic growth by Rostow (1960) is an example of a linear-stage model. According to Rostow, the transition from underdevelopment to development can be viewed or understood as a series of stages that all countries must proceed through (Todaro, 1994, 70; Franko, 1999, 17).

Rostow's Argument

In the process of economic development, according to Rostow:

> It is possible to identify all societies, in their economic dimensions, as lying within one of five categories: the traditional society, the preconditions for take-off into self-sustaining growth, the take-off, the drive to maturity, and the age of high mass consumption ... These stages are not merely descriptive. They have an inner logic and continuity... They constitute, in the end, a theory about economic growth and a more general, if still highly partial, theory about modern history as a whole (Rostow, 1960, 1–12; Todaro, 1994, 70).

> The traditional society operates within limited production functions. Its central feature is a ceiling on the level of the attainable output per head. This is followed by the establishment of preconditions in a period of transition where the traditional

society is transformed to enable it … 'to exploit the fruits of modern science, to fend off diminishing returns, and thus to enjoy the blessings and choice opened up by the march of compound interest' (Bauer, 1972, 15).

The take-off stage, occurs 'when the old blocks and the resistances to steady growth are finally overcome… growth becomes its normal condition' (Bauer, 1972, 478). In this period 'new enterprising men come forward, willing to take risks in pursuit of profit' (Hunt, 1989, 97). Rostow believed that the 'take-off' would be induced by the mobilization of domestic and foreign savings in order to generate sufficient investment to accelerate economic growth. Rostow maintained that when an economy increased its savings rate above 10 percent it would be able to pass from take-off to self-sustaining growth (Behrman and Srinivasan, 1988, 2112). In fact, Rostow believed that 'capital constraint' was the main obstacle to economic development (Todaro, 1994, 73; Franko, 1999, 17).

Rostow's central proposition is the 'take-off' to sustained development. He defines it as an industrial revolution driven by radical change. That is, in this stage a leading industry with sufficient forward and backward linkages expands and spreads its effects to the whole economy and in so doing prepares the way for additional industrial expansion (Mason, 1982, 118).

The take-off is followed by the *drive to maturity*, which is completed when maturity is achieved (in Rostow's view, some 60 years after take-off begins):

the make up of the economy changes unceasingly as techniques improve, new institutions accelerate, older industries level off. The economy finds its place in the international economy: goods formerly imported are produced at home; new import requirements develop, and the new export commodities to match them… [In this stage] …an economy demonstrates the capacity to move beyond the original industries (Bauer, 1972, 478).

Rostow, along with Schumpeter and Hirschman, viewed the economy as being in continuous disequilibrium, rising only to fall as other 'production functions' take their place. In the 'drive to maturity' there is considerable similarity in concept between Rostow's successive production functions and Schumpeter's 'creative destruction' (Mason, 1982, 123).

Finally, the age of *high mass consumption* comes 'where in time, the leading sectors shift towards durable consumer's goods and services; a phase from which Americans are beginning to emerge' (Bauer, 1972, 479) in the 1970s.

Rostow believed that while all the advanced countries had passed the stage of take-off into the self-sustaining growth, undeveloped countries were still in the 'traditional society' or 'preconditions' stage. Thus, underdeveloped countries had to follow certain rules of development to take off into self-sustaining growth (Todaro, 1994, 70). In short, there is a well-defined pattern of development that should be pursued by undeveloped countries. For example, in order to pass into the take-off stage a country would need to raise investment to a minimum of 10 percent of national income, develop leading high-growth sectors, and create a supportive institutional framework and infrastructure (Hung-Chao, 1991, 896–7). 'Once these conditions are met, a nation can achieve "sustained, self-sustaining growth" leading eventually to great wealth' (Hung-Chao, 1991, 897).

Critique of Rostow's Stage Theory

Rostow's theory had many shortcomings, however, as many countries viewed Rostow's stages as a basis for the analysis of problems of development and for policy prescriptions such as 'aid-financed investment' policies promoted by the World Bank. He believed that Western nations could provide Third World countries with aid to fill the 'financing gap' between the necessary investments for take-off and national savings. Currently, however, extensive literature and country-based evidence, such as from Latin America and Africa, show that more savings and investments are not sufficient conditions for high growth (Hunt, 1989, 107; Easterly, 2002, 34–5).

Savings and investment alone are not sufficient

Rostow claimed that a crucial factor that serves to lift an economy toward a sustained growth path is a significant increase in the share of savings and investment in national income. The proposed rate of 10 percent appears simplistic, in hindsight, since many countries have more than satisfied this criterion but have not 'taken off' (Behrman and Srinivasan, 1988, 2112). Many countries referenced by the World Bank (1993) as having a savings rate much higher than 10 percent have yet to enter into a period of sustained growth (Behrman and Srinivasan, 1988, 2112).

Furthermore, Rostow's theory, like many other Western-based economic theories, assumed the existence of necessary factors but failed to take into account the particular set of conditions in a country. For investment to work and generate economic growth, a country must possess the necessary structural and institutional conditions, that is, well-integrated commodity markets, money markets, infrastructure facilities, established and enforced property rights and so on (Todaro, 1994, 73, 84). Solow and more recently the new growth theoreticians have argued that capital cannot be the ultimate source of growth, but that technology and endogenous growth conditions are also necessary (Malecki, 1997; Easterly, 2002, 69).

Influence of public policies

Linear-stage theories maintain that 'a chain of causality runs from the mode of production within a given society' to economic development and growth (Mason, 1982, 118). This means that there is a unique ladder of ascent confronting each society. However, there are some factors that influence the development process: a country's resource endowments and size, its public policies and objectives, its institutions, the availability of capital and technology, the international trade environment and the presence of skilled labor. Under this rationale the state acts only in subordinate ways in that it only affects the outcome in a secondary way. However, there are cases where public policies have deeply influenced the process of growth in ways that were not historically inevitable (Mason, 1982, 119–120). An efficient government that possesses the ability to plan and administer development projects can make a difference in outcomes. South Korea is an example. Contrary to South Korea, however, is India, where many economists attribute and agree that a large measure of blame for stagnant economic growth in the past is due to both bureaucracy and faulty development policies including excessive protection via industrial licensing (Mason, 1982, 131).

Small number of key variables

Rostow claimed that his model both explained the course of economic history and produced predictions for the future that, in turn, could serve as bases for far-reaching and appropriate policies. His theory suggests that there are a small number of readily discernible critical variables (which he vaguely described) to resolve the problem of economic development. However, simple models and loosely defined variables cannot effectively serve to guide solutions to the complex problems often found in developing countries (Bauer, 1972, 482). Experience with economic development strategy and policy in many Third World countries over the past few decades shows how far from reality this approach can be.

Manufacturing is a necessary condition

Manufacturing is both a definition and condition of economic progress for Rostow. The manufacturing sector sets in motion 'a chain of further modern sector requirements and its expansion provides the potentiality of external economy effects, industrial in character' (Bauer, 1972, 485). Thus, the Rostow view proposes that manufacturing activity is a necessary condition for continued economic advancement. However, the case of India raises doubts as it may be argued that India passed, in part, from an agricultural society to a service society without developing a strong export-based manufacturing sector.

Neglect of social, cultural, psychological and institutional factors
Rostow places great emphasis on the growth of inputs, particularly capital accumulation, and in the allocation of resources as the primary sources of economic growth. At the same time, he neglects cultural, social and psychological factors that influence human economic behavior (Mason, 1982, 121). Many scholars have argued that the impressive economic growth of East Asian Countries cannot be totally explained without considering specific cultural attributes and values such as thrift and hard work promoted by Confucianism (Chuen-Chau, 1997, 64; Leipziger, 1997).

Moreover, as with many other Western economic theories, Rostow makes many assumptions about conditions in non-Western countries. That is, he places all undeveloped countries in the same context. However, Western countries, for the most part, emerged from societies that had hundreds of years of social, political and cultural development (Mason, 1982, 129; Bauer, 1972, 488). 'These theories of development can thus be criticized as ethnocentric, biased in favor of a particular economic growth pattern, ideologically based on Western assumptions and values; and dogmatic in their insistence upon a contiguous progression through historical stages' (Chilcote, 1984,11).

With regard to Rostow's stages and the development process for the developed countries, the focus is on industrialization as the catalyst. But time and environments change and to assume stability is to commit the classical longitudinal fallacy.

Inability to adopt and/or use new technology
Even if technology that is available via imports to latecomers (such as illustrated in East Asian countries via reverse engineering) creates a distinct advantage for latecomers, developing countries have often not been able to spread technological effects (for example productivity enhancement) to the domestic economy. The emergence of leading sectors does not always mean significant domestic links and nation-wide real income effects. The absence of solid policies (especially distributive ones) and endogenous growth conditions are some of the reasons why this advantage has been unevenly exploited by developing countries (Mason, 1982, 128). India is an example of this, where growth in some sectors has not meant economic development for the country as a whole or for all groups, all sectors and/or for all regions.

Stage Theory Conclusions

There is little doubt that Rostow's stages of growth model offers insight into the circumstances under which different societies have experienced rapid acceleration in economic development (Bauer, 1972, 489). Moreover, by examining the experience of some countries, such as South Korea, there is little doubt that some of Rostow's factors can be identified. For example, Korea's large investment in national income was a critical part of its rapid ascent. However, in Rostow's view, South Korea did not meet the 'maturity' criteria. Moreover, instead of achieving maturity as incrementally envisioned over a 60-year period established by Rostow, it achieved maturity in less than 15 years (Todaro, 1994, 123). Also, as with other countries that have shown rapid or highly compressed sudden growth, it is difficult to identify the level of uniformity emphasized in Rostow's formulation (Mason, 1982, 127). So not only is there the need to recognize the potential for temporal compression in the development process, but also to true leapfrogging due to technology or dynamic returns to the simultaneous integration of multiple factors of production such as technological investments and human capital expansion.

Since Rostow's book on the stages of economic development, there have been significant changes in the prospects of many countries. Many of those that were mentioned by Rostow as having few of the 'preconditions to take off', such as South Korea and Singapore, now satisfy most of the maturity stage criteria. That many others classified in the take-off stage are ready to achieve 'self-sustaining maturity', such as Argentina, calls into question the theory's reliability (Mason, 1982, 127; Todaro, 1994, 125). The lessons of a historic perspective may or may not be valid in the near-term environment, but not to recognize this would be to accept the principle of uniformitarianism and to commit the associated fallacy that the past is the guide to the present and future.

GROWTH POLE THEORY

Introduction

Balanced growth or 'big push' advocates have argued that small market economies were victims of a cycle-hindering growth. 'The small size of the market was responsible for the limited amount of production and income, and for the perpetual poverty and stagnation' (Franko, 1999, 17). To break this cycle, countries need to develop a wide range of industries simultaneously if they want to achieve sustained growth. That is, an economy needs a 'big push' coordinated by government to allocate resources (Franko, 1999, 17; Perkins et al., 2001, 101). One problem with this view is that it is discouraging advice for a poor country; for example, India in mid-century because it is expected to start up the development process across a wide range of industries simultaneously or resign itself to stagnation (Perkins et al., 2001, 101).

Hirschman (1958), in a broadening and explication of the work of Perroux (1950), provided a contrary thesis. He argued that 'unbalanced growth rather than 'balanced growth' was the principal strategy for development (Franko, 1999, 17). He believed that by 'promoting a few key sectors with strong linkages, then moving on to other sectors to correct the disequilibrium generated by these investments, and so on, was actually the right approach' (Krugman, 1994, 42).

Growth Pole Theory: A Review

Hirschman set out his strategy as follows: 'underdeveloped countries need special "pressure mechanisms" or "pacing devices" to bring forth their potential ...[as]... development depends not so much on finding optimal combinations for given resources and factors of production as on calling forth and enlisting for development purposes resources and abilities that are hidden, scattered or badly utilized' (Rostow, 1990, 391).

Hirschman argued that when 'one thinks in terms of a missing component, be it capital, entrepreneurship, or technical knowledge, he is likely to believe that the problem could be solved by injecting that component from the outside or by looking for ways and means of producing it within a country' (Hirschman, 1958, 7, 10). Instead, he argued, what is needed is a 'binding agent' which will bring together the 'scattered' or 'hidden elements' (factors, resources or abilities) needed for successful development (Hirschman, 1958, 10). With this view, bottlenecks are the main causes of underdevelopment. Thus, policy makers' attention should be guided to major resource bottlenecks as revealed by the market and 'induce investment' or 'pressure' in branches of production that possess substantial backward and forward linkages (Hunt, 1989, 60). Hirschman argued that the market was the main inducement or policy and, as such, it was an approach that indicated a strategy of backward-linked industrialization, starting with import substitution in consumer goods production (Hunt, 1989, 129).

Hirschman believed that countries 'could and did concentrate their energies on a few sectors during the early stages of development' (Perkins et al., 2001, 102). A country should specialize in what it could do at least cost and import the rest. All that is needed is to ensure that the domestic industry can compete effectively with imported products. Here the main point is that trade and import substitution are ways 'to begin industrialization on a limited and selective basis rather than with a balanced big push' (Perkins et al., 2001, 102).

The major concept in Hirschman's strategy is that of linkages or what is called 'spread effects'. An industry creates backward linkages when it uses inputs from other industries which, in turn, allow them to grow at a faster rate (Krugman, 1994, 43). That is:

> Industries are linked to other industries in ways that can and should be taken into account in deciding on a development strategy. Industries with backward linkages use inputs from other industries... Initially, this demand may be supplied by imports, but eventually local entrepreneurs will see that they have a ready market for domestically made machinery... [equipment or goods]... Planners interested in accelerating growth, therefore, will emphasize industries with strong backward linkages because these industries will stimulate production in additional sectors resulting in the production of powerful multiplier effects. (Perkins et al., 2001, 102–3)

'Forward linkages occur in industries producing goods that then become inputs into other industries' (Perkins et al., 2001, 103), 'they involve the ability of an industry to reduce the costs of potential downstream users of its products and thus, again, push them over the threshold of profitability' (Krugman, 1994, 43). From a national development perspective this too produces a positive multiplier effect.

'Both forward and backward linkages set up pressures that lead to the creation of new industries, which in turn create additional pressures, and so on' (Perkins et al., 2001, 103). These pressure points can be built (intentionally or unintentionally) by private entrepreneurs seeking new profit opportunities or through government action (Perkins et al., 2001, 103). As Francois Perroux, the father of growth pole theory noted, those sectors leading development not only generate strong economic linkages (backward and forward) but also a political economy of their own that supports, protects and guides complementary public infrastructure investments.

In Perroux and Hirschman's view, unbalanced growth was inevitable because:

> economic progress does not appear everywhere at the same time and that once it has appeared powerful forces make for a spatial concentration of economic growth around the initial starting points .... There can be little doubt that an economy, to lift itself to higher income levels, must and will first develop within itself one or several regional centers of economic strength. This need for the emergence of 'growing poles' or 'growth poles' [a term used for both regional and sectoral targeted growth] ... in the course of the development process means that international and interregional inequality of growth is an inevitable concomitant and condition of growth itself... Thus, in the geographical sense, growth is necessarily unbalanced' (Hirschman, 1958, 183–4).

In Hirschman's view, advocating for the presence of unbalanced growth was reasonable because extreme imbalances would be avoided through the very concept of linkages where 'an advance at one point sets up pressures, tensions and compulsions toward growth at subsequent points' (Hirschman, 1958, 184). Thus, Hirschman suggests that pressures force a country toward more balanced growth: 'because of the interdependence of the economy in the input–output sense, the expansion of one sector or sub-sector ahead of the other could be relied on to set forces in motion (relative price changes and public policies in response to complaints about shortages) that would tend to eliminate the initial imbalance' (Rostow, 1990, 391; Perkins, Radalet et al., 2001, 101). An initial impulse of planning in the form of an investment project will take its own course (that is, invisible hand) with market forces responding to demand and supply (Myrdal, 1968, 1935). All this, however, is conditioned in Hirschman's view to the presence of entrepreneurship as '… it takes innovators like Ford … to establish a new basic industry or to perceive the development potentials of the more backward regions of a developing country' (Hirschman, 1958, 184). Yet, since Hirschman believed that decision-making and entrepreneurial skills in underdeveloped countries were scarce, progressive sectors were easily neglected. 'Government should therefore concentrate scarce resources in a few sectors rather than in the entire economy' (Franko, 1999, 17).

Many economists such as Prebisch or Singer were influenced by these ideas. This produced support for an operational import substitution industrialization (ISI) strategy promoted in many countries of Asia and especially in Latin America that had its theoretical justification in the unbalanced growth concepts of supportive sectors with linkages and justifying government intervention to support them as essential for economic development (Hunt, 1989, 61).

Critique of Growth Pole Theory

Hirschman (like Rostow) concentrates on physical investments and outputs, which he assumes to be the vehicles for development, where supplies come relatively easy and the lack of decision-making risks can be overcome. Again, like Schumpeter and Rostow, he placed great value on entrepreneurship. While the lack of entrepreneurship is certainly a serious obstacle for development, it is also the case that many undeveloped countries have serious supply and institutional limitations, which cannot be overcome by entrepreneurial efforts alone. Moreover, in these countries decision-making is also constrained by the political and economic climate of the country (Bauer, 1972, 480).

In Hirschman's view, intersectoral unbalanced growth seems to be easy to overcome; however, in many countries, such as India, unbalanced growth also has economic and political expression between regions and different ethnic groups. Such differences and their regional manifestation, though embedded in a sectoral structure are pervasive and difficult to overcome. The lack of spillovers from successful regions to those not so successful has created great inequality, and growth in only some regions has constrained more broad-based development (Syrquin, 1988, 211).

Regional economists, regional scientists and economic geographers have long understood that as economic activities grow and concentrate at a location, the relative importance of that location grows. In turn, as more activity is concentrated at a location, the location becomes more attractive also because of the many activities that are occurring there. In short, economic benefits derive from agglomeration. This is the assumption upon which much of growth pole theory is erected and the vigorous interest that has emerged in industrial clusters as a primary focus of local and regional as well as national growth policy (Porter, 1990). Agglomeration or agglomerative forces are viewed as arising from one of two sources. The Jane Jacobs (1969, 1984) school argues that the attraction arises from the spillover effects of multiple and diverse activities that make up the urban milieu. Such attraction arises from so-called urban economies as it derives from the diversity of activities in the urban context. However, another tradition that began with Marshall (1920), later amplified by Arrow (1962), and even later rediscovered by Romer (1986) and others such as Porter (1990) argues that interdependent industries are attracted to each other and thus create what are called 'location economies'.

THE EXPORT-ORIENTED INDUSTRIALIZATION (EOI) STRATEGY

Introduction and Description of EOI

From the 1930s to the mid-1970s, the growth strategy known as ISI dominated economic planning and policy in Latin America and Asia. ISI was a deliberate effort by structuralists to free developing countries from their dependence on developed countries. This strategy required that governments play an active role in the economy. The main tools used in this strategy were import licensing, tariffs, overvalued exchange rates and direct government investment in key industries (Cardoso and Helwege, 2000). A main shortcoming of this strategy was 'its failure to stimulate the sustained productivity growth that is the hallmark of the long run economic development in the most advanced economies' (Stern, 2001: 53). In India ISI started in the Nehru years (1947–64) as a reflection of Gandhian principles and it was reinforced under Prime Minister Indira Gandhi in the mid-1960s and 1970s. However, a large fiscal deficit (8.4 percent of gross domestic product (GDP)) in 1985 and the exhaustion of foreign reserves by 1991 forced the government of Rao to adopt reform, whereby liberalization and market-oriented strategies were put in place (World Development Report, 1997).

After the failure of ISI and the related Keynesian welfare state theory in many countries of Latin America and Asia, along with a growing consensus about the benefits of liberalization, most of these countries engaged in market-oriented strategies. By the mid-1980s and early 1990s most Latin American and Asian countries followed policies promoted by multilateral agencies such as the World Bank and the International Monetary Fund (IMF) that were based on a new school of thought known as 'export-oriented industrialization' (EOI). The main proponents of EOI among others were Krueger et al. (1985), Balassa (1981) and Bhagwati (1985). EOI is based on the idea that the integration of a country into the world market through export trade will encourage economic growth and development (Dussel, 2000, 13; Dussel, 2001, 124).

The above is considered under the assumption that export-oriented production of manufacturing maximizes the efficient allocation of factors of production and specialization among nations according to their respective comparative cost advantages and that this would stimulate competitiveness. Thus, successful EOI ensures that goods and services are produced where it is cheapest to do so: price is seen as the fundamental 'signal' (Dussel, 2000, 12, 16).

The EOI Argument

The main arguments for the implementation of EOI lie in its capacity to create spillovers. That is, exports create a dynamic effect on overall economic growth. According to EOI trade allows countries to allocate resources more efficiently (according to their comparative advantage), have access to foreign capital (for example, foreign direct investment (FDI)), and enables the learning of new techniques and processes. Furthermore, it increases familiarity and access to new production technologies and new goods invented abroad (Dussel, 2000, 14). As a result, a country that seeks an outward orientation should be able to benefit from technological spillovers generated by trade and better participate in the international flow of goods and technologies (Keller, 1996, 200).

Critique of EOI

For many countries, the promotion of EOI was seen as a way for 'catalyzing endogenous industrial development' suggesting concrete linkages, higher foreign currency, jobs, upgraded personnel and a genuine transfer of technology (Wilson, 1992, 40; Sklair, 1993, 196). However, in many cases, EOI has not successfully created endogenous industrial development (Wilson, 1992, 7).

Several schools of thought such as neostructuralists (Taylor 1988) new neoclassical theories (Krugman, 1994) and new growth theory (Pack, 1994; Romer, 1994) have rejected the assumption of EOI that market-oriented strategies are sufficient for economic development. Growth or development 'is significantly correlated (or explained) by factors other than capital and labor, such as human capital conditions' (Dussel, 2000, 20). Under new growth theory, the production function (based on capital and labor) is expanded to include research and development, technological advances, physical capital (infrastructure) and human capital or education. These variables are seen as central indicators of 'endogenous growth conditions', and are expected to generate spillovers and externalities, including economies of scale (Malecki, 1997; Cimoli 2000). For this school, the 'East Asian miracle' is seen largely as a result of increases in labor skills (through education) and capital investment (Krugman, 1994; Malecki, 1997; Nelson and Pack, 1999).

Further, a great number of studies conducted in the USA, Japan and the UK have found that increases in output are not attributable to capital investments but mainly to improvements in human capital including the quality of labor, education and training, and experience. Capital investment growth accounts for less than half of all such growth (Malecki, 1997, 38). Also, Romer (1990) shows that growth and growth differentials between nations are the result of using and producing ideas and knowledge, and that such variables should be considered in the production function in order to achieve sustainable growth.

The different experience in the newly industrialized countries (NICs) compared to many other countries, such as India with the EOI strategy, shows that it requires the presence of endogenous growth conditions in order to be successful. The EOI strategy has been almost homogeneously beneficial in terms of its capacity to increase the volume of exports. However, when a country lacks endogenous growth conditions such a strategy cannot be successful because the export sector draws its dynamism from abroad rather than from the local national economy. Endogenous growth conditions have been recognized to be essential for a successful integration into the world economy. The lack of these conditions could (and usually will) impede the ability of the domestic sector of a given country to respond fast and to upgrade its production in ways that reflect the new needs of the global economy (Cimoli, 2000; Dussel, 2000).

SOME DEVELOPMENT ISSUES IN INDIA

Since India's trade policy reform in the 1990s, it has experienced positive growth results. For example, India's average annual rate of real per capita income growth increased from about 1 percent in the 1960s and 1970s to about 3 percent in the 1990s (Stern, 2001, 54, 2002, 3, 11). Also, trade liberalization 'has resulted in productivity gains associated with increased competition, innovation and acquisition of new knowledge and technologies, all of which have contributed to raising living standards in the country' (Stern, 2002, 10). In short, India economic development performance suggests improvement has been achieved.

However, many have questioned how much India's recent economic growth has been pro-poor. Data shows that the decline of poverty since the beginning of the reform period has been at least 1 percent per year (Stern, 2001, 54, 2002, 3, 11). However, such reduction has only occurred in some states. Considerable differences in sectors and geographic imbalances of growth explain why India's economic growth has not made a greater impact on the poor (Gaurav and Ravallion, 2002, 1). 'Initial conditions mattered. States that started the period with better infrastructure and human capital development – with more intense irrigation, greater literacy, and lower infant mortality rates – had significantly greater long-term rates of consumption growth and poverty reduction' (Gaurav and Ravallion, 1996, 1). Those states that lacked such conditions have generally been bypassed by India's economic growth. Moreover, it is argued that the slowdown of the reforms in the past few years, rigid labor policies and the presence of subsidies and barriers to domestic entry have not only slowed the pace of growth and poverty reduction but they have also reduced India's possibilities for greater insertion into the international market (Stern, 2002, 15, 46).

In other words, economic growth does not necessarily mean economic development and better conditions for a country as a whole. In India, as in Mexico and other developing countries like the Philippines, the economic growth generated by EOI has concentrated in some regions and when initial conditions are missing great inequalities are created. Evidence shows that the EOI strategy by itself is not a sufficient condition for achieving sustainable economic growth.

CONCLUSION

This short chapter attempts to provide an overview of recent and contemporary economic development theory, practice and outcomes in an effort to set the stage for the variety of analyses presented in subsequent chapters of this book. As such it has been general but at the same time it has attempted to identify the critical elements of the past 60 or so years of economic development practice and policy in general and to some extent as applied to the Indian experience. At the same time it has not been a definitive treatment either generally or more specifically as it applies to India. What it does accomplish it to show some of the major elements of development practice and the Indian development trajectory and to surface some of the more important questions that are discussed in later chapters of the book. These include questions about distributive effects of past and current Indian development efforts, the potential that India may be able to leapfrog steps in the usual development process, institutional reform, liberalization, growing and building forward and backward linkages to the ICT industry, and more generally the role of technology in development. As such, this chapter attempts to describe broadly the development context within which India is embedded and to target the important questions that are being asked and, in turn, considered in later chapters.

REFERENCES

Arrow, K.J. (1962), 'The economic implications of learning by doing', *Review of Economic Studies*, **29**, 155–73.
Balassa, B.A. (1981), *Structural Adjustment Policies in Developing Countries*, Washington, DC: World Bank.
Bauer, P.T. (1972), *Dissent on Development. Studies and Debates in Development Economics*, Cambridge, MA: Harvard University Press.
Behrman, J. and T.N. Srinivasan (eds) (1988), *Handbook of Development Economics*, vol 3, Amsterdam and New York: North-Holland and Elsevier Science.
Bhagwati, J.N. (1985), *Essays in Development Economics*, Cambridge, MA: The MIT Press.
Chilcote, R. (1984), *Theories of Development and Underdevelopment*, Colorado: West Point Press.
Cardoso, E. and A. Helwege (2000), 'Import substitution industrialization', in M.P.J. Jeffrey Frieden and Michael Tomz (eds), *Modern Political Economy and Latin America: Theory and Policy*, Boulder, CO: Westview Press, pp. 155–64.
Chuen-Chau, L. (1997), 'Hong Kong: a unique case of development', in D.M. Leipziger (ed.), *Lessons from East Asia*, Ann Arbor, MI: The University of Michigan Press, pp. 35–81.
Cimoli, M. (2000), 'Conclusions: an appreciative pattern of the Mexican innovation system', in M. Cimoli (ed.), *Developing Innovation Systems: Mexico in a Global Context*, London: Continuum, pp. 278–92.

Denison, E. (1967), *Why Growth Rates Differ: Postwar Experience in 9 Western Countries*, Washington, DC: Brookings Institution.

Dussel, E.P. (2000), *Polarizing Mexico: The Impact of Liberalization Strategy*, Boulder, CO: Lynne Rienner Publishers.

Dussel, E.P. (2001), 'Integration and polarization: Mexico's economy since 1988', in P.A.M. and L.F. Punzo (eds), *Mexico beyond NAFTA: Perspectives for the European Debate*, London: Routledge, p. 124.

Easterly, W. (2002), *The Elusive Quest for Growth*, Cambridge, MA: The MIT Press.

Franko, P. (1999), *The Puzzle of Latin American Economic Development*, Lanham, MD: Rowman and Littlefield.

Gaurav, D. and M. Ravallion (1996), *Why Have some Indian States Done Better than Others at Reducing Rural Poverty*? Washington, DC: World Bank.

Gaurav, D. and M. Ravallion (2002), *Is India's Economic Growth Leaving the Poor Behind*? Washington, DC: World Bank.

Higgins, B. and Savoie (eds) (1988), *Regional Economic Development: Essays in Honor of Francois Perroux*, London and Boston: Allen & Unwin.

Hirschman, A. (1958), *The Strategy of Economic Development*, New Haven, CT: Yale University Press.

Hung-Chao, T. (1991), 'The stages of economic growth', *The Journal of Asian Studies*, **50** (4), 897–9.

Hunt, D. (1989), *Economic Theories of Development: An Analysis of Competing Paradigms*, Savage, MD: Barnes & Noble.

Jacobs, J. (1969), *The Economy of Cities*, New York: Random House.

Jacobs, J. (1984), *Cities and the Wealth of Nations: Principles of Economic Life*, New York: Random House.

Keller, W. (1996), 'Absorptive capacity: on the creation and acquisition of technology development', *Journal of Development Economics*, **49**, 199–227.

Krueger, A., V. Corbo and F. Ossa (eds) (1985), *Export Oriented Development Strategies: The Success of Five Newly Industrialized Countries*, Boulder, CO: Westview Press.

Krugman, P. (1994), 'The fall and rise of development economics', in R. Lloyd and Donald A. Schön (eds), *Rethinking the Development Experience: Essays Provoked by the Work of Albert O. Hirschman*, Washington, DC: Brookings Institution, pp. 39–58.

Leipziger, D.M. (ed.) (1997), *Lessons from East Asia*, Ann Arbor, MI: The University of Michigan Press.

Malecki, E.J. (1997), *Technology and Economic Development: The Dynamics of Local, Regional and National Competitiveness*, Harlow: Longman.

Marshall, A. (1920), *Principles of Economics: An Introductory Volume*, London: Macmillan and Co.

Mason, E. (1982), 'Stages of economic growth revisited', in C. Kindleberger and G. Di-Tella (eds), *Economies in the Long View: Essays in Honour of W.W. Rostow*, vol 1, New York: New York University Press, pp. 116–40.

Myrdal, G. (1968), *Asian Drama: An Inquiry into the Poverty of Nations*, vol III, New York: Pantheon.

Nelson, R. and H. Pack (1999), 'The Asian miracle and modern growth theory', *The Economic Journal*, 109 (July), 416–36.

Pack, H. (1994), 'Endogenous growth theory: intellectual appeal and empirical shortcomings', *Journal of Economic Perspectives*, **8** (1), 55–72.

Pastor, R. (2001), *Towards a North American Community? Lessons from the Old World to the New World*, Washington, DC: Institute for International Economics.

Perkins, Radalet, Snodgrass, Gillis and Roemer (eds) (2001), *Economics of Development*, New York: W.W. Norton & Company.

Perroux, F. (1950), 'Economic space: theory and applications', *Quarterly Journal of Economics*, **64** (1), 89–104.

Porter, M. (1990), *The Competitive Advantage of Nations*, New York: The Free Press.

Romer, P.M. (1986), 'Increasing returns and long-run growth', *Journal of Political Economy*, **94** (5), 1002–1037.

Romer, P. M. (1990), 'Endogenous technological change', *Journal of Political Economy*, **98**, S71–S102.

Romer, P.M. (1994), 'The origins of endogenous growth', *Journal of Economic Perspectives*, **8** (1), 3–22.

Rostow, W. (1960), *The Stages of Economic Growth: A Non-Communist Manifesto*, London: Cambridge University Press.

Rostow, W. (1990), *Theories of Economic Growth from David Hume to the Present: With a Perspective on the Next Century*, New York: Oxford University Press.

Sklair, L. (1993), *Assembling for Development: The Maquila Industry in Mexico and the United States*, San Diego, CA: Center for the US–Mexican Studies, University of California, San Diego.

Solow, R.M. (1956), 'A contribution to the theory of economic growth', *Quarterly Journal of Economics*, **70**, 65–94.

Stern, N. (2001), *Building a Climate for Investment, Growth, and Poverty Reduction in India*, India: The Export–Import Bank of India.

Stern, N. (2002), *A Strategy for Development*, Washington, DC: World Bank.

Syrquin, M. (1988), 'The agricultural transformation', in H. Chenery and T.N. Srinivasan (eds), *Handbook of Development Economics*, Amsterdam and New York: North-Holland and Elsevier Science, pp. 205–73.

Taylor, L.J. (1988), *Varieties of Stabilization Experience: Toward Sensible Macroeconomics in the Third World*, London: Oxford University Press.

Tinbergen, J. (1959), *Selected Papers*, L.H. Klaasen, L.M. Koyck and H.J. Witteveen (eds), Amsterdam: North Holland.

Todaro, M.P. (1994), *Economic Development*, New York: Longman.

Wilson, P.A. (1992), *Exports and Local Development: Mexico's New Maquiladoras*, Austin, TX: University of Texas Press.

World Bank (1993), World Development Report, New York and Oxford: Oxford University Press.

World Bank (1997), *World Development Report. The State in a Changing World*, New York: Oxford University Press

3. Information and communication technology and economic development: the Indian context

**Tojo Thatchenkery, Roger R. Stough,
Govindasamy Balatchandirane and
Rupa Ranganathan***

India has emerged as one of the fastest growing economies in 2003–04 with its gross domestic product (GDP) rising by 8.2 percent (Central Statistical Organization Report, June 30, 2004). India's technological capabilities and rising exports in information technology (IT) and pharmaceuticals have driven the country to become a significant outward investor of capital (The World Investment Report, the United Nations Conference on Trade and Development, September 22, 2004.). According to the report, India's top 15 software and service companies have all invested abroad, mostly in developed countries, while the country's business process outsourcing firms are setting up affiliates in Mexico and the Philippines. Such developments have raised India's standing in the world. More specifically, the IT exports have brought about a heightened awareness of India in different parts of the world.[1] The IT growth has also challenged traditional modes of economic development. This chapter explores the relation between ICT and the economic development of India.

A NASSCOM–McKinsey study (2002) ranks India above many developed countries in software capability. In 2001, according to the World Bank projections, growth as a percentage of annual growth was 3.9 percent when the average annual percentage of GDP growth for all developing countries was 5 percent. India is growing slower than other developing countries but is continuing to grow much faster in the software arena. This appears to be an interesting scenario. While the growth of the IT services sector has been nearly eightfold between 1994 and 2001, India's overall growth has not been nearly so remarkable (Hira, 2003). Other countries that have successful development strategies have moved through a fairly predictable set of development stages from producing low-value labor-intensive goods initially to high value and technologically advanced goods and services. India's success with state-of-the-art information technology and software in the global market, in contrast, appears to be different from the other development success stories.

Is India's development strategy different from the rest of the world? Did India leapfrog into its current stage of development skipping the interim stages of development and, if so, is this a replicable model for some other emerging economies of the world? If India does indeed have a thriving ICT sector, will the rest of the economy benefit from it?

GROWTH OF THE INDIAN ICT INDUSTRY

The growth of the Indian IT industry has been impressive. The Indian IT industry which produced just a few million dollars worth of goods and services in the mid-1980s produced US$ 15.6 billion in 2002–03 and $ 20 billion in 2003–04 (NASSCOM, 2004). The IT industry accounted for 1.22 percent of GDP in 1997–98, 3.09 percent in 2002–03, and 3.8 percent for 2003–04. This increase in the share of the IT sector in the national economy is due to exports as the domestic market for IT products is small and underdeveloped. IT exports have accounted for as much as 60 percent of the total IT industry, a figure that is expected to reach 62 percent in 2003–04.

There are a few large companies that control much of the exports of the Indian software industry. The top five firms account for 32 percent of the total software exports. The IT industry in India is concentrated in the three southern states of India – Tamil Nadu, Karnataka and Andhra Pradesh. Almost 90 percent of the software development and export activity are confined to four metropolitan areas in India, namely Mumbai, Bangalore, Chennai and Delhi (Joseph, 2003) as depicted in Table 3.1.

The Indian software industry has grown at a compound annual rate of over 50 percent in the 1990s, the highest for any country during this period. The revenues have risen from $175 million to $8.7 billion during the decade. Indian nationals account for 45 percent of H1-B visas issued by the USA every year and a large proportion of them go to software engineers. India is home to some 650 000 software developers or about 10 percent of the world's developer population. The Indian software developer population is growing at an annual compound rate of 32 percent, which means that in the next three years the Indian developers will be the largest in the world. Among the Fortune 500 companies, over 250 outsource their software-related work to India. Some of the best performing and most admired industries in India are in IT-related industries. Table 3.2 below shows India's IT industry output.

Table 3.1   Software exports of IT clusters and their rankings

IT cluster	Software exports in 2003–04 in US$ million	Software exports in 2004–05 in US$ million	Current ranking
Bangalore	3934	5115	1
National capital region (Delhi, Noida and Gurgaon)	2097	2559	2
Chennai	1657	1988	3
Hyderabad	1092	1630	4
Pune	967	1353	5
Mumbai	913	1278	6

Source: *Business Today*, November 7, 2004 (figures for 2004–05 are estimates).

Table 3.2   Estimates of India's IT industry output (billion $)

Year	Domestic segment	Export segment	Total
1990–91	0.41	0.11	0.51
1991–92	0.47	0.16	0.63
1992–93	0.59	0.22	0.80
1993–94	0.78	0.33	1.11
1994–95	1.15	0.44	1.59
1995–96	1.64	0.62	2.26
1996–97	2.00	1.13	3.12
1997–98	2.52	1.67	4.19
1998–99	3.07	2.50	5.57
1999–00	3.95	3.73	7.69
2000–01	5.74	6.95	12.69
2001–02	5.65	8.80	14.45

Source: Chandrasekhar (2002).

Table 3.2 illustrates the following: first, the IT industry in India has grown at a fast pace in the years following the adoption of liberalization policies. Between 1990–91 and 2001–02, the annual compound rate of growth of output was 37.4 percent. In other words, IT output has been doubling every 2.2 years. Second, this rapid pace of growth was enabled by IT exports, which have been growing at 54 percent per annum. This translates to a doubling of the exports in this industry every 18–24 months. The share of exports in IT industry output had risen from 20 percent to 28 percent between 1990–91 and 1995–96 and rose to 61 percent in 2001–02. Third, the ratio of gross IT sector output to GDP has risen from 0.38 percent in 1991–92 to 1.88 percent in 1999–2000 and to 3 percent in 2001–02 (Chandrasekhar, 2002). The software exports accounted for 4.9 percent of India's export revenues in 1997 and rose to 20.4 percent in 2003–04 (NASSCOM, 2003). By the year 2008, the IT industry is expected to contribute 7 percent of India's GDP. This would account for 30 percent of the foreign exchange inflows. Over four million jobs are estimated to be created in this industry. Notwithstanding the competition from other countries, India will remain the pre-eminent destination for IT and IT-enabled services. The latter is expected to move up the value chain and move from the level of call centers to higher levels of activities so that the revenue generated in the ICT sector alone is likely to reach $20 billion by 2008 (NASSCOM–McKinsey, 2002).

A number of aspects seem to have propelled India towards the creation of a dynamic IT sector, which include a large English-speaking educated labor force, comparatively low labor costs, absence of barriers to setting up back offices, and reasonable availability of infrastructure in places like Bangalore, Hyderabad and Chennai. The talent pool of IT professionals in India is vast. Some projections for 2001–02 placed them at 520 000 (Singh, 2003). About 700 engineering colleges are estimated to produce over 150 000 graduates every year. In this regard India is second only to the USA.

India's presence in the software industry dates back to 1970 when the Tata Consultancy Services (TCS), which was a part of the TATA conglomerate, entered the IT business sector (Krishnan and Matta, 2003). The foundation for the intellectual capital for software industry was laid by the establishment of the Indian Institute of Science (IISc) in 1909 through the pioneering vision of J.N. Tata, one of India's most famous industrialists and patriots. Since then, it has grown into an internationally reputed premier institution of research with more than 2 000 active researchers working in most areas of science and technology. The Indian Institutes of Technology (IITs) and the Indian Institutes of Management (IIMs), established soon after India's independence in 1947, provided the intellectual power necessary to develop a strong knowledge base in technology and innovation management. During the last five decades, the Indian Institutes of Technology (IITs) have produced thousands of engineers, many of whom now occupy senior positions in global technology and corporate industry.

Role of IT in India's Economic Development

The success of a few countries like India has spurred a considerable amount of writing on the potential role IT can play in economic development (Adeya, 2002; Arora and Athreye, 2002; Bhatnagar and Schware, 2000; Chandrasekhar, 2003; Kapur, 2002; Kumar, 2001; Richter and Parthasarathi, 2003; and Tessler et al., 2003). Some have argued that the Indian case could be studied as a useful 'model' for other developing countries (Tschang, 2001).

What is the relationship between ICT and economic development? Can India follow the ICT route to achieving development? At an intuitive level, we can argue that ICT helps with economic development. ICT also helps to reduce the barrier for access to information, consequently, knowledge. It can help to disseminate vast amounts of information in fields such as education and health-care by reducing the cost of procuring critical and latest knowledge. Furthermore, the various innovations in ICT may lead to investment in infrastructure. The enhancement of communication services through ICT may promote the interaction of producers and consumers, allowing the transmission of market information and promotion of enterprises (Kenny, 2002).

ICT played a key role in providing decision support systems to managers and public administrators and has helped in the monitoring of development programs through the use of Geographical Information Systems (Bhatnagar, 2000). It has brought more transparency to the way the governments work and to some extent has streamlined unsatisfactory customer service functions such as billing and accounting. ICT seems to be improving accountability and transparency in the governance and allowing greater access of services to the poor (D'Costa, 2003).

According to Porter (1990), a country is likely to have competitive advantage in an industry when firms in that industry are under pressure to constantly innovate. This would imply that India and other developing countries would be condemned to mediocrity (Krishnan et al., 2003). This has proved to be erroneous as many countries like Japan, Korea and Taiwan have had successes in the automobile industry, consumer electronics, semiconductors and software, respectively (Krishna et al., 2000). The reason for this was that these firms did not absorb old technologies but improved technologies to become global players (Krishnan et al., 2003). While the lack of resources can be an impediment to industrialization, newcomers have benefited from existing technologies and have not been locked into organizational and institutional inertia (Krishnan et al., 2003). Studies show that when ICT is introduced to countries that have reached a certain stage of development, the effect of the introduction of ICT is only marginal (Dey, 2002). However, for developing countries, the biggest advantage of ICT lies in the fact that they can benefit from the lessons learned and not reinvent the wheel, as in the example of India's export-oriented software services.

India's Leapfrogging Hypothesis

Academics argue that India seems to have followed a very different pattern of development (Stough et al., 2003). According to development theory, in the first stage, labor intensive low-capital goods like clothing, shoes and toys are produced in an effort to build wealth through export. In the second stage, investments are made in heavy industry (for example, steel and shipbuilding). In the third stage, the focus is on production of higher-value consumer goods (consumer durables such as computers, TVs, washers and dryers). In the fourth stage, production and economic activity focus on the creation of technology or innovation-based goods and services (ICT, biotechnology, bioinformatics, pharmaceuticals and so on). This is the model that most countries have followed in their path to developed status. From the perspective of stage development theory, India's development is vastly different because for a country to have a competitive higher-end services industry, it needs to develop an export-competitive industry in agriculture where low- to high-end manufacturing of services has created advanced infrastructure (Stough et al., 2003).

ICT in India: The Impact on Economic and Social Development

Academics who are critical of the leapfrogging hypothesis believe that ICT is an enabler of economic activity rather than the leading edge of it. ICT serves as a catalyst in the role of economic development (Mir and Mir, 2003; Bhatnagar, 2003). The next section of the chapter examines how ICT can enhance the existing trajectories of economic and human development. Though the notion that ICT impacts the economy in various ways is intuitively appealing, quantifying any such impact is challenging. Existing data remains sketchy and establishing the pathways of influence of ICT on a number of variables and segregating the impact of ICT alone on them is complicated. Despite these limitations, it is possible to provide anecdotal or descriptive evidence of the impact of ICT on various sections of the Indian economy.

ICT and Regional Growth

The ICT industry growth in India is centered on a few clusters. The city of Bangalore in the state of Karnataka is one such center. The tax collections in the state of Karnataka last year were well above those for earlier years. If the contribution of Bangalore is removed from the total collections, the tax collections for the rest of the state show negative growth. This shows how much weight the single city of Bangalore accounts for in the overall tax collections for the state (NASSCOM, 2004).

In terms of job creation, the IT industry has directly created tens of thousands of jobs. For India as a whole, just three IT companies, TCS, Infosys and Wipro, created 14000 new jobs in the three-month period ending September 2004. A sizable percentage of such jobs are in the city of Bangalore. A whole range of new jobs have been created to cater to the IT industry, which has been rapidly growing in the city. For example, computer hardware sellers have opened offices in Bangalore who cater not only to the sales but also to the after-sales service for the tens of thousands of computers and related machinery. There has been a boom in the catering sector, the hospitality sector and the transportation companies and so on. Many companies prefer to have their employees picked up and dropped at home after work to ensure that there is no delay in the shift work they maintain 24 hours a day. This has resulted in such companies engaging a fleet of transport vehicles. It is estimated that every IT job creates three more jobs indirectly in the transport, catering and maintenance services (NASSCOM, 2004).

The consumer goods industry in Bangalore, too, got a major boost in the last ten and a half years. Sales of a whole range of consumer durables including expensive items such as automobiles have risen significantly. Some of the largest shopping malls and stores in India have come up in Bangalore in recent years. Likewise, the leisure industry too has been booming.

From a regional development point of view, the cities of Southern India are thriving because they have formed industrial clusters where a number of firms and institutions coexist to reap the benefits of being close to each other in location. Extensive market, technical and competitive information within these clusters have accumulated over a period of time and as a result, firms prefer to be in close proximity to reap the positive externalities. Clusters in Bangalore and Hyderabad have helped firms to increase productivity, drive innovation and stimulate the formation of new firms to increase competition and improve quality (Ramachandran and Ray, 2003). Bangalore has attracted 40 percent of the 112 foreign direct investment (FDI) ventures established in India (Ramachandran and Ray, 2003). Hyderabad is another city that has adopted a strategic policy towards ICT. Andhra Pradesh aims at being the 'most connected state' and has adopted a policy called 'AP First' which addresses the factors required for a strong ICT sector. Improvements have been made in the area of infrastructure and institution creation, resource development, and state participation as a customer and business incentive (Biswas, 2004). The State has created a hi-tech city, which has a campus-style facility of over 55000 square feet to encourage clustering of firms. The

State government has provided fiber optics and established satellite links to improve telecom facility (Biswas, 2004).

ICT and Education

A large amount of anecdotal evidence shows the innovative ways in which ICT helps to improve educational services in India. IFC, an arm of the World Bank, has invested $1.6 million in a project called 'Hole in the Wall' that teaches a web-based curriculum to children in urban and rural slums. Intel and Microsoft have launched a teacher computer literacy program in India called 'Teach the Future' with the training of over 10 000 teachers in 20 cities across India. Schools Online have launched internet training centers with 10 computers each in over 50 schools in the larger cities of India. A nonprofit organization in the state of Tamil Nadu has launched a site called Zooonline.com to increase awareness of zoos and wildlife. A Delhi-based non-governmental organization (NGO) with funding from British Telecommunications (BT) has launched an Internet awareness campaign in the poorest slums of Delhi to educate the local population on employment opportunities (D'Costa, 2003). The state of Karnataka has launched a site called EducationBangalore.com to provide users with access to test scores, exams and course information. They hope such attempts will promote computer literacy and help citizens to recognize and take advantage of various educational and employment opportunities not available until now (World Economic Forum, 2002). Another southern state, Kerala, has committed itself to make 60 million students computer-literate. Over 6 000 computers have been set up in over 2 000 schools. Through the assistance of Intel and Microsoft, over 60 000 teachers are being trained to provide computer education at primary and secondary school levels.

ICT has also been helping in rural education. The Sarvodaya Ashram Resource Center in the northern state of Uttar Pradesh has launched an initiative to improve female education. In collaboration with CARE, an international aid agency, the government has designed innovative techniques to help rural women get basic education (Kappal, 2002). Another organization has established a plan called Schoolnet Limited to help schools in poor areas realize the power of the Internet by providing a few hours of Internet access. The Zee Interactive Learning Services established by Zee TV provides e-learning materials to students, especially in rural areas (World Economic Forum, 2002).

Internet kiosks have been set up all over India and are marketed to rural farmers and schools. There have been successes in providing telephone lines to the less empowered with allocation of $630 million from the private sector alone. NIIT and Aptech, two large private IT training institutions, have provided computers and maintained labs in rural areas that would not otherwise afford a computer connection. Improvement in infrastructures of villages were made with the active participation of the local population in order to set up the networks (Hawkins 2001).

ICT and Health

ICT has helped provide health-care in rural India in modest ways. One of the first such attempts, the Indian Healthcare Project, began in 1994 as a collaborative effort between Apple Computers, Government of India and Computer Maintenance Corporation of India. The Indian rural health-care system is estimated to provide services to 630 million people in 32 states. The health-care workers were burdened by paperwork and data collection responsibility, which took their focus away from the primary task of providing health-care to people. Using the Newton Message Pad, the Auxiliary Nurse Midwife personnel could collect demographic data and help with the immunization of the villagers (Graves and Reddy, 2000).

Another example of ICT helping in health-care comes from *the India HealthCare Delivery Project*, jointly organized by the Government of Andhra Pradesh and World Bank. This project enables auxiliary midwives to eliminate redundant paperwork and enter data through computers, cutting down paperwork and data gathering time by about 40 percent (World Bank, 2002).

The third example comes from a village near the city of Madurai in southern India which has internet kiosks with web cams which transmit the pictures of diseased eyes of the villagers to a better equipped eye hospital in Madurai. The doctors examine these pictures and prescribe the appropriate medication or call the people who are really ill to come in for consultation for a nominal fee that the villagers can afford (Jain, 2003).

ICT and Governance

One of the most significant areas where ICT holds great promise for India is governance. Transparency in communication between the public and the governmental representatives is a basic requirement for good governance. Vested interests have developed that thrive by preventing this communication. Negotiators operate between the citizenry and government officials with the promise to get things done for a fee. This could be something as simple as getting a copy of a land registration. The end result is a bureaucracy that has an incentive to keep the system of graft or corruption continuing uninterrupted. It blocks access to information, making the public dependent on the bureaucrat even for the most basic transactions such a paying utility bills.

One of the most efficient approaches to bring transparency and reduce corruption in public governance has come about through ICT. It has also helped the public save time, effort and money. One widely cited example of the usage of ICT in governance has been the adoption of SMART technologies in Andhra Pradesh. The term 'SMART' is the acronym for simple, moral, accountable, responsive and transparent. Andhra Pradesh is the first state to adopt a state-wide computerization program covering all levels of the administrative spectrum from the smallest to the largest office. The government made extensive use of IT and introduced computers at all levels of the state government to improve citizen services.

With the digitization of tax information several states in India that had year-long backlog are now able to meet the needs of the citizens in a matter of minutes. In addition to creating better efficiency in administration, ICT has helped in the elimination of a good part of corruption in the bureaucracy. ICT is facilitating greater communication with public officials through the setting-up of computer networks, making the Internet accessible to the people.

ICT and Rural Development

ICT holds great promise in the area of rural development. It is possible to classify these into three categories: decision making for the public administrators, improvement of services to citizens and empowering citizens with knowledge and information (Bhatnagar, 2003). One of the best examples of ICT improving the quality of rural India comes out of the work of a nonprofit organization called Drishtee (2002) which has created a need identification survey that is undertaken at the district level. The data has been rendered electronic and is widely accessible by administrators. It enables villagers to have access to government programs and benefits, market-related news, and information on private exchanges and transactions. Drishtee has created over 50 000 information kiosks in six years which serve 500 million people. The organization has trained members of households who are mainly village entrepreneurs who use inexpensive and very simple software. They own these kiosks which are financed through government-sponsored programs. These kiosks have led to a new breed of IT-literate village populations with the number of kiosks rising to 45 000 in 2003.

Drishtee is also allowing the filing of grievances online which are accessed by district and local officials. These kiosks exist in large states such as Haryana, Punjab, UP, Bihar, Rajasthan and Orissa and use standalone, extremely user-friendly software that gets updated whenever the kiosk is connected to the district server. The district server holds vital information such as market prices.

'Gyandoot' is a program that uses ICT for development in rural areas of Madhya Pradesh, a large state in central India. Computers in several village centers in one of the districts of the state were wired for the Internet which made several government services available to the people to establish better relationships between the rural people and traders of agricultural commodities. The Internet helped with stock market information, online complaint resolutions, obtaining essential certificates and several other types of transactions. Gyandoot won the Stockholm Challenge Award for 2000, which focuses on the benefits ICT can bring to society at large.

One of the most widely cited problems in Indian agriculture is the lack of technology and credit availability. The farming community does not have adequate information regarding agricultural techniques, market prices, and supply and demand of commodities. The agricultural sector is replete with the suboptimal use of resources and distorted price signals. Several efforts to deal with this information asymmetry have been launched in India which are cooperative relationships with local universities, businesses and government. An example is a project called Indiagriline, the AgriPortal, created in collaboration with an agricultural university, the National Horticultural Board, and the Indian Institute of Technology, Chennai. An online information database assisted in the dissemination of information regarding the latest developments in agricultural science and technology. The content is in the local language known as Tamil.

Learning from the few projects cited above suggests that ICT did have an impact on rural development, though on an isolated incident basis. For example, one village in a state may have good access to information while another one languishes. So there is a digital divide, not just between the cities and villages of India, but also between one village and another in the same state.

ICT AND ECONOMIC DEVELOPMENT IN INDIA: PROSPECTS AND CAUTION

A discussion of the role that ICT may have played in the economic and social development of India is tied to the strengths and weaknesses of India's IT industry. During the 1980s, the Indian software exports were at the low-end of the value chain (Arora et al., 2000). The high value-added software development was hampered by a small domestic market. As a result, Indian software exports have historically focused more on services than product development. The situation has changed today because Indian software firms are increasingly providing final 'products' and complete solutions and are active in customized software. Firms that began to export in the 1980s offering low-wage, low value-added services have since moved to high-end work. But in the 1990s, a majority of firms have struggled: rising wages have blunted the low-wage strategy, while social constraints on the state have limited the institutional support for valorizing skills either through innovation or local markets. Parthasarathi and Joseph (2002) argue that this has hindered the transformation of Bangalore into a Silicon Valley-style region that defines technologies. He believes that the path to an effective developmental state is not well defined and that multiple trajectories are possible. It also shows how a specific development trajectory influences the ability of firms and regions to exploit the opportunities provided by new technologies and industries. Abundant and skilled labor is providing job opportunities but one of the problems with the ICT-led development is that these jobs do not generally utilize all the skills that labor brings to the job. Several Indian software experts are working in low-skilled jobs that do not enrich their skills.

A growing concern among ICT industry leaders is the inadequate investment in research and development (R&D) in India. The USA and other Organization for Economic Co-operation and Development (OECD) countries invest heavily in R&D and attempt to deploy innovative techniques to use ICT for productivity growth. India's R&D is relatively low which means that India will lag as a creator of new technology but will tend to be a recipient that uses technology at lower-end jobs. The massive brain drain coupled with the poor training in some Indian institutions will not attract high-skilled employment to India. There are of course exceptions to this rule. Infosys, Wipro, TCS and Satyam Computers are some of them. They are changing the landscape of the Indian software industry. However, many firms are still contracted as back offices, working on low-end, low-skill activities that do not generate much knowledge externalities in Indian society. Further, domestic firms do not really interact with larger multinational corporations (MNCs), and as a result, there is little knowledge sharing and trust between the firms. ICT indeed has the capacity to be the driver of development but the challenge is that the ICT industry in India has an enclave-like development where there is an expansionary trajectory that is not yet wide enough to include other sectors (D'Costa, 2003).

The East Asian countries like Taiwan, China and South Korea have turned to using ICT as one of the largest contributors to the economy. They have concentrated on developing the domestic market. India and these countries have all had government-sponsored intervention in the development stage but the difference has been the fact that India did not competitively follow a performance-based system which has rendered Indian industries to be uncompetitive. Even though these countries benefit from large amounts of outsourcing, the East Asian nations, unlike India, are not as dependent on the foreign market, since they have a home-grown ICT industry to rely on (D'Costa, 2003). While India's development strategy has been focused on links with the rest of the world, China has concentrated on making products for the domestic market. The structure of the Chinese market is composed of firms that work on high-end as well as low-end activity. The advantage is that the Chinese market is growing rapidly in the areas of manufacturing, business and consumer markets (Tschang and Xue, 2003). While China's development strategy has been focused on domestic firms and their competition with MNCs, India has concentrated its efforts on providing services to the MNCs and on exports. The smallness of the Indian domestic market is thus an area of serious concern.

There is an absence of absorptive capacities where there are local knowledge gaps that prevent the acquisition and adaptation of new technologies (Mir and Mir, 2003). Although ICT has penetrated some sectors of the economy, there are a number of sectors that are still lagging. Mir also argues that there is a lack of domestic demand of ICT within India. ICT is mainly exported and only as little as 20 percent is consumed locally. Economic theory posits that for a sector to develop fully and for that sector to contribute towards economic growth, there needs to be a demand nationally and internationally. This demand is what leads to the integration of ICT in every sector of the economy, this integration being key to development.

Stemming from the enclave-like development pattern in India, D'Costa argues that the ICT growth pattern in India leads to uneven development in India. Some areas benefit from ICT more than others. The southern states of Andhra Pradesh, Karnataka and Tamil Nadu are leaders in ICT. They benefit from generating large amounts of employment in the high-skilled sector because of ICT. Areas around the industrial centers in these states have generated some of the highest rates of primary education (D'Costa, 2003). However, other areas will be left behind. The southern state of Kerala, despite having the highest literacy rate in India, is lagging behind. Bihar, one of the poorest states of India, has very little penetration of ICT.

Economic development is characterized by removing social exclusion with an increase in access to government and property rights by those who are marginalized by the system. The traditional path of development has been favored over an ICT-driven approach because the ICT approach focuses on the elite of the nation relying on the benefits induced by the economic activities of the elite to trickle down to the poor (Mir and Mir, 2003).

Currently there are few competitors to India thanks to the vast pool of IT professionals, cost advantages, the linkages with Indian IT professionals in the Silicon Valley, and the availability of human talent over the entire spectrum of IT-related services. Currently two-thirds of Indian software companies are engaged in developing end-user application products and services. However, there are a number of countries wanting to replicate the Indian experience and so India cannot have the luxury of resting on its laurels.

High-technological sophistication and intellectual capital, quick time responses, short life term of the technologies, a rapidly changing global market, high-export dependency and absence of true knowledge sharing are some of the hallmarks of IT industries. Nations like India need to learn from each other. Delay in rapid learning and knowledge sharing may mean that large opportunities are lost to other competitor nations looking for a share of the global IT industry services market. In other words, the new economy by its very nature can offer no models. For general economic development, developing nations like India had the luxury of learning from a number of nations who were ahead of it in terms of economic development. The IT sector is one where the rules are in constant flux and different from conventional ones. A hesitation to rapidly learn and stay on top of the developments may mean a lost opportunity for many years.

A strong role by the government in providing incentives and removing obstacles is essential to develop IT industry in any part of the world. This is because unlike the manufacturing sector, software creation does not need any heavy investment in land, machinery and so on. Anybody anywhere can set up an IT company. Strong local incentives are key to development. It is ultimately the quality of the human capital that determines the growth of this industry. Without the creation of high-quality human capital, other advantages do not add much value. Any country that wants to be a significant IT services provider has to have a strong higher education sector.

Quality of services is equally important. The large concentration of IT companies with the highest level of quality certifications in the world is in locations like Bangalore and Hyderabad. The private sector should interact with the university system because the latter could offer valuable research that is required for product innovation. At the same time, the autonomy of the educational institutions must be maintained. If it is lost, universities and research centers could end up becoming extension centers of private industry.

CONCLUSION

ICT in India harbingers change at various levels – social, political and economic. There has been an increase in the monitoring and accountability of governments. ICT has brought the rural areas much closer to the markets and has improved business transactions. There has been an increased flow of information thereby increasing productivity and innovation. Marginalized communities have been able to mobilize and collaborate to bring about social change. Thanks to the significant job creation, income levels for some sections of the population have risen. The confidence generated by this sector has energized whole sections of the population and prompted a major political party to campaign for India's national elections in 2003 on the theme of 'India shining'.

More transformation is possible. To capitalize on this potential, an integration of the sectors segregated is essential. The large, educated, computer-savvy population could be employed in ICT-applied jobs in different sectors of the economy. ICT will bring sweeping changes in society provided it is integrated with other sectors and not treated as a sector that is independent of the rest. ICT is a means and not an end.

While quantification of the benefits of ICT is a challenge, ICT has contributed to economic growth. The development trajectory of India has been different from the traditional development pattern with increasing reliance on the ICT sector. The main lesson, however, is that ICT, more than being an engine of growth, is a powerful facilitator and catalyst of growth.

NOTE

* The views expressed in this chapter are those of the authors and should not be attributed to the World Bank.
1. In this article we use the terms IT and ICT as interchangeable, as used by NASSCOM, the National Association of Software and Service Companies, the apex body for IT companies in India, which includes hardware, peripherals, networking, training, domestic and export market for software and services.

BIBLIOGRAPHY

Adeya, Catherine (2002), 'ITs and poverty: a literature review', www.network.idrc. ca/ev.php?URL_ID=24718&URL_DO=DO_TOPIC&URL_SECTION.
Arora, A. and S. Athreye (2002), 'The software industry and India's economic development', *Information Economics and Policy*, **14**, 253–73.
Arora, A., V.S. Arunachalam, J. Asundi and R. Fernandes (2001), 'The Indian software service industry', *Research Policy*, **30**, 1267–87.
Bhatnagar, Subhash (2000), 'Information technology and development: foundation and key issues', in *Information Communication Technologies in Rural Development*, World Bank Institute, Washington, DC: World Bank.
Bhatnagar Subhash (2002), *Information Communication Technology and Development: Foundation and Key Issues*, Washington, DC: World Bank Institute, World Bank.

Bhatnagar, Subhash (2003), 'Economic impact of E-government in India', proceedings of the International Conference on Information Communication Technology and Economic Development, the Indian Institute of Science, 2–5 March, Bangalore, India.

Bhatnagar, Subhash and Robert Schware (eds) (2000), *Information Communication Technologies in Rural Development*, Washington DC: World Bank Institute, World Bank.

Biswas, Radha (2004), 'Making a technopolis in Hyderabad, India: the role of government IT policy', *Technological Forecasting and Social Change*, **71** (8), 823–35.

Chakravarty, Rupak (2000), 'IT at milk collection centers in cooperative dairies: the national dairy development board experience', in *Information Communication Technologies in Rural Development*, Washington DC: World Bank Institute, World Bank.

Chandrasekhar, C.P. (2002), 'Promoting ICT for human development in Asia: realizing the millennium development goals India', in *Country Paper Regional Human Development Report*, United Nations Development Programme: Regional Bureau for Asia and the Pacific

Chandrasekhar, C.P. (2003), 'The diffusion of information technology and the implications for development: a perspective based on the Indian experience', www.networkideas.org/featart/feb2003/IT_Bangalore_Paper.pdf.

D'Costa, Anthony (2003), 'Uneven and combined development: understanding India's software exports', *World Development*, **31**, 211–26.

Dey, Atanu (2002), 'A brief note on ICT and economic development', paper presented at the Sri Lanka Silicon Valley Initiative, Across World Communication Office, Santa Clara, CA, June 26.

Drishtee (2002), 'Drishtee: connecting India village by village', www.drishtee. com.

Graves, Mike and Kumar Reddy Naresh (2000), 'Electronic support for rural health-care workers', in *Information Communication Technologies in Rural Development*, Washington, DC: World Bank Institute, World Bank.

Hawkins, Robert (2001), 'Ten lessons for ICT and education in the developing world', A UNDP report, Chapter 4, New York: UNDP.

Hira, Ron (2003), 'Utilizing immigration regulations as a competitive advantage: an additional explanation for India's success in exporting information technology services', proceedings of the International Conference on Information Communication Technology and Economic Development, the Indian Institute of Science, 2–5 March, Bangalore, India.

Jain, Mukti (2003), 'Putting the I see into ICT', *a news item on BBC about e-villages*, www.bbc.co.uk/radio4/factual/evillages3.shtml.

Joseph, K.J. (2003), 'Perils of excessive export orientation: the case of India's sector', proceedings of the International Conference on Information Communication Technology and Economic Development, the Indian Institute of Science, 2–5 March, Bangalore, India.

Kappal, Ritu (2002), 'Educating rural girls using technology', paper presented at the Second Annual Baramati Initiative on ICT and Development: Creating the Infrastructure for the Future, Vidya Pratishthan's Institute of Information Technology, 31 May–June, Pune, India.

Kapur, Devesh (2002), 'The causes and consequences of India's IT boom', India Review, **1** (2), 91–110.

Kenny, Charles (2002), 'Information and communication technologies for direct poverty alleviation: costs and benefits', *Development Policy Review*, **20** (2), 141–57.

Krishna, S., Abhoy K. Ojha and Michael Barrett (2000), 'Competitive advantage in the Indian software industry: an analysis', in Chrisanthi Avgerou and Geoff Walsham (eds), *Information Technology in Context: Studies from the Perspectives of Developing Countries*, Aldershot: Ashgate, pp. 182–97.

Krishnan, R.T., A. Gupta and V. Matta (2003), 'Biotechnology and bioinformatics: can India emulate the software success story?', proceedings of the International Conference on Information Communication Technology and Economic Development, the Indian Institute of Science, Bangalore, India, 2–5 March.

Kumar, Nagesh (2001), 'Indian software industry development in international and national development perspective', *Economic and Political Weekly*, **36** (45) 4278–90.

Mir, Raza and Ali Mir (2003), *Catalysis, not leapfrogging: an institutional argument for a limited role of ICTs in India's development*, paper presented at the Conference on ICT Leapfrogging India's Development, March 1–3, Bangalore.

NASSCOM (2003), *The IT Industry in India: Strategic Review 2003*, New Delhi: National Association of Software and Service Companies.

NASSCOM (2004), *The IT Industry in India: Strategic Review 2004*, New Delhi: National Association of Software and Service Companies.

NASSCOM–McKinsey (2002), *Report: Strategies to Achieve Indian IT Industry's Aspiration*, New Delhi: National Association of Software and Service Companies.

Parthasarathi, A. and K.J. Joseph (2002), 'Limits to innovation with strong export orientation: the case of India's information and communication technologies sector', *Science, Technology & Society*, **7** (1), 13–49.

Porter, Michael (1990), *The Competitive Advantage of Nations*, New York: Free Press.

Ramachandran, K. and Sougata Ray (2003), 'Creating IT industrial clusters: learning from strategies of early and late movers', proceedings of the International Conference on Information Communication Technology and Economic Development, The Indian Institute of Science, Bangalore, India, 2–5 March.

Richter, Frank-Jugen and Parthasarathi Banerjee, (eds), (2003), *The Knowledge Economy in India*, Hampshire: Palgrave Macmillan.

Singh, Nirvkar, (2003), *India's information technology sector: what contribution to broader economic development?*, OECD Development Centre, technical paper no 207, March, www.oecd.org/dev/Technics.

Stough, Roger, Kingsley Haynes and Maria Salazar, (2003), Economic development theory and practice: the Indian development experience, proceedings of the International Conference on Information Communication Technology and Economic Development, the Indian Institute of Science, Bangalore, India, 2–5 March.

Tessler, Shirley, Avron Barr and Nagy Hanna (2003), 'National software industry development', *The Electronic Journal on Information Systems in Developing Countries*, **13** (10), 1–17.

Tschang, Ted (2001), 'The basic characteristics of skills and organizational capabilities in the Indian software industry', ADB Institute working paper no 13, Tokyo, February.

Tschang, Ted and Xue Lan (2003), 'The development of software industry in China and a comparison with that of India', proceedings of the International Conference on Information Communication Technology and Economic Development, the Indian Institute of Science, 2–5 March, Bangalore, India.

World Bank (2002), 'Using informatics and communications technology to reduce poverty in rural India', in *Prem Notes No. 70*, Washington, DC: World Bank.

World Economic Forum (2002), 'Global digital divide initiative: steering committee on education', Educational ICT Pilot Initiatives: India Country Report, annual meeting 2002, January 31–February 4.

4. Recent developments in India's service economy and the role of the information technology industry

Cherian Samuel*

Structural change in an economy is usually measured in terms of changes in the sectoral – primary (agriculture), secondary (industry), and tertiary (services) shares of output/value added/employment. From a purely mathematical viewpoint, the economic structure at any given time is dependent on initial conditions of sectoral shares and the growth rates between the initial and final time periods. From this perspective, a study of structural change in an economy should ultimately focus on explaining the initial conditions and the subsequent sectoral growth rates.

This chapter attempts to study recent structural changes in the Indian economy, with particular emphasis on the services sector. In turn, it also tries to identify the role of the information, communications and technology (ICT) industry in the recent growth of the Indian service economy.

This chapter is divided into four parts: part one surveys the literature on structural changes in economies; part two presents the data analysis on structural change; part three looks at different aspects of the Indian information technology (IT) industry; and part IV concludes the study.

I THE SERVICE ECONOMY

For estimating the gross domestic product (GDP), the whole economy is usually partitioned into primary, secondary and tertiary sectors. These sectors are used interchangeably with agriculture, industry and services. The GDP estimates of the primary sector, that is agriculture, forestry and logging, fishing and a part of the secondary sector, that is mining and quarrying, registered manufacturing and construction are based on the production approach. In the remaining part of the secondary sector: unregistered manufacturing, electricity, gas and water supply and the tertiary sector: trade, hotels and restaurants, transport, storage, communication, banking and insurance, real estate, ownership of dwellings, business services, public administration and defense and other services, the GDP is estimated based on the income approach. Some analysts (Ghosh, 1991) have noted this as being the key factor affecting growth in the service sector in developing countries like India in recent years.

Theories of Structural Change

As noted by Ansari (1995), there are at least four theoretical explanations for structural change: (i) Cambridge view; (ii) Dutch-disease view; (iii) Bacon–Eltis view; and (iv) Secular trend view.

The Cambridge view attributes structural change to a growing inability of the export sector to pay for rising imports (Cornwall, 1977; Singh, 1977; Thirlwall, 1978). The balance of payments constraint eventually makes it necessary to cut down the growth in output to match growth in exports.

The Dutch-disease view explains structural change in terms of resource movement and spending effects (Corden and Neary, 1982). In a three-sector model, the resource sector and the manufacturing sector are assumed to be the booming and lagging sectors, respectively. Both of these sectors together comprise the tradeable sector. The service sector is considered non-tradeable. A rise in the resource sector causes the marginal product of labor to rise in the booming sector. This leads to a movement of resources away from the manufacturing and the service sectors. The excess demand for services due to the inward shift of the supply curve in this sector leads to a further movement of resources away from the manufacturing sector. The spending effect is caused by a rapid rise in real income following the boom. This creates additional demand for services causing a further shift of resources away from the manufacturing sector.

Bacon–Eltis (BE) view explains structural change as an outcome of the rapid expansion in the public sector. Since government spending tends to be biased towards services, resources shift away from the goods sector, including the industrial sector. At the same time, the public is not willing to pay for increased government expenditure in terms of higher taxation. The net result is that increased government spending is matched by a reduction in savings, investment and net exports. All this, along with the demand for higher wages by trade unions, tends to 'squeeze' the resource availability in the manufacturing sector.

According to the secular/structuralist view, changes in structure that accompany economic growth are a transition from a low-income agrarian economy to an industrial urban economy with substantially higher income. The main features of the transformation, identified by Kuznets (1965) as the core of modern economic growth on the basis of long-term experience in advanced countries, can be identified in the shorter time series of a large number of developing countries (Syrquin and Chenery, 1989).

Structural change is a manifestation of the society's attempt to reallocate available resources in response to changing tastes and income. As income rises above the subsistence level, the proportion of income spent on goods which have high primary content falls. At this stage, both secondary and tertiary sectors grow at the expense of the primary sector. As incomes rise even higher, the tertiary sector grows at the cost of the secondary sector,[1] because the secondary sector has reached a certain minimum level of growth (Chenery, 1961; Kasper, 1978). Changes in population, innovation and international competition are other factors that drive structural change.

Relevance to Less Developed Countries (LDCs)

The Cambridge view has little relevance to LDCs, since it primarily tries to explain the decline of the manufacturing sector. Likewise, the Dutch-disease view has limited validity, since most of the LDCs have not experienced significant resource booms. In contrast, the BE and secular view seem relevant for LDCs, supported by empirical evidence (Ansari, 1995).

History suggests that while both the secondary and primary sectors have experienced a relative decline in the developed countries (DCs), the manufacturing sector has shown a steady increase in its share of the GDP in LDCs. In this case, only the primary sector has experienced significant declines in its GDP share. Also, the developed countries have experienced a relative increase in the GDP share of the service sector in phase III of their development. In contrast, the service sector in LDCs has become the largest sector in terms of its GDP share, while still in their second phase of development. Evidence presented later in the chapter supports some of these findings.

Indian Evidence

Bhattacharya and Mitra (1990) show that the services sector in India is growing faster than the commodity-producing sector. The relative disparity between growth rates in services and the commodity sector has widened. They argue that the pattern of service growth in India appears to be different from experiences elsewhere. The service sector has become the predominant sector even before the economy became a highly industrialized one[2] and the share of services in national income is much larger than its share in employment. Thus, in general, the growth of the service sector in India would appear to be independent of the commodity sector.

The Bhattacharya and Mitra study also suggests that the tertiary sector in India has been growing faster than the demand generated for services by the commodity sector due to strong exogenous factors. Had the growth in services employment been higher, one could have attributed employment as a basic factor behind the growth of services income. The growth of services employment lags far behind income and hence cannot be regarded as a major cause for the faster growth of services income. Probably, the rise in salary and wage rates and mark-ups are more important contributors to service income growth.

II TYPOLOGY OF STRUCTURAL CHANGE

Table 4.1 presents the elements of an analytical framework for studying structural changes in an economy by looking at the relative importance of agriculture, industry and the services sectors over time. This could be based on value added, GDP or employment. Most of the empirical evidence presented in this chapter is based on value added. In addition to this time-series approach, we can also take a cross-section approach that compares different economies – say based on income levels – at a given time.

Table 4.1   Typology of structural change

		Economic structure in the final time period					
		I	II	III	IV	V	VI
Economic	I						
structure in	II						
the initial	III						
time period	IV						
	V						
	VI						

Broadly speaking, economic growth is expected to transform countries from type I/II to type V/VI structures, with type III/IV as intermediate states. Agriculture is the leading sector in type I/II economies; industry in type III/IV economies; and services in type V/VI economies. While economic structures in LDCs are often characterized as type I/II, they are usually type V/VI in DCs. In general, observed economic structures in countries at a given point are a function of the initial economic structure and growth rates over time. A more detailed discussion of this framework is presented in the Appendix.

The six states of an economic structure based on percentage shares of agriculture (primary), industry (secondary) and services (tertiary) sectors in the value added/GDP/ employment can be defined as follows:

Type I – agriculture>industry>services; type II – agriculture>services> industry
Type III – industry>services>agriculture; type IV – industry>agriculture >services
Type V – services>agriculture>industry; type VI – services>industry> agriculture

The agriculture sector corresponds to International Standard Industrial Classification (ISIC) divisions 1–5 and includes forestry, hunting and fishing, as well as the cultivation of crops and livestock production. The industry sector corresponds to ISIC divisions 10–45 and includes mining, manufacturing (ISIC divisions 15–37), construction, electricity, water and gas. The services sector corresponds to ISIC divisions 50–90 and includes wholesale and retail trades (including hotels and restaurants), transport, government, financial, professional and personal services such as education, health-care and real estate services. Also included are imputed bank service charges, import duties and any statistical discrepancies noted by national compilers as well as discrepancies arising from rescaling.

Empirical Evidence: India versus Others

Tables 4.2–4.7 present the evidence on structural change for India (Table 4.2) and a group of comparison countries. India was a type II economy in 1960 and a type VI in 2000. India was already a type II economy at the beginning of the study period in 1960 and therefore the data does not capture the type I →type II transformation of the economy, wherein services became more important than industry. Over the 40-year period from 1960 to 2000, most of the gains from the decline of agriculture (45%→25%) accrued to services (36%→ 48%); but industry also gained (19%→27%).

The Indian experience is quite different from the Chinese (as shown in Table 4.3), where sectoral shares have remained remarkably stable. China was a type III economy in 1960 as well as 1999. From 1960 to 1999, the small loss in agriculture (22%→18%) has been captured entirely by industry (45%→49%). In the case of China, the dominant share (45 percent) of industry at the beginning of the study period in 1960 – compared to India's 19 percent – was indeed quite remarkable.[3] Quite clearly, industry has led the way in China's blazing economic growth in recent years.

Table 4.2   Structural changes in the Indian economy: 1960–2000

India	1960	1961	1962	1963	1964	1965	1966	1967	1968	1969	Av.
Agriculture, value added (% of GDP)	45	44	42	44	46	44	45	48	46	46	45
Industry, value added (% of GDP)	19	19	20	20	19	20	20	18	19	20	19
Manufacturing, value added (% of GDP)	13	14	15	15	14	14	14	12	13	13	14
Services, etc., value added (% of GDP)	36	36	37	36	35	36	36	34	35	34	36

India	1970	1971	1972	1973	1974	1975	1976	1977	1978	1979	Av.
Agriculture, value added (% of GDP)	46	44	44	47	44	41	39	40	39	37	42
Industry, value added (% of GDP)	20	21	21	20	21	22	23	23	24	25	22
Manufacturing, value added (% of GDP)	14	14	15	14	16	15	16	15	17	17	15
Services, etc., value added (% of GDP)	34	35	35	33	35	37	38	36	37	38	36

India	1980	1981	1982	1983	1984	1985	1986	1987	1988	1989	Av.
Agriculture, value added (% of GDP)	39	37	36	37	35	33	32	32	32	31	34
Industry, value added (% of GDP)	24	25	26	26	26	26	26	27	26	27	26
Manufacturing, value added (% of GDP)	16	16	16	16	16	16	16	16	16	17	16
Services, etc., value added (% of GDP)	37	38	39	38	39	40	42	42	41	41	40

India	1990	1991	1992	1993	1994	1995	1996	1997	1998	1999	2000	Av.
Agriculture, value added (% of GDP)	31	32	31	31	30	28	29	28	28	26	25	29
Industry, value added (% of GDP)	28	26	27	26	27	28	27	27	27	26	27	27
Manufacturing, value added (% of GDP)	17	16	16	16	17	18	17	17	16	15	16	16
Services, etc., value added (% of GDP)	41	42	42	43	43	44	44	45	46	48	48	44

Source: World Development Indicators (World Bank, 2003).

Table 4.3   Structural changes in the Chinese economy: 1960–1999

China	1960	1961	1962	1963	1964	1965	1966	1967	1968	1969	Av.
Agriculture, value added (% of GDP)	22	36	39	40	39	38	38	40	42	38	37
Industry, value added (% of GDP)	45	33	32	33	35	35	38	34	31	36	35
Manufacturing, value added (% of GDP)	–	–	–	–	–	29	32	28	26	30	29
Services, etc., value added (% of GDP)	33	32	29	27	26	27	24	26	27	26	28

China	1970	1971	1972	1973	1974	1975	1976	1977	1978	1979	Av.
Agriculture, value added (% of GDP)	35	34	33	33	34	32	33	29	28	31	32
Industry, value added (% of GDP)	40	42	43	43	43	46	45	47	48	47	45
Manufacturing, value added (% of GDP)	34	35	36	36	36	38	38	39	41	40	37
Services, etc., value added (% of GDP)	24	24	24	24	23	22	22	23	24	21	23

China	1980	1981	1982	1983	1984	1985	1986	1987	1988	1989	Av.
Agriculture, value added (% of GDP)	30	32	33	33	32	28	27	27	26	25	29
Industry, value added (% of GDP)	49	46	45	45	43	43	44	44	44	43	45
Manufacturing, value added (% of GDP)	40	39	37	37	35	35	35	35	35	34	36
Services, etc., value added (% of GDP)	21	22	22	22	25	29	29	29	30	32	26

China	1990	1991	1992	1993	1994	1995	1996	1997	1998	1999	Av.
Agriculture, value added (% of GDP)	27	24	22	20	20	21	20	19	19	18	21
Industry, value added (% of GDP)	42	42	44	47	48	49	50	50	49	49	47
Manufacturing, value added (% of GDP)	33	33	33	35	34	35	35	35	34	34	34
Services, etc., value added (% of GDP)	31	33	34	33	32	31	30	31	32	33	32

Source: World Development Indicators (World Bank, 2003).

Panagariya (2002) has suggested that the differences in the composition of GDPs of these two countries are important explanations of why India lags behind China. These differences in GDP composition matter because, under liberal trade policies, developing countries are much more likely to be able to expand exports and imports if a large portion of their output originates in industry. Not only is the scope for expanding labor-intensive manufacturing greater, a larger industrial sector also requires imported inputs thereby offering greater scope for the expansion of imports. Stimulating industry growth remains a key challenge for India.[4]

Table 4.4 presents data for all low-income countries as a reference point. As a group, low-income countries could be described as having a type II structure in 1960 and a type VI structure in 2000, like India. Over the 40-year period from 1960 to 2000, most of the gains from the decline in agriculture (48%→24%) accrued to industry (16%→32%) and services gained (36%→ 44%) as well. This pattern of structural change is broadly consistent with the secular view, wherein the decline in agriculture is mostly taken up by industry.

Table 4.5 presents data for all middle-income countries. In aggregate terms, middle-income countries could be described as having a type VI structure in 1960 and 2000. Over the 40-year period from 1960 to 2000, most of the gains from the decline in agriculture (24%→9%) accrued to services (43%→55%); while industry also gained (33%→36%) but marginally so.

Table 4.6 presents data for South Asia, where most countries have low-income economies.[5] In aggregate terms, South Asia had a type II structure in 1960 and a type VI structure in 2000. Between 1960 and 2000, most of the gains from the decline of agriculture (46%→25%) accrued to services (37%→49%); and industry also gained well (18%→26%). This pattern is very similar to the Indian experience and the South Asia data is dominated by India. South Asia is also different from other countries in that agriculture is still important for these countries, accounting for 25 percent of value added in 2000.

Table 4.7 presents data for the world as a reference. On an aggregate basis, the global economy had a type VI economic structure in 1972 and 1999, like middle-income countries. Between 1972 and 1999, both agriculture (10%→5%) and industry (40%→31%) experienced relative declines, captured solely by services (50%→64%). This relatively high share of services at the global level reflects the dominance of the data by middle and high-income countries.[6]

In terms of structural characteristics at the beginning and end of the time periods, the Indian experience is similar to that of low-income and South Asian countries. However, in terms of the nature of the structural change itself – wherein the gains from the decline of agriculture have accrued

Table 4.4 Structural change in low-income economies: 1960–2000 (%)

Low-income countries	1960	1961	1962	1963	1964	1965	1966	1967	1968	1969	Av.
Agriculture, value added (% of GDP)	48	46	48	48	48	47	45	47	45	45	47
Industry, value added (% of GDP)	16	17	16	17	18	17	17	17	18	19	17
Manufacturing, value added (% of GDP)	11	12	12	11	11	11	11	11	11	12	11
Services, etc., value added (% of GDP)	36	37	36	36	35	36	38	37	37	36	36

Low-income countries	1970	1971	1972	1973	1974	1975	1976	1977	1978	1979	Av.
Agriculture, value added (% of GDP)	44	42	41	42	39	37	36	37	36	34	39
Industry, value added (% of GDP)	19	20	21	22	25	25	26	25	26	27	24
Manufacturing, value added (% of GDP)	12	12	12	12	13	13	13	13	14	14	13
Services, etc., value added (% of GDP)	37	38	37	36	36	38	39	38	38	38	38

Low-income countries	1980	1981	1982	1983	1984	1985	1986	1987	1988	1989	Av.
Agriculture, value added (% of GDP)	34	33	32	33	31	31	31	30	30	29	31
Industry, value added (% of GDP)	29	28	28	28	28	27	27	29	30	30	28
Manufacturing, value added (% of GDP)	14	14	14	14	15	15	15	16	16	18	15
Services, etc., value added (% of GDP)	38	39	40	39	41	42	43	41	40	41	40

Low-income countries	1990	1991	1992	1993	1994	1995	1996	1997	1998	1999	2000	Av.
Agriculture, value added (% of GDP)	29	28	28	28	27	26	26	26	26	26	24	27
Industry, value added (% of GDP)	30	28	31	30	31	31	31	31	30	30	32	31
Manufacturing, value added (% of GDP)	18	17	18	18	19	19	19	18	18	18	18	18
Services, etc., value added (% of GDP)	41	44	41	42	42	42	43	43	43	44	44	43

Source: World Development Indicators (World Bank, 2002).

Table 4.5   Structural change in middle-income economies: 1960–2000 (%)

Middle-income countries

	1965	1966	1967	1968	1969	Av.
Agriculture, value added (% of GDP)	24	22	22	23	21	23
Industry, value added (% of GDP)	33	35	34	34	35	34
Manufacturing, value added (% of GDP)	23	24	23	23	24	
Services, etc., value added (% of GDP)	43	43	44	44	44	43

Middle-income countries

	1970	1971	1972	1973	1974	1975	1976	1977	1978	1979	Av.
Agriculture, value added (% of GDP)	20	20	20	20	20	19	19	18	17	17	18
Industry, value added (% of GDP)	36	37	37	38	39	40	40	40	40	41	40
Manufacturing, value added (% of GDP)	25	25	26	26	26	26	27	27	27	27	27
Services, etc., value added (% of GDP)	43	43	43	42	41	41	41	41	43	42	42

Middle-income countries

	1980	1981	1982	1983	1984	1985	1986	1987	1988	1989	Av.
Agriculture, value added (% of GDP)	16	16	16	16	16	15	15	14	14	14	14
Industry, value added (% of GDP)	42	41	41	41	41	40	40	41	40	41	40
Manufacturing, value added (% of GDP)	27	27	27	27	27	27	27	27	27	27	27
Services, etc., value added (% of GDP)	42	43	43	43	43	45	45	45	46	46	45

Middle-income countries

	1990	1991	1992	1993	1994	1995	1996	1997	1998	1999	2000	Av.
Agriculture, value added (% of GDP)	13	12	11	11	11	11	11	10	10	10	9	10
Industry, value added (% of GDP)	39	38	38	39	39	38	37	36	36	35	36	36
Manufacturing, value added (% of GDP)	–	25	24	24	24	24	24	24	23	24	25	24
Services, etc., value added (% of GDP)	47	49	50	50	50	51	52	53	54	55	54	54

Source: World Development Indicators (World Bank, 2002).

Table 4.6   Structural change in South Asia economies: 1960–2000 (%)

South Asia	1960	1961	1962	1963	1964	1965	1966	1967	1968	1969	Av.
Agriculture, value added (% of GDP)	46	45	43	44	45	44	44	47	46	45	45
Industry, value added (% of GDP)	18	18	19	19	19	19	19	18	18	19	19
Manufacturing, value added (% of GDP)	13	13	14	14	13	14	13	12	12	13	13
Services, etc., value added (% of GDP)	37	37	38	37	36	37	37	36	36	35	36

South Asia	1970	1971	1972	1973	1974	1975	1976	1977	1978	1979	Av.
Agriculture, value added (% of GDP)	45	43	44	46	43	41	39	40	39	37	42
Industry, value added (% of GDP)	20	21	20	20	21	22	23	23	23	24	22
Manufacturing, value added (% of GDP)	14	14	14	14	15	15	15	15	16	17	15
Services, etc., value added (% of GDP)	35	36	36	34	36	37	38	37	38	39	37

South Asia	1980	1981	1982	1983	1984	1985	1986	1987	1988	1989	Av.
Agriculture, value added (% of GDP)	38	37	35	36	34	33	32	31	32	31	34
Industry, value added (% of GDP)	24	24	25	25	25	25	25	25	25	26	25
Manufacturing, value added (% of GDP)	16	16	16	16	16	16	16	16	16	16	16
Services, etc., value added (% of GDP)	38	39	40	39	41	42	43	43	43	43	41

South Asia	1990	1991	1992	1993	1994	1995	1996	1997	1998	1999	2000	Av.
Agriculture, value added (% of GDP)	31	31	30	30	29	28	28	28	27	26	25	28
Industry, value added (% of GDP)	27	26	26	26	26	27	26	26	26	26	26	26
Manufacturing, value added (% of GDP)	17	16	16	16	17	17	17	16	16	15	16	16
Services, etc., value added (% of GDP)	43	43	44	44	44	45	45	46	47	48	49	46

Source: World Development Indicators (World Bank, 2002).

Table 4.7 Structural changes in the world economy: 1972–1999

World

	1972	1973	1974	1975	1976	1977	1978	1979	Av.
Agriculture, value added (% of GDP)	10	11	10	10	10	9	9	8	10
Industry, value added (% of GDP)	40	40	40	39	40	39	39	39	40
Manufacturing, value added (% of GDP)	–	–	–	–	–	–	–	–	
Services, etc., value added (% of GDP)	50	49	49	51	51	51	52	52	51

World

	1980	1981	1982	1983	1984	1985	1986	1987	1988	1989	Av.
Agriculture, value added (% of GDP)	8	8	8	8	8	7	7	7	7	7	7
Industry, value added (% of GDP)	40	39	38	38	38	38	37	37	37	37	38
Manufacturing, value added (% of GDP)	–	–	–	–	–	–	–	–	–	–	
Services, etc., value added (% of GDP)	52	53	54	54	54	55	56	56	56	56	55

World

	1990	1991	1992	1993	1994	1995	1996	1997	1998	1999	Av.
Agriculture, value added (% of GDP)	7	6	6	6	6	6	6	5	5	5	6
Industry, value added (% of GDP)	36	36	35	34	34	33	33	32	32	31	34
Manufacturing, value added (% of GDP)	–	–	–	–	–	22	22	22	22	–	22
Services, etc., value added (% of GDP)	57	58	59	60	61	61	62	62	63	64	61

Middle-income countries

	1990	1991	1992	1993	1994	1995	1996	1997	1998	1999	2000	Av.
Agriculture, value added (% of GDP)	13	12	11	11	11	11	11	10	10	10	9	10
Industry, value added (% of GDP)	39	38	38	39	39	38	37	36	36	35	36	36
Manufacturing, value added (% of GDP)	–	25	24	24	24	24	24	24	23	24	25	24
Services, etc., value added (% of GDP)	47	49	50	50	50	51	52	53	54	55	55	54

Source: World Development Indicators (World Bank, 2003).

mainly to services – the Indian experience is closer to that of middle-income countries and the world.

Nature of the Service Economy: India versus Others

As noted above, in India as well other developing economies – with the exception of China – services became more important than industry, even at the beginning of the study period in 1960. The nature of the service economy in India and other countries is examined below. More specifically, the investigation focused on whether there are fundamental differences between DCs and LDCs with regard to the nature of their service economies, by looking at the Indian and the US experience.

Tables 4.8 and 4.9, based on the United Nations (UN) national accounts database, present empirical evidence on the nature of the service economy in India and the USA. Due to data limitations, further disaggregation of International Standard Industrial Classification (ISIC) industry categories is not possible. Within the context of the Indian IT industry, the paucity of data at more disaggregated levels limits to some extent our ability to fully understand the implications of the dynamics of the computer (ISIC code 72[7]) industry for the larger Indian economy.

Table 4.8 shows the sectoral share data and its components for India in 1993 and 1998. Consistent with the previous evidence, services has grown at the expense of agriculture. Within services, the top three sub-sectors in 1998 (and 1993) are: (i) wholesale and retail trade; repairs; hotels and restaurants (31 percent); (ii) financial intermediation; real estate and business services (26 percent); and (iii) transport, storage and communication (16 percent). It is interesting to note that the IT industry is part of (ii), which made up a little more than a quarter of the value added in services.

For comparative purposes, Table 4.9 shows the results for the USA. Between 1993 and 1996, there was a minor decline in services (73%→70%) that was captured by industry (26%→28%). Within services, the top three sub-sectors for 1996 are: (i) financial intermediation; real estate and business services (37 percent); (ii) transport, storage and communication (24 percent); and (iii) public administration and defense; compulsory social security (15 percent).

A comparison of the data for India and the USA suggests: (i) over the years, Indian agriculture has declined in importance and services have become a leading sector of the economy. However, it is still a major contributor to economic activity in India, accounting for 26 percent of the value added in 1998 compared to only 2 percent for the US economy in 1996. In contrast, services is the dominant sector in the US economy, accounting for 70 percent of value added in 1996; (ii) sectors G, H and I – wholesale and retail trade; repairs; hotels and restaurants; transport. Storage and communication are more important for India than the USA; (iii) sectors J and K – financial intermediation; real estate and business services are more important for the USA than India. IT industry is a sub-sector of this J and K sector.

Table 4.8   Value added by Indian industries (at constant 1993 prices, tens of millions of Indian rupees)

	1993	%	1998	%
Gross value added	799,957	100%	1,109,990	100%
A, B. Agriculture and	244,157	31%	292,653	26%
industry	217,178	27%	310,388	28%
C. Mining and quarrying	20,282		25,421	
D. Manufacturing	135,909		201,701	
E. Electricity, gas and water				
supply	19,864		28,716	
F. Construction	41,123		54,550	
services	338,622	42%	506,949	46%
Composition of services	338,622	100%	506,949	100%
G, H. Wholesale and retail trade;				
repairs; hotels and restaurants	102,128	30%	156,151	31%
I. Transport, storage and				
communication	52,389	15%	80,367	16%
J, K. Financial intermediation;				
real estate and business services	90,349	27%	131,016	26%
L. Public administration and				
defense; compulsory social security	43,636	13%	63,072	12%
M, N, O. Education; health and				
social work; other community,				
social and personal services	50,122	15%	76,341	15%
P. Private households with				
employed persons	N/A		N/A	

Source: National Accounts Statistics, Main Aggregates and Detailed Tables, United Nations (1998).

Overall, these results suggest that as countries move up the income scale, the relative importance of intermediation, real estate and business services increases. Interestingly, the IT industry belongs to this sub-sector.

Table 4.9   Value added by US industries (at constant 1992 prices, tens of millions of US dollars)

	1993	%	1996	%
Gross value added	631,840	100%	715,470	100%
A, B. Agriculture and	10,410	2%	11,420	2%
industry	162,520	26%	202,660	28%
C. Mining and quarrying	9,760		10,310	
D. Manufacturing	111,070		145,330	
E. Electricity gas and water supply	17,960		20,280	
F. Construction	23,730		26,740	
Services	458,910	73%	501,390	70%
Composition of services	458,910	100%	501,390	100%
G, H. Wholesale and retail trade;				
repairs; hotels and restaurants	102,450	22%	119,570	24%
I. Transport, storage and				
communication	37,570	8%	40,340	8%
J, K. Financial intermediation;				
real estate and business services	168,040	37%	185,290	37%
L. Public administration and defense;				
compulsory social security	72,850	16%	73,120	15%
M, N, O. Education; health and				
social work; other community,				
social and personal services	68,640	15%	71,650	14%
P. Private households with employed				
persons	N/A		N/A	

Source: National Accounts Statistics, Main Aggregates and Detailed Tables, United Nations, (1998).

III   INDIAN IT SECTOR

By now, there has been significant research on India's IT industry in general and software exports in particular (Chakraborty and Jayachandran (2001); Joseph and Harilal (2001); Arora and Athreye (2001). These studies have emphasized a need : (i) for a structural transformation of India's IT export sector, in terms of upward movement in the software value chain; (ii) to reduce the current dependence on the US market that accounts for over 60 percent of India's export earnings; and (iii) to broaden the product variety, since India's software exports are skewed towards custom software work and programming services (currently, development and sale of prepackaged software are a negligible share of software exports). They contend that the software industry has not become the leading sector in India's economic growth, due in part to its poor linkages with the rest of the economy. In turn, this poor linkage is a consequence of the 'service' rather than 'product' orientation of the industry and its external rather than inward direction.

Leapfrogging Possibilities

On the basis of the dynamism shown by the Indian IT industry in general and the software sector in particular, there has been some speculation as to whether India is currently in a position to leapfrog some of the stages of economic development experienced by the developed countries that now exist.

As noted by Panagariya (2000), while virtually all countries stand to gain from the opportunities offered by the Internet, developing countries may gain more than developed countries. Developing countries are far behind in terms of IT infrastructure. Given the cost savings offered by Internet technology and the relative ease with which it can be provided, they can now leapfrog, skipping several stages of technological development, which the developed countries had to go through. However, many developing countries are currently constrained in benefiting from e-commerce, due to the poor state of their telecommunications infrastructure.

Likewise, Das (2001) suggests that India, with its vast intellectual capital – two million low-cost English-speaking graduates each year – is in an excellent position to provide 'knowledge workers' to the global economy and to benefit from the knowledge revolution. With competitive advantages in agriculture and the new knowledge economy, it may be right for India to skip much of the industrial revolution. Das (2002) went one step further in arguing that the export of software and IT services are to India today what textile exports were to Britain in the early 19th century,

In contrast, Miller (2000) is of the view that it is still premature to determine whether or not the Internet will become a 'leapfrogging' technology for India, enabling it to radically improve economic growth. The use of the Internet in India is not yet widespread either by consumers or businesses. Consumer use has been constrained by the relatively low number of PCs, unreliable telecommunications and electric power infrastructure, and a financial system that has not encouraged the use of consumer credit to support commercial transactions. While there is more progress in the corporate use of the Internet, infrastructural inadequacies also exist there.

IV CONCLUSIONS

Our data set of LDCs that begins in 1960 and ends in 2000 does not capture the whole spectrum of structural change where the focus of economic activity moves from agriculture to industry to services. However, the coverage is sufficient to handle more than a cursory assessment.

Over the 40-year period, there is a steady convergence of economic structures to a situation where services become the leading sector, followed by industry and agriculture. What seems to distinguish countries is the speed of convergence. For instance, middle-income countries already had this economic structure in 1960. In contrast, most developing countries progressed to this structure, only towards the end of the study period in 2000.

In the case of India, most of the gains from the decline of agriculture from 1960 to 2000 have accrued to services, with the rest going to industry. To the extent that industry in India never became a dominant sector, following the decline of agriculture, as in China, structural change in India has been different from the classic pattern. Also, India is yet to experience the 'deindustrialization' phase that developed countries went through from the 1950s to the 1980s, where the decline of the industry sector is absorbed by the service sector so that it could become a truly dominant sector. Differences in GDP composition may be a key explanation for India lagging behind China.

While the pattern of structural change observed in India is similar to the experience of other South Asian and middle-income countries, it is at variance with the experience of the low-income economies that follow the classic pattern of structural change, as described and documented by Kuznets (1965) and others.

In the absence of more disaggregated data, our analysis of the nature of the service economy in India and the USA (based on UN data on national accounts) did not reveal significant differences. In turn, this has complicated the depth of comparative assessment of the quality of structural change in India, in relation to other countries.

The presence of numerous infrastructural constraints may prevent the Internet from becoming a leapfrogging technology. However the study suggests the need for generating more data to better tests and/or establish linkages between growth of the IT and service sectors. More comparative structured research is needed with China and other LDCs to further test structured change hypothesis there and to document any patterns of best practices or lessons learned from the change processes.

Future Research Questions

It will be interesting to explore the experiences of China and other LDCs with dominant industrial sectors so that other countries can replicate the lessons learned.

The study also suggests the need for generating more data to establish the linkages between growth of the IT industry and the services sector.

APPENDIX: A FRAMEWORK FOR ANALYZING STRUCTURAL CHANGE

The framework in Table 4.1 can be used for describing the changes in economic structures over time due to GDP growth.[8]

Initial State I

Type I→II
While agriculture remains the leading sector, services become more important than industry due to its faster growth rate. This is usually found in LDCs with slow industrial growth rates.

Type I→III
Industry becomes the leading sector and services become more important than agriculture due to their faster growth rates. This is usually found in LDCs with rapid industrial and service growth rates.

Type I→IV
Industry becomes the leading sector and agriculture continues to remain more important than services due to its faster growth rate. This is usually found in LDCs with rapid industrial and agricultural growth rates.

Type I→V
Services become the leading sector and agriculture continues to remain more important than industry due to its faster growth rate. This is usually found in LDCs with rapid service and agricultural growth rates.

Type I→VI
Services become the leading sector and industry becomes more important than agriculture due to its faster growth rate. This is usually found in DCs with rapid service and industrial growth rates.

Initial State II

Type II→I
While agriculture remains the leading sector, industry becomes more important than services due to its faster growth rate. This is usually found in LDCs with slow service growth rates.

Type II→III
Industry becomes the leading sector and services become more important than agriculture due to its faster growth rate. This is usually found in LDCs with rapid industrial and services growth rates.

Type II→IV
Industry becomes the leading sector and agriculture continues to remain more important than services due to its faster growth rates. This is usually found in LDCs with rapid industrial and agriculture growth rates.

Type II→V
Services become the leading sector and agriculture, more important than industry, due to its faster growth rate. This is usually found in LDCs with rapid service and agricultural growth rates.

Type II→VI
Services become the leading sector and industry, more important than agriculture, due to its faster growth rate. This is usually found in LDCs with rapid service and industrial growth rates.

Initial State III

Type III→IV
While industry remains the leading sector, agriculture becomes more important than services due to its faster growth rate. This is usually found in LDCs with slow service growth rates.

Type III→V
Services become the leading sector and agriculture, more important than industry, due to its faster growth rate. This is usually found in LDCs with rapid service and agricultural growth rates.

Type III→VI
Services become the leading sector and industry, more important than agriculture, due to its faster growth rate. This is usually found in DCs with rapid service and industrial growth rates.

Initial State IV

Type IV→III
While industry remains the leading sector, agriculture becomes more important than services due to its faster growth rate. This is usually found in LDCs with slow service growth rates.

Type IV→V
Services become the leading sector and agriculture, more important than industry, due to its faster growth rate. This is usually found in LDCs with rapid service and agricultural growth rates.

Type IV→VI
Services become the leading sector and industry, more important than agriculture, due to its faster growth rate. This is usually found in DCs with rapid service and industrial growth rates.

Initial State V

Type V→VI
While services remain the leading sector, industry becomes more important than agriculture due to its faster growth rate. This is usually found in LDCs with slow agricultural growth rates.

Initial State VI

Type VI→V
While services remain the leading sector, agriculture becomes more important than industry due to its faster growth rate. This is usually found in LDCs with slow industry growth rates.

Type III→I, III→II, IV→1, IV→II, V→I, V→II, V→III and V→IV are unusual cases, since they represent reversals from the usual agriculture–industry–services transformation.

Type I→I, II→II, III→III, IV→IV, V→V, VI→VI; in all cases, there is no significant structural change, as the different sectors grow at similar rates.

NOTES

* The views expressed in this chapter are those of the author and should not be attributed to the World Bank.
1. Within the context of the developed countries, the relative decline of the secondary/industry sector also has been characterized as deindustrialization (Feinstein, 1999).

2. Data shown later supports this hypothesis.
3. China is often referred to as the hub of global manufacturing in current writings. The data here suggests that the dominance of industry in the Chinese economy goes back a long way.
4. Panagariya (2002) recommends the following measures for stimulating industry growth: (i) bring all tariffs down to 10 percent or less; (ii) abolish the small-scale industries reservation; (iii) institute and exit policy and bankruptcy laws; and (iv) privatize all public sector undertakings.
5. South Asia consists of eight countries: Afghanistan, Bangladesh, Bhutan, India, Maldives, Nepal, Pakistan and Sri Lanka. Of these, only two – Maldives and Sri Lanka – are middle-income countries. The other six are low-income countries.
6. We do not have any data for high-income economies. It is also interesting to note that decline of both agriculture and industry found for the world is indicative of the 'deindustrialization' that is taking place in middle and high-income countries.
7. ISIC has three levels of disaggregation: category, division and group. The computer industry belongs to category 'K' – Real estate, renting and business activities; division '72' – Computer and related activities; and groups '721' – Hardware consultancy, '722' – Software consultancy and supply, '723' – Data processing, '724' – Data base activities, '725' – Maintenance and repair of office, accounting and computing machinery, and '729' – other computer-related activities.
8. The analysis here is based on the assumption of positive economic growth. The conclusions are valid even if economic growth is negative.

REFERENCES

Ansari, Mohammed I. (1995), 'Explaining the service sector growth: an empirical study of India, Pakistan, and Sri Lanka', *Journal of Asian Economics*, **6** (2), 233–46.

Arora, Ashes and Suma Athreye (2001), 'The software industry and India's economic development', WIDER discussion paper no 2001/20.

Bhattacharya, B.B. and Arup Mitra (1990), 'Excess growth of tertiary sector in Indian economy – issues and implications', *Economic and Political Weekly*, November 3, 2445–50.

Bhattacharya, B.B. and Arup Mitra (1990), 'Excess growth of the tertiary sector', *Economic and Political Weekly*, June 1, 1423–24.

Chakraborty, Chandana and C. Jayachandran (2001), 'Software sector: trends and constraints', *Economic and Political Weekly*, August 25, 3255–61.

Chenery, Hollis (1969), 'Economic growth and structural change', Center for International Affairs, Harvard University, Cambridge, MA.

Corden, Max and Peter Neary (1982), 'Booming sector and de-industrialization in a small open economy', *The Economic Journal*, **92**, 825–48.

Cornwall, John (1977), *Modern Capitalism: Its Growth and Transformation*, London: Martin Robinson.

Das, Gurcharan (2001), 'India – skipping the industrial revolution' (adapted from 'India Unbound'), *The Globalize*.

Das, Gurcharan (2002), 'Playing to win', *Times of India*, January 13.

Feinstein, Charles (1999), 'Structural change in the developed countries during the 20th century', *Oxford Review of Economics and Policy*, **15** (4), 35–55.

Ghosh B.N. (1991), 'Development of tertiary sector', *Economic and Political Weekly*, February, 881–3.

Government of India (2002), *Economic Survey*, Ministry of Finance.

Joseph K.J. and K.N. Harilal (2001), 'Structure and growth of India's IT exports – implications of an export-oriented growth strategy', *Economic and Political Weekly*, August 25, 3263–70.

Kasper, Wolfgang (1986), 'Structural change for economic growth', *Economic Affairs (U.K.)*, **6**, 8–13.

Kuznets, Simon (1965), *Economic Growth and Structure: Selected Essays,* New York: Norton.

Miller, Robert R. (2000), 'Leapfrogging? India's information technology industry and the Internet', International Finance Corporation (World Bank) discussion paper no 2, Washington, DC, USA.

Panagariya, Arvind (2000), 'E-commerce, WTO and developing countries', *World Economy*, **23** (8), 959–78.

Panagariya, Arvind (2002), 'Why we lag behind China', *Economic Times*, May 22.

Singh, Ajit (1977), 'U.K. industry and the world economy: a case of de-industrializaton?', *Cambridge Journal of Economics*, 1, 113–17.

Syrquin, Moshe and Holis Chenery (1989), 'Three decades of industrialization', *World Bank Economic Review*, **3** (2), 145–81.

Thirlwall, Tony (1978), 'The UK's economic problems: a balance of payments constraint?', *National Westminster Bank Quarterly Review*, February, 24–32.

United Nations (1998), *National Account Statistics*, New York: UN.

World Bank (2002), *World Development Indicators*, Washington, DC: World Bank.

World Bank (2003), *World Development Indicators*, Washington, DC: World Bank.

5.   An analysis of factors responsible for the Indian information technology sector growth: signaling quality

Aparna Sawhney

INTRODUCTION

The emergence of the Indian information technology (IT) industry in the global economy in the 1990s has inspired academicians, industry analysts and policy makers alike, as one of the most amazing achievements of a developing country (Heeks and Nicholson, 2002; Krishna et al., 2000; Heeks, 1996; Bajpai and Shastri, 1998; Moitra, 2001). The growth of the IT industry, one of the fastest growing industries in the country, has been driven by the export of software services. The export revenue from software services consistently grew at more than 50 percent per year during 1995–2001, and the earnings constitute the bulk of India's overall invisible receipts. Indeed, the software industry's spectacular growth has encouraged other industrializing countries in Asia to replicate the Indian Silicon Valley phenomenon in a bid to accelerate their development process.

The software industry is still small compared to other traditional industries, like textiles, in India and accounts for approximately 2 percent of the country's gross domestic product (GDP). However, given its current growth rate, it could account for over 7 percent of GDP by year 2008 (NASSCOM–McKinsey, 2002). The software services industry is a mature sector in India (compared to other developing countries), and consists of some of the largest software services exporting firms. While initially firms largely provided on-site services, currently offshore delivery is the preferred business model, especially since global business outsourcing has been increasing. The National Association of Software and Service Companies (NASSCOM) of India estimates that one in every four global giants outsources their software requirements to Indian companies. The software industry has largely three segments: IT services; product and technology services; and IT-enabled services. The IT services have constituted the largest segment of the Indian industry (about 70 percent of total export revenue in 2001–02). Within IT services, on-site services had been the most important component (with Indian professionals providing services on customer site abroad), but growth in this mode of supply has been overtaken by offshore services. The offshore services exports registered a growth of 64 percent between 2001 and 2002, while the on-site IT services grew by barely 7 percent during the same period (NASSCOM, 2002). This trend is likely to continue especially with increasing restrictions on labor movement in the USA and Europe.

The increase in offshore services represents a remarkable achievement that Indian software companies have been successful in by establishing an image of quality and reliability in the world market. By the same token, however, offshore service provision has increased the onus on Indian firms to maintain this reputation. This chapter provides an analysis of the factors supporting the growth of the Indian software services industry, focusing on firm-level strategies[1] that helped in establishing an image of reliability and quality.

In any service sector, it is important for firms to establish trust and reliability with clients to retain and expand business. Towards achieving this goal, the Indian firms have aggressively pursued international quality certifications, particularly SEI CMM,[2] and more recently CMMi,[3] PCMM,[4] and Six Sigma quality assurance. Indeed, more than half the world's SEI CMM level 5 and CMMi certified firms are located in India. These initiatives illustrate the efforts by Indian firms to signal quality in the global market, especially in the wake of competition from new entrants in other developing countries, and the increase in outsourcing.

The following sections describe the growth of the software services export industry in India, the different factors that supported this development, and analyze the Indian software service providers' pursuit of quality parameters and nurturing client relationship in a bid to inculcate trust and signal reliability of services.

THE SOFTWARE SERVICES EXPORT INDUSTRY IN INDIA

India is considered to be one of the first-tier major software exporting countries (the other two being Ireland and Israel; Heeks and Nicholson, 2002), and the industry made a modest beginning in the mid-1970s. In the 1980s the industry was still obscure in the global market, and gained significance only in the 1990s. Most Indian firms began with the maintenance of legacy systems and moved to lower-end software development services including low-level design and coding of software components (Arora and Asundi, 1999). Firms established in the late 1990s, however, entered into the niche markets for specialized services and product development.

The total software exports from India have increased from less than $5 million in 1980 to more than $9.6 billion in 2002–03. In particular during 1995–2001, the annual growth rate in export earnings was more than 50 percent. In 2001–02 the growth rate plummeted, mainly due to the slowdown in the USA, which is the single largest importer of Indian software exports. The following year, in 2002–03, the exports picked up and the growth rate rose to 27 percent. Table 5.1 gives the value of software exports for the last seven years 1995–96 to 2001–02, and the corresponding annual growth rates.

Table 5.1 Indian software exports growth, 1995–2003

Year	Export value (US $million)	Year-on-year annual growth (%)
1995–96	747	53
1996–97	1,099	47
1997–98	1,759	60
1998–99	2,626	49
1999–2000	4,015	53
2000–01	6,341	57
2001–02	7,174	13
2002–03	9,600	27

Source: RBI Annual Report (various years).

The growth of the Indian software service industry has been concentrated in certain cities or cyber cities, like Bangalore, Mumbai, Delhi and Hyderabad. The different cities or growth centers have specialized in different service segments, including IT software services or IT-enabled services, for the global market.

The export destination market is also marked by geographical concentration. While the customer base of the export services consists of more than 255 Fortune 500 companies across the world, the USA alone accounts for more than half the total exports by value, followed by Europe. In 2001–02, the Americas (the USA, Canada and Latin America) accounted for 63 percent, Europe for 26 percent, Japan for 4 percent, and the rest of the world for 7 percent of the total Indian software exports (NASSCOM, 2002). Not surprisingly, the performance of the Indian software service industry is largely determined by the USA, and the slowdown in the US economy was reflected in the sharp fall in the growth rate of the Indian exports during 2001–02.

Currently the export competition from other developing countries like China, Russia and the Philippines is intense. Indian firms are thus focusing on value-added higher-end services (the larger firms are moving away from the low-value services) to boost the export growth rate. In particular, firms are expanding the IT-enabled services sector, which is now considered to be a high-growth sector (NASSCOM–McKinsey, 2002).

The change in the pattern of software service exports reflects the maturing of the Indian industry. While the firms had begun with an emphasis on body shopping, where movement of workers overseas to the client site had been important, now firms specialize in offshore services. For instance, in 1991–92 on-site services accounted for 95 percent of the total software exports by value, and offshore services for barely 5 percent. By 2001–02, the shares of on-site and off-site services in total software exports (by value) were about 50 percent each (NASSCOM, 2002). Firms are now mature in offshore delivery of services, especially in handling large project implementation. Recently, Indian companies have also made a modest headway in segments such as packaged software support and installation, product development and design services and embedded software solutions. More importantly the software industry has a reputation of high quality and reliability through a track record of on-time delivery.

FACTORS SUPPORTING THE GROWTH OF THE INDIAN SOFTWARE INDUSTRY

The Indian software export industry has had the first-mover advantage in the global market, and the timing of the central government's liberalization policy has been advantageous. India's liberalization process began in the late 1980s, but more earnestly in 1991. The intellectual capital in the IT industry was waiting to be tapped at competitive costs, and the software service industry's take-off began in 1991–92. Several strong enabling factors helped in the take-off of this sector, and are discussed in this section.

The most important factor supporting the development of the software service industry has been the availability of low-cost technically skilled labor. The second factor has been a large pool of English-speaking labor, and the time zone that made IT services from India convenient (in off-shore service provision). Third, policies adopted and incentives provided by the central and some state governments to encourage the industry's development and exports (for example, development of software technology parks to boost the sector's growth) also played an important role. Indeed the concurrence of all these factors, coupled with the foresight of Indian entrepreneurs, explains the astounding journey that this industry has witnessed in the global market.

Some of these enabling factors can be found in other developing countries too and are not unique to India, suggesting that other developing countries have the same potential advantages to replicate the Indian success story, especially with regard to the availability of cheap, skilled labor.

In India, however, apart from the advantage of relatively cheap skilled English-speaking labor, the quality and reputation of reliability established by the Indian software industry has been an important aspect. The latter attributes have afforded an advantage that is quite unique to India and have helped to sustain the growth of the software services export industry in India in the last few years in the face of competition from other developing countries like China and the Philippines. To signal the quality and reliability of the IT services, export firms have aggressively pursued international quality SEI CMM and more recently CMMi (CMM integrated), certified quality analyst and Six Sigma quality assurance. The different factors supporting the growth of the industry are discussed briefly below.

Low-cost Technically Skilled Labor

The availability of relatively cheap software programmers, technicians and engineers in India is perhaps the most important factor supporting the growth of the IT export industry. In 2002, according to NASSCOM, the average annual cost per employee in India was about US$5,800 which was supported by high-quality engineers and a 10-year track record in project management skills. This cost advantage, however, is not unique to India, and other developing countries like China and Philippines offer serious competition in this regard. Other close competitors to India in terms of labor costs are Russia and the Czech Republic, with per employee costs of US$6,000 and $6,400, respectively.

The pool of employees trained at the diploma, undergraduate and post-graduate level come from more than 200 universities (over 900 colleges). In the year 2000, there were about 130000 such trained people at the degree/diploma level, including those from several IITs (Indian Institute of Technology), graduates from polytechnics and other colleges.

Early Bird Advantage

Perhaps the most significant aspect of the growth of the Indian software service export industry is its timing. The emergence of the Indian software enterprises in the 1980s seems to the biggest advantage to India. At the time, the shortage of skilled programmers and IT professionals had just begun to emerge, especially in the USA. The early bird advantage is especially important in view of the increasing restrictions on outsourcing of projects in developed countries like the USA. For the greater part of the 1990s, the Indian software service providers found it reasonably easy to provide on-site services for clients in these countries. Currently, however, a stringency in labor laws and visa restrictions for foreign service providers in the industrialized countries has limited the scope of this kind of work. This makes off-site work and quality assurance of long-distance provision of service all the more important.

The low-capital investment required in establishing software services firms also played a role in attracting a large number of entrepreneurs. Moreover, the on-site services provided abroad by the domestic firms helped a large number of start-up companies to fund long-term projects (Krishna et al., 2000). This path of growth of the Indian firms is somewhat unique, since the scope of initial growth through onsite-service provision is now constrained.

Established Relationships

In a service-oriented business, a close relationship with clients is a valuable asset for the service-providing firms, both to ensure future contracts as well as to establish a reputation of reliability. In this regard, the Indian firms have maintained a long-term strategic relationship with their clients in the USA and Europe. Indeed, the majority of the export contracts are with old customers. A firm survey indicated that over 93 percent of the most important export contracts of Indian software service exporters involved a company that the firm knew earlier (Arora et al., 2001).

Language Skills

The relatively good English language skills of Indian computer programmers have played an important role, besides their intellectual skills, in the growth of the Indian software services exports industry. Indians continue to have the language advantage since English is the predominant mode of instruction in the country, compared to other developing countries, which are now emerging as the second-tier exporters including Russia, China and the Philippines.

Cultural Factors

Education is considered important among Indians and in particular the education system in the country emphasizes mathematics and science.

This has resulted in producing a large number of science and engineering graduates every year in the country. Moreover, activities requiring mental skills are regarded as more respectable among Indians as opposed to those requiring physical labor. The software service industry certainly offered the preferred careers to Indians requiring language and logical skills. Analysts have called this the 'natural propensity of Indians to succeed' in professions demanding mental abilities (Krishna et al., 2000).

Government Support

The liberalization policy undertaken by the Indian government since the mid-1980s, and more prominently beginning in 1991, has worked well for the Indian IT sector since the domestic intellectual capital was waiting to be tapped at a competitive cost in the world market. The initial growth of the Indian software export industry, however, occurred largely without any government aid, and it was only later in the 1990s when the industry began to make strides in the international market that the government began to support the development through tax benefits and software export park development. Some analysts have termed the role of the government in the growth of software industry as a mixture of 'benign neglect and active encouragement' (Arora et al., 2001). While the government initially did not push the software industry to grow, it did simplify the administrative processes for obtaining the numerous clearances and permits for operating a software export firm. In particular, in 1990, the Ministry of Communications and Information Technology formulated the scheme of Software Technology Parks (STPs)[5] to promote and facilitate the software exports. The scheme offered fiscal incentives (tax breaks) and the STPs were provided with state-of-the-art infrastructure facilities to encourage the investment in this segment. This is important especially since infrastructure, in terms of power and communication lines, is otherwise poor in a developing country like India.

The IT Bill in 2000 provided a legal framework for the recognition of electronic contracts, prevention of computer crimes, electronic filing and documents. The government has thus provided both infrastructure and institutional support for the development of the software services export industry in India.

Access to Technology

In the decades of the 1970s and the 1980s, access to technology in India was a limiting factor in the growth of the IT industry, which is characterized by rapid technological changes. During the 1990s, the liberalization and deregulation drive in India made access to foreign technology easier and now the availability of technology is helping the development of off-site services.

Organizational Skills

The organizational structure of the Indian software services firms is considered to be innovative and adaptive to global market demands, and thus comparable to some of the best international companies (Krishna et al., 2000). This characteristic of the industry is in sharp contrast to the traditional Indian businesses, and can be attributed to the exposure that software professionals obtained through their service provision abroad. In other words, the on-site work certainly seems to have had a positive spillover in developing a world-class organizational structure among the Indian firms.

Adapting to Global Market Trends

The Indian software firms have followed the global market trends closely to ensure that growth continues to grow. With competition increasing in the lower-end software services from other developing countries, the larger firms are now moving up the value-ladder. Although the industry as a whole still largely caters for the lower end of the services, the bigger Indian players including Infosys, Tata Consultancy Services, Satyam and Wipro, have made conscious efforts to get away from this low-end and low-value service provider image and move towards the higher-end services. This is especially pronounced in the case of Infosys (the second largest Indian computer services firm), which has become rather selective in terms of both clients and type of work.

Entrepreneurial Dynamism

The Indian software firms are dynamic with a strong entrepreneurial capacity to distinguish themselves in the world market. Entrepreneurial dynamism explains the industry's initial growth without any government aid, and the continued relentless drive signals high-quality standards in the global market by acquiring certifications in the last few years. The firms began to move beyond ISO 9000 towards software industry-specific quality certifications including Software Engineering Institute Capability Maturity Model (SEI CMM), Capability Maturity Model Integration (CMMi), People Capability Maturity Model (PCMM) and so on. Of course the early bird advantage (the established image in the USA and Europe) has complemented this entrepreneurial effort to differentiate themselves from other competitors in the market.

INDUSTRY FOCUS ON QUALITY

The signaling of quality and reliability of software services has been an important strategy of the Indian firms in order to retain and expand clientele. Given that off-site work has gained significance (as opposed to on site services)[6] in the last few years, quality assurance is an essential business strategy. In order to promote the quality movement, the Indian government too has undertaken various initiatives. These initiatives have encouraged software developers to attain the certifiable quality standards for their products and services. For example, the Indian Ministry of Information Technology entered into a licensing arrangement with the Software Engineering Institute, Carnegie Mellon University, USA, in order to encourage the quality drive. As an incentive to quality certification, the Directorate General of Foreign Trade in the Ministry of Commerce provides special software licenses to eligible companies that have acquired the quality status of ISO 9000, SEI CMM Level 2 and above or equivalent certifications.

The strategy of differentiation adopted by the Indian firms is also a feature typical of a mature and competitive industry. Independent agencies like Gartner rank India significantly ahead of its competitors in terms of suitability for off-shoring IT services based on parameters like quality, depth of talent pool, cost structure, and overall process capability and quality (NASSCOM-McKinsey, 2002). The focus on quality by export firms has taken two paths: strategic customer relationship management and quality certifications.

Strategic Customer Relationship Management

Strategic customer relationship management ensures client satisfaction in terms of the quality of work provided. For instance, Satyam Computers, a well-known computer software services company in India adopted a major initiative in 1999–2000 under which the top 20 strategic customers were assigned to dedicated management teams such that top management attention was focused on increasing market shares in each of these relationships. In contrast, China was evaluated to lack 'project management skills and front end consulting skills' by McKinsey (NASSCOM-McKinsey, 2002, p. 142).

Quality Certifications

These quality certifications assure global customers that Indian firms are serious about quality benchmarking. A strong base of ISO 9000 certification existing in the country has helped the game of signaling quality by the Indian firms. More recently, however, the Indian firms have aggressively pursued SEI CMM certification, SEI CMMi and PCMM. Firms have also undertaken Six Sigma and zero-defect initiatives. By March 2003, about 51 Indian software firms had been assessed at SEI CMM level 5 (more than half the worldwide figure) and about four firms at CMMi level 5. On the other hand, by 2002 China did not have a single company above CMM level 3 (NASSCOM–McKinsey, 2002).

The Game of Signaling and Certification Strategy

The attempt by the Indian firms to differentiate themselves from competitors in other developing countries is well captured in the race for quality certification. The ISO 9000 quality certification became popular in India in the early 1990s, and the large base of ISO-certified firms helped the industry to adopt other forms of quality certifications in the latter half of the 1990s. In particular, firms chose software management specific quality certification especially those associated with the capability maturity models. Indeed, certification is perceived as such a significant measure of quality assurance among the Indian firms that when a new process or management quality certification comes into the market, they are among the first to aggressively obtain these signals of quality.

An earlier study of ISO-certified Indian software companies found that quality certification for Indian firms was important in signaling reliability to potential customers, rather than improving quality of software or profitability *per se* (Arora and Asundi 1999). At the time ISO 9001 was more popular; the study found that many firms had ISO certification alone, and some had added TickIT or CMM (typically level 3 or higher), and very few had the latter but not ISO certification. The ISO certification was used as a tool for marketing and distinguishing from others. Moreover, importers in industrialized countries often asked for certification from suppliers from developing countries like India.[7] This suggests that clients from industrialized countries consider certification as an important indicator of quality and reliability of service providers abroad in lieu of a better measure. Quality certification was thus perceived by Indian exporters as a credible signal in the global market.

A survey of software and services companies conducted by NASSCOM in March 2002 showed that 95 percent of the top 300 companies in India had already obtained or were in the process of obtaining some form of international quality standard certification. In particular, 216 of these firms had already acquired quality certifications (ISO 9000 or SEI and other certification) and 70 more were expected to be certified by the end of 2002.

Currently, the quality certification of SEI CMM signifying excellence and maturity in software project management skills is by far the most popular quality model in the world and among Indian software firms. By 2002, about 100 Indian firms had been assessed for SEI-CMM at different levels (see Table 5.2).

Table 5.2   Distribution of Indian software firms by quality assessment, *
             May 2002*

SEI quality assessment level	Number of certified companies as of May 31, 2002
SEI CMMi	3
SEI CMM level 5	42
SEI CMM level 4	22
SEI CMM level 3	24
SEI CMM level 2	3
PCMM level 5	2
PCMM level 4	1
PCMM level 3	5
PCMM level 2	4

Note: * Several companies have multiple certifications.

Source: NASSCOM (2002).

Quality certification seems to have paid off to the extent that Indian firms with quality certification at CMM level 3 or above have been found to have a higher revenue per employee than non-certified firms (Arora et al. 2001, p. 1285). The higher revenue per employee among the large certified firms also reflects the higher value-added software services provided by these firms. Thus quality certification seems to have allowed the Indian firms to take on larger projects and grow.[8]

The focus now, however, has shifted towards the knowledge environment within an organization including innovation, best practices in human resources management, business excellence and moving up the value chain. Besides SEI CMM certifications, the People-CMM and CMMi certifications are used as quality indicators in the industry. Four Indian companies, Wipro,

Infosys, EmSys and Polaris Software Lab have already obtained CMMi level 5 certifications. Not surprisingly, the Indian software firms have tried to keep ahead in this new quality certification wave too. The race to be ahead in the quality certification signaling game by the Indian firms is evident in the different forms of certification prevalent in the industry, and is summarized in Box 5.1.

BOX 5.1   INDIAN COMPANIES AS FIRST MOVERS IN GLOBAL QUALITY CERTIFICATION

The world's first ...
Company to be certified at level 4 of PCMM in August 2001: *TCS*.
Software company to be awarded CMMi level 5 (Version 1.1) in 2002. Also world's first company to be awarded PCMM level 5: *Wipro*.
Organization assessed by BVQI and certified for the new ISO 9001:2000 International Standards, under the Tick IT scheme: *Satyam Computers*.
Company to acquire SEI CMMi level 5 (Version 1.02) in 2001: *Polaris Software*.
Systems company to implement and assessed for using *all components* of the CMMi version 1.1 level 5 model in 2003: *Embedded Systems & Software* (EmSyS), business unit of Electrical & Electronics Division of L&T (Mysore facility).

Another interesting feature in the race of quality certification by the Indian firms is the multiplicity of certification by a single firm. Since there is a belief that quality certification is an important market signal, and firms pursue new certification models with ardor, they typically end up acquiring a multiplicity of quality certification (see Table 5.3).

The quality profile of the top six Indian firms in Table 5.3 shows that even large firms with more established global market reputation, including Infosys and Tata Consultancy Services, have continued to acquire quality certification. Moreover, the multiplicity of quality certifications of these firms implies that the signaling role of quality certifications is perceived by even the larger firms to be important. Since the bigger Indian players adopt this strategy, it becomes all the more pertinent for the smaller and newer firms to jump onto the quality bandwagon, since the latter lack the advantage of an established market reputation.

Table 5.3   Multiple quality certifications: profile of the top six Indian companies

Company	Revenue*	Quality certifications
1. Tata Consultancy Services	792	SEI CMM level 5; P-CMM level 4
2. Infosys Technologies	521	Tick IT; SEI CMM level 5, CMMi level 5
3. Wipro Ltd	469	Six Sigma, SEI CMM, PCMM, CMMi
4. Satyam Computer Services Ltd	348	ISO 9001, Tick IT, SEI CMM level 5
5. HCL Technologies	269	SEI CMM level 5, ISO 9001
6. Patni Computer Systems	149	SEI CMM level 5, ISO 9001

Note: *Revenue in US$ million for the financial year 2002.

Source: NASSCOM, and individual company websites.

While quality certification is used as a signal to potential international clients, it is true that Indian firms are indeed moving towards larger and more complex projects. Thus upgrading software development methods and project management skills through CMM level 5 and other concepts like CQA (Certified Quality Analyst), Certified Software Test Engineer (CSTE) program, and Six Sigma are helping these firms to climb up the value chain. For instance, Wipro claims to have a holistic approach to quality with the 'most mature' six-sigma program in the industry and that 91 percent of their projects are completed on schedule (much above the industry average of 55 percent).

It is important to note here that the high frequency of obtaining newer quality certification supports the *market signal* role of certification. A market signal is meant to convey information about the product/service quality of a seller so as to obtain a higher price or remuneration, and to be strong a signal must be easier for the higher-productivity seller to give than the lower-productivity seller (Spence, 1974). For instance a particular quality certification *à la* Spence, say SEI CMM level 5, will stop being a signal if firms that are not as good in quality and management start acquiring the certification. Poor performance of a CMM level 5 certified firm would then make the signal non-credible in the market! In case that happens, the players (firms) would move away from non-credible signals and opt for other forms of more credible market signals.

In the light of this, the current trend among larger Indian firms to move beyond SEI CMM towards Six Sigma and Quality Function Deployment illustrates the dynamic characteristic of the process of market signaling. The bigger players, in their bid to stay ahead and differentiate from the lesser players, continue to obtain newer forms of certification which, in turn, drives the smaller players to race for the same signals to indicate that they are just as reliable.

CONCLUSION

Despite the poor infrastructure in India, the IT industry has succeeded in achieving phenomenal export growth due to the presence of several enabling factors. The most significant among them are entrepreneurial dynamism of the software firms, the availability of relatively cheap skilled labour and an early bird advantage in entering the global market.

Moreover, since the growth of the services trade is largely based on client–vendor relationship, the success of the IT industry is partly attributable to the reputation that has been established in the global market, a feature unique to India compared to other exporters like China, the Philippines and Russia. The latter countries share some of the same cost advantages as India, especially in terms of relatively cheap technically skilled labor. The Indian firms, however, have the advantage of established client relationships in developed countries, and have been relentlessly pursuing firm-level certification to signal quality and reliability in the global market to differentiate themselves from competitors.

The race to signal quality among the Indian software firms has been so intense that whenever a new management or process certification comes up in the industry, the firms make a beeline for it. While quality certifications are not considered as a credible signal among several clients (specially in the USA), such a consideration has not affected the Indian firms *as a whole* from continuing to pursue certifications. It is also true that the pursuit of quality has indeed helped Indian software service providers to move on to larger and more complex projects. Thus the market signaling role of quality certification is an aid in climbing the service value ladder, and a move away from the highly competitive lower-end market where other developing countries are fast emerging.

NOTES

1. Although the multinational companies contribute significantly to the total software exports from the country (25 percent of total Indian exports in 2001–02), this chapter only considers

the domestic firms since building a quality reputation in the international market is more pertinent for the latter than for the former.

2. The Software Engineering Institute (SEI) established in 1984 at Pittsburgh, USA, had instituted the Capability Maturity Model for Software (CMM) as a framework that describes the key elements of an effective software process. The CMM is composed of five maturity levels. Each maturity level provides a layer in the foundation for continuous process improvement. Achieving each level of the maturity model institutionalizes a different component in the software process, resulting in an overall increase in the process capability of the organization.

3. The purpose of the Capability Maturity Model Integration (CMMi) is to guide organizations in the task of improving their processes and their ability to manage the development, acquisition and maintenance of products and services. CMMi places proven practices into a structure that helps organizations assess their maturity and process area capabilities, establish priorities for improvement and guide the implementation of these improvements.

4. People CMM or PCMM is a process targeted at managing and developing an organization's work force and adopts the maturity framework of the CMM for software. The aim of PCMM is to radically improve the ability of software organizations to attract, develop, motivate, organize and retain talent needed to continuously improve software development capability. PCMM consists of five maturity levels that lay successive foundations for continuously improving talent, developing effective teams, and successfully managing the people assets of the organization.

5. The STP scheme is a 100 percent export-oriented scheme for the development and export of computer software using data communication links or in the form of physical media including export of professional services.

6. The composition of exports as noted earlier shows that outsourcing has increased and on-site deployment has declined. This is coupled with restrictions on movement of labor into developed countries.

7. Many firms looking to outsource in India ask NASSCOM for a list of the top 20–25 firms and those that are quality certified (Arora and Asundi 1999).

8. The size of firms, namely large versus small, is an important factor in receiving higher-value contracts. The top 20 Indian software companies accounted for almost half of the total software service exports in 2001–02 (Nasscom 2002).

REFERENCES

Arora, Ashish, V.S. Arunchalam, Jai Asundi and Ronald Fernandes (2001), 'The Indian Software Services Industry', *Research Policy*, 30, 1267–87.

Arora, Ashish and Jai Asundi (1999), 'Quality certification and the economies of contract software development: a study of the Indian software industry', National Bureau of Economic Research, working paper no 7260, Cambridge, MA.

Bajpai, Nirupam and Vanita Shastri (1998), 'Software Industry in India: A Case Study', Harvard Institute for International Development discussion paper no 667, Harvard University.

Heeks, Richard and Brian Nicholson (2002), 'Software Export Success Factors and Strategies in Developing and Transitional Economies', Institute for Development Policies and Management Development Informatics working paper no 12, University of Manchester, UK.

Heeks, Richard (1996), *India's Software Industry*, Thousand Oaks, CA: Sage Publications.

Krishna, S., Abhoy Ojha and Michael Barrett (2000), 'Competitive Advantage in the Software Industry: An Analysis of the Indian Experience', in C. Avegeron and G. Walsham (eds), *Information Technology in Context: Studies from the Perspective of Developing Countries*, Aldershot: Ashgate Publishers, pp. 182–97.

Moitra, Deependra (2001), 'India's Software Industry', *IEEE Software*, January/February, 77–80.

National Association of Software and Service Companies (NASSCOM) (2002), *Software Industry in India 2001–02*, New Delhi: NASSCOM.

NASSCOM-McKinsey (2002), *Strategies to Achieve the Indian IT Industry's Aspirations*, New Delhi: NASSCOM and McKinsey Report.

Reserve Bank of India (RBI) (various years) *Annual Report*, New Delhi: RBI.

Spence, Michael (1974), *Market Signaling*, Cambridge, MA: Harvard University Press.

PART II

Knowledge spillovers and innovation in the
ICT sector

6. Diffusion innovation: a pattern of information communication technology innovation in the Indian economy

Mary Mathew

INTRODUCTION

Documented descriptions of the impact of information and communication technology (ICT) in India, predominantly focuses on software exports (Arora et al., 2001; D'Costa, 2003; Heeks, 1996; Schware, 1992). Undoubtedly, software exports are a successful result of Indian ICT and India's software exports do show rapid growth (NASSCOM, 2003). An analysis of Indian ICT innovation *per se* is missing in earlier literature. Furthermore , innovation itself, irrespective of ICT, is defined in many ways in the literature. This chapter presents evidence of a larger view of innovation with less emphasis on the magnitude of software exports and more on the implications of the pattern of sectors in which exports occurs. This evidence is analyzed in the context of ICT adoption in a developing country. Admittedly, software is the trigger that magnifies innovations (Quinn et al., 1997). This chapter looks at Indian ICT with a positive approach, emphasizing the presence of innovation termed as diffusion innovation.

The adoption of ICT in India has led to a rapid urban spread of the technology and consequently has enhanced social communication and enabled improvements in its domestic economic activity. The adoption of ICT in a developing country, such as India, refers to the transference of innovation from first-generation innovators (USA), where ICT is in itself the technical innovation and a set of inventions generated from the research and development (R&D) laboratories of the USA. Diffusion of this adopted innovation refers to the process by which knowledge of an innovation spreads throughout a population and is communicated through certain channels among the members of a social system (Rogers, 1983). Diffusion innovations therefore can be referred to as those innovations that arise during and after the adoption stages of ICT in countries that have little R&D activity in ICT. ICT, having spread into the Indian population, is accepted and absorbed by the society, facilitates newly acquired ways of life and business, and then creates technological innovations and inventions in the very same technology. By mastering its appropriate use, users progress into R&D contributing to prior art. This results in next generation innovations and inventions of ICT, and the birth of second-generation innovators. Hence in diffusion innovation one sees two states; the first being the adoption of ICT into the larger population, and the second being indigenous R&D and inventiveness in ICT.

LITERATURE

Chronologically analyzing the term 'innovation', its meaning is clarified as 'novus' or new. Researchers in the field emphasize that innovation is newness, both in the case of products or outcomes and processes (Gopalakrishnan and Damanpour, 1994). So, while newness is at the core of innovation, the *degree and pattern* of newness is a constant source of concern for researchers. Innovativeness, on the other hand, is differentiated from innovation; it is felt that innovativeness is a degree of newness (Garcia and Calantone, 2002). Some definitions of the term 'innovativeness' are: new to the world; new to the industry; new to the scientific community; new to the organization; and new to the customer (Garcia and Calantone, 2002).

Innovation has been classified into radical, incremental, product and process innovations. Radical innovation is a product, process or service with either unprecedented performance features or familiar features that allow significant improvements in performance or cost. They can create dramatic change and transform markets or industries (Leifer et al., 2000). However, deep structural adjustments are required for radical innovations (Lipsey and Bekar, 1995), and these can influence the entire economy. For example innovations to the automobile have a deep-seated impact on the transportation sector in general. Radical product innovations involve introducing and applying significantly new technologies or ideas into markets that either do not exist or require dramatic changes (Dewar and Dutton, 1986; Ettlie et al., 1984). Incremental innovations are said to be extensions of current product features and are relatively minor improvements to existing processes (Dewar and Dutton, 1986; Ettlie et al., 1984). Describing national innovation systems, researchers define such systems as a network of agents, a set of policies or a set of institutions that introduce new technology into the economy ... the key aspects of such a system are the extent to which the economy acquires technology from abroad, the amount of domestic technological effort it undertakes and the level of technical human capital it requires (Dahlman, 1994; Nasierowski and Arcelus, 2003). Stressing the importance of understanding how innovation is labeled and defined, researchers Garcia and Calantone (2002) state that innovation comprises the technological development of an invention, combined with market introduction of that invention to end-users through adoption and diffusion.

Much research has also divided innovation into outcomes and processes (Gopalakrishnan and Damanpour, 1994). While outcomes deal with new products, process theorists on innovation understand how innovations emerge over time. Process innovations comprise diffusion generation and adoption (Gopalakrishnan and Damanpour, 1994). Diffusion process innovations are the diffusion of ideas, products, processes or practices to members of a social system. Generation process innovations, a more powerful typology, are defined as problem-solving and decision-making processes. Idea generation, project definition, problem-solving, design and development, production and marketing, and commercialization all categorize the generation process. On the other hand, adoption process innovation refers to the adoption of innovations from the environment and the resulting changes in a given organizational system (Gopalakrishnan and Damanpour, 1994). Diffusion innovations, however, are beyond mere process innovations; they are innovations that will trigger R&D activity.

Some writers feel that IT innovations are a distinct class, even though they may have administrative and technological properties (Drury and Farhoomand, 1999; Swanson, 1994). Information technology (IT) innovation includes newness in hardware, software, and systems (Drury and Farhoomand, 1999).

Diffusion Innovation

The diffusion innovation model presumes that innovation is formed in a social system that is a learning system. The system adopts and learns to use ICT for its economic activity. In learning the advantages of usage, the system learns to create the required support systems to augment the further use of ICT in economic activity. The system then sees the advantage of technically inventing newer generations of the technology to accelerate usage and explore new markets, thus learning to master ICT by engaging in R&D. ICT has the potential to show such dynamic and self-organizing characteristics in economies, such that even when economies start from an almost homogeneous or almost random state, they spontaneously form large-scale patterns (Krugman, 1996).

The pattern of ICT adoption, proliferation and active R&D is characteristic of diffusion innovation. Diverse applications of ICT result in diffusion throughout various industries; this is far more important than the production of ICT industries *per se* (Wang, 1999). Researchers feel that the demand-side, that is, the use of ICT, or pattern of ICT usage, is perhaps more important in considering ICT innovations in an economy than other, general macroeconomic effects (Koski et al., 2002). This implies that evidence of the adoption of ICT into Indian industry verticals (like banking or sectors that did not use ICT earlier) is a critical requirement for diffusion innovations.

ICT diffusion innovations in the Indian economy can be seen in terms of typical definitions of innovation, namely, a new industry, new business, new market, new organization and new intellectual capital. These diffusion innovations are classified into four stages. Figure 6.1 shows these stages. The first three refer to the pattern of adoption. These are socioeconomic innovations at the national level that emerge during technology adoption. First seen are *adaptation-diffusion innovations*: the transfer of ICT to sectors not previously influenced or administered by ICT, also known as traditional sectors or non-ICT sectors. Second, we see *infrastructure-diffusion innovations*: supportive infrastructure innovations, mainly in the communications, telecommunications and connectivity areas that augment adaptation diffusion innovations. The third stage is more subtle but powerful: *human-skill-diffusion innovations* in the human capital knowledge base.

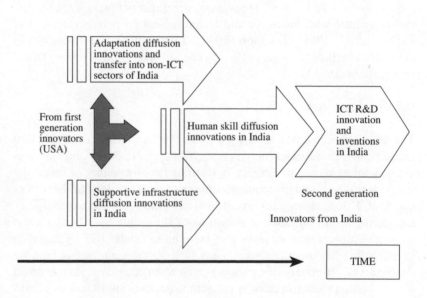

Figure 6.1   Diffusion innovations of the two stages

This stage brings growth to human capital, namely to knowledge, skills and competencies. This stage is a pre-requisite for the fourth stage, which emerges as human capital masters ICT. Success of the first three stages of ICT diffusion innovations in terms of adaptation-diffusion innovations, infrastructural diffusion innovations and human-skill-diffusion innovations will trigger the fourth the *technical ICT innovations and inventiveness*. After the initial adoption success with ICT entry, ICT generation innovations and inventions, in the form of intellectual property, product, process and service, typically emerge. This last or fourth stage refers to the ultimate state in which R&D supports technological innovation and inventions.

Evidence of ICT Diffusion-innovations in India

ICT developed in India as it did in other countries. The difference between India and other countries is with the pattern and degree of innovation in the first stage of diffusion. This pattern and degree of innovation will trigger or result in second-stage diffusion innovations, namely R&D activity and technological innovation and inventions. When this happens, diffusion innovation has its desired influence of technological capability-building. While countries may vary in the pattern and degree of socioeconomic innovations, this variation will determine the speed of movement into the fourth stage of diffusion innovations. Secondary data are used to illustrate evidences of the four diffusion innovations in India as seen in Figure 6.1.

Evidence of Adaptation Innovations in Non-ICT Sectors

Globally, ICT is seen as a pervasive technology that supports various sectors, providing effectiveness, efficiency, economic opportunity and empowerment, all designed with a built-to-last approach (Accenture, 2001). Tables 6.1–6.4 show India's status regarding proliferation of ICT in previously non-ICT sectors. The proliferation into verticals in Indian industry, namely, banking services, retailing, government support and education, are discussed. The following paragraphs discuss each table in turn.

Table 6.1 shows that banking, financial services and insurance sectors make a fairly high contribution to international exports, as well as to the domestic market. India's export business in banking, for example, helped ICT to enable domestic banking. This is a radical change from the way India operated prior to ICT adaptations in the banking, financial and insurance sectors. Business models in software services and business process outsourcing activities are new ICT-enabled ways to serve markets now practiced by Indian professionals for domestic requirements. ICT-enabled business process outsourcing is a business model seen in both

Indian exports and domestic markets. The other important segments in the domestic market are IT/telecom and governmental ICT interventions. As competition increases, a number of banks are looking at IT deployment as a comprehensive IT strategy rather than fragmented investments. This sector contributes about 22 percent to India's software and services exports.

Table 6.1   Verticals in Indian ICT

Percentage of contribution (%)	International exports (2001–2002)	Domestic market (2002–2003)
Banking, financial services and insurance	35	21
Manufacturing	12	15
Telecom equipment	12	–
Telecom service providers	3	–
IT/Telecom	–	22
Government	1	14
Retail	4	–
Utilities	2	–
Transportation	1	–
Healthcare	3	–
Energy	–	6
Small office/home	–	11
Education	–	11
Others	27	–

Source: NASSCOM, 2003.

India has about 300 banks with 68 200 branches and administrative offices functioning in various states across the country. The possibilities of banking software applications are: retail or core banking market (52 percent), corporate (21 percent), treasury (10 percent), securities (7 percent) and asset management (10 percent) (Glancy and Chitra, 2003).

Table 6.2 shows the status of computerization in public sector banks. About 28 percent of public bank branches are fully computerized. Service branches that service the public banks are closer to being fully computerized. Looking more closely at the banking sector shows incremental changes with computerization but radical changes with regard to customer account accessing, specifically introduction of automated teller machines (ATMs). 2 490 ATMs have been installed in India showing the entry of ICT in the 24-hour service delivery systems of the banking sector, a service that is radically new to the Indian customer.

Table 6.2   Computerization activity in Indian banking

Computerization activity	Number of banks/branches
Total number of branches in public banks	46 528
Partial computerization at branch level	16 526
Number of fully computerized branches	13 078
Number of existing service branches	385
Number of partially computerized service branches	63
Number of fully computerized service branches	318
Total ATMs installed	2 490
Online terminals at corporate sites installed	5 980
Debit card (as ATM cards) issued	3 062 628

Source: RBI, September, 2002 (Glancy and Chitra, 2003).

Looking at IT-enabled services (ITES), we see a new advantage for India in business process outsourcing and IT-enabled services where annual cost of a full-time employee (FTE) is concerned. ITES in India is a promising revenue generator, a new service to the Indian market, helping India to develop radically new skill sets. Table 6.3 shows the Indian cost of manpower advantage in a world where cost is a key determining factor in choosing ITES outsourcing vendors. Telecom infrastructure inadequacy in India rings an alarm and has been doing so for a long time (Heeks, 1996). Nevertheless, the total expenses are certainly less for India, making ITES more attractive. The overall cost for a FTE in India is just 20 percent of the corresponding cost in the USA. While personnel and general and administrative (G&A) expenses range from 12 percent to 14 percent of the costs in the USA, property rentals are 33 percent of US costs. The cost of telecom infrastructure is higher in India (155 percent) since the communication channels are international.

Table 6.3   Comparison of operating costs for the ITES sector in India and the USA

US$ cost per FTE	USA	India	India as % of US cost
Personnel	42 927	6 179	14
G&A expense	8 571	1 000	12
Telecom	1 500	2 328	155
Property rentals	2 600	847	33
Depreciation	3 000	1 500	50
Total expenses	58 598	11 854	20

Source: Industry Sources, Merrill Lynch (NASSCOM, 2003).

The ITES sector was estimated to grow by about 65 percent (NASSCOM, 2003) in the years 2002–2003. This rapid growth is seen in service lines, where India has about 103 companies operating, and web sales/marketing, which has about 100 companies (NASSCOM, 2003). The business outsourcing market shows a large number of employment openings. Content development and customer care brought in the maximum revenue, US$ 450 million and US$ 400 million, respectively, in 2002 (NASSCOM, 2003). Outsourcing finance, administration and payment services are also revenue earners. These service delivery models are new to the country and new to the skill sets of Indian employees.

Additionally, ICT-enabled domestic retailing is a new experiment radical to the buying methodologies of Indian customers. The diffusion of smart cards is evident in Indian projects being executed. Smart cards in India are reaching the rural area through state and central government initiatives. Since, unlike magnetic stripe cards, these cards do not need online infrastructure; they have growth potential where online infrastructures are poor. It is estimated that the smart card market in India is $5.1 billion and with a compound annual growth rate (CAGR) of 39.8 percent (Srikanth and Glancy, 2003). Notable smart card projects are the loyalty PetroCard by BPCL, the Employees Provident fund organizations (2.6 subscribers) together with Siemens, Rajasthan's milk collection project smart card, Kerala's ration card project (public distribution monitor) and the BEST smart card for transportation on the Mumbai buses. In the year 2005, it is estimated that the sectoral percentage of unit shipment by application of the smart card markets will be 59.6 percent for telecom, 23.7 percent in banking and retail, 0.72 percent in transportation, 0.05 percent in healthcare and 15.5 percent in the government sector (Srikanth and Glancy, 2003).

The Indian Farmers Fertilizers Cooperative Ltd launched ICT-enabled Agri-Kiosks to provide farmers with information on agriculture, the fertilizer industry, agrochemicals and the cooperative sector. Also noticeable is the Gyandoot project (from the Hindi word for 'messenger of information' or 'purveyor of knowledge') that produces *suchanalayas*, or kiosks, and provides employment to the village youth trained to use such kiosks. Kiosk usage in India is 40 percent for governmental uses, 30 percent in banking and finance, 25 percent in telecom and travel and 5 percent for other activities (Chitra, 2003). Information accessibility for decision-making is helping rural sectors that were earlier information-impoverished. Quoting Dr V. Kurien, the leader who revolutionized the milk cooperative movement,

> computers were not created to solve the problems of poverty. Hence it is futile
> to expect that the world will be a better place if all had access to the computer

and internet. But information is power and it stands to reason that if this power is shared equitably, all will benefit (Srikanth, 2003).

ICT-triggered socioeconomic innovations have fueled new energy into Indian socioeconomic dynamics. ICT-enabled rural uplift programs are very new and very radical for the Indian villager. As is the case in most countries that use ICT, it has the potential to reduce the 'information have-nots' (Halal, 1993).

Besides rural government support activities, the education sector, also important for all-round socioeconomic growth, is experiencing incremental changes. India has 0.44 PCs per 1 000 people in the educational sector. The vision for 2006 is to have 5 per 1,000 in this sector (Phatak, 2003a). Table 6.4 shows the Skoch-2000 (Phatak, 2003b) estimates in education PC penetration.

Table 6.4   The computer per 1,000 in Indian education

	1998	1999	2000	2001	2002	2003	Cumulative
PCs sold in education	31 000	44 500	62 000	63 054	89 852	150 518	440 924
Education PCs per 1000	0.03	0.04	0.06	0.06	0.09	0.15	0.44

Source: 'An Education PC for India', Skoch-2000 (Phatak, 2003b).

Attempts are being made to increase ICT education at the state level. However, considering that literacy programs themselves are not very effective, ICT literacy may not have the desired impact. Training and education in ICT experienced a drop in growth in 2002–2003. The revenues in training and education are close to $270 million, NIIT and Aptech being the highest revenue generators (NASSCOM, 2003).

Evidence of Infrastructure Diffusion Innovations

Despite the apparently polarized strategies of 'IT manufacturers look inside' (Fichardo, 2003) and software projects 'gun for volumes and target niche areas' (Mishra, 2003) being used, India's target estimates indicate that cross-border software service exports will remain at the helm of the ICT revenues, rather than the domestic revenues (NASSCOM, 2003). ICT's specific contribution to the GDP *per se* is negligible. Nonetheless, the level of discussion and fascination it has created in every urban Indian household is stunning; it does not compare with any other technological intervention the country has seen in its history. ICT's capacity to reach every member of an Indian household is now a realization. Indians as a people are charmed by TV, radio, telephone, computers and now the internet and internet telephony. Although inter-country comparisons do show higher radio and TV penetration in other countries, the subjective and felt need to watch TV or listen to the radio is pervasive. Purchasing power and literacy, however, could be the stumbling blocks for poor radio diffusion density in India.

India recently witnessed a spate of FM licenses renewing the possibility of radio broadcasting in cities. Since achieving independence, India had only six channels under the state-owned All India Radio. Currently, with privatization, the government is permitting 150 new FM channels across 40 cities.

The National Telecom Policy of 1999 (NTP99) enabled improvements in the telecom infrastructure in India through reforms and deregulations. The highlights of the NTP99 were the movement from a fixed license fee to revenue-sharing, opening up domestic long distance and initially opening up International Long Distance (NASSCOM, 2003).

Table 6.5 shows the revenue and estimated revenue for the telecom sectors. Evidence of diffusion innovation telecommunication infrastructure is seen considering the progress in revenues. Leased-line and voice is estimated to bring in the largest amounts of revenue, about US$ 11,727 million. Cellular users bring in a revenue of about US$ 2,692 million. The reasons for poor teledensity are stated to be inefficiency, inadequate infrastructure, outdated technology, lack of quality services and high mobile service tariffs.

Table 6.5   Indian telecom sector revenue in million dollars

	2000–2001	2001–2002	2003–2004 (estimated)
Population (millions)	1 027	1 047	1 086
Wire line services	2 725	3 110	366
Cellular	1 163	1 458	2 692
WILL-CDMA			175
National Long Distance	3 310	3 167	2 420
International telephony	1 436	1 263	1 437
Leased lines	26	72	193
Leased – line and voice	8 661	9 072	11 727

Source: Morgan Stanley (NASSCOM, 2003).

Looking at software development in the telecom sector, Table 6.6 shows the revenue from telecom software services in 2002. Among the telecom software service giants, Wipro garnered in the maximum revenue of $244 million dollars in 2002; the second major player was TCS. The other software companies that create telecom software are Infosys, Hughes and Subex. There is evidence that much of the Indian software development of business corporations is also in the telecom sector, thus indicating the possibilities of increasing markets and competition in the telecom arena in India. Incremental innovation in the form of new business areas, new technology and markets in the telecom sector describes the Indian ICT's infrastructural innovations.

Table 6.6   Indian telecom software services revenue (2002)

Company	Revenue in million dollars
Wipro	244
TCS	167
Infosys	106
Hughes Software	52
Subex	4

Source: Pasha, 2003.

Innovations in Human Skill Diffusion Innovations

ICT can be viewed as the connecting link between previously separate technologies. As technological evolutions have become increasingly interrelated and complex, ICT specialization enables firms to fuse together different kinds of technology across national boundaries in an intra-firm network (Anderson, 1998). With Indian software experts manning and maintaining the best of US business back-ends, tacit knowledge transfer of business models to Indians is evident. In the process, a traditional economy, earlier unaware of skills in customer service and customer schedules, suddenly thrives on the US experience of newer methods of management theory and business practices. This learning adds to the knowledge base of the developing economy. Hence India learned to manage banks, for example, in a manner it would never have, if it were not for software services projects in international banks. Hence transfer of this knowledge to domestic services via the tacit knowledge gained from international business organizations is the skill gain that only software export businesses could make possible. Bestowed with logical and abstract intelligence, an eagerness to earn higher incomes and work long hours, and a capacity to be 'flying geeks' (Goldstein and O'Connor, 2002), the Indian software developers fit very easily into the ICT professional's mold. The business process analysis, project management and quality skills are all part of a learning that came with software exports. With 48 Indian companies having acquired the Capability Maturity Model (CMM) level 5 certification (most of them in Bangalore) (NASSCOM, 2003), ICT will likely continue to contribute innovations in the knowledge base and the abilities of Indians to solve problems. With the possibility of collaborating with China (Tschang, 2002), India has certainly come a long way towards co-evolution (Smits, 2002) skill sets in its human capital.

The evidence of ICT business in non-ICT sectors, infrastructure and human capital skills build-up illustrates the success of diffusion innovations required for R&D preparedness. This success leads further to the next stage of technical R&D.

Generation of Technological Innovations and Inventions in Indian ICT

There is strong evidence that the Indian human intellectual capital is now capable of high-end R&D. Foreign multinational corporation (MNC) R&D is investing in the intellectual capital in India. Indian ICT professionals have opportunities to work in state-of-the-art R&D facilities and contribute to intellectual property generation with recognition and rewards. The recent years have seen a spate of R&D investors in India. Table 6.7 shows the R&D investors and their profiles. The development at the higher end of R&D work is, however, concentrated in Bangalore. This provides for a strong ICT R&D investment thrust in the Bangalore cluster. Of all the cities in India, Bangalore has become the most dynamic hi-tech cluster.

The R&D centers of Oracle and SAP in India are the largest outside their respective parent locations of USA and Germany. With many companies carrying out significant portions of their R&D work in India, software products are emerging. Sun has brought out products such as portal servers, web servers, identity servers and meta-directories from India. Texas Instruments has at least 20 fully developed products, including Ankur Digital Signal Processor, Sangam, a bridge router for DSL and Zeno, which runs multimedia applications. The local SAP products look at global markets and channel marketing solutions that help chip manufacturers negotiate prices with dealers online, such as dealer portals for the automotive sector, mobile laptop solutions, oil and gas upstream solutions and even a product on value added tax (VAT). The organization i2 delivers about eight manufacturer-industry templates and retail solutions.

This trend in becoming an R&D hub has shown promise for India. An increase in 'porous societies' with knowledge-intensive intermediaries (Smits, 2002) and disintermediation and discoveries of 'knowledge societies' are now characteristic of Indian ICT. These are indeed indications of technological innovation.

Table 6.7   MNC R&D investors

Company name	Location and year of establishment	Current number of employees	Area of R&D
Texas Instruments	Bangalore, 1984	900	VLSI and embedded software enabling or within a chip
Oracle India Development Centre	Bangalore, 1994 Hyderabad, 1999	2700 (4000 by this year end)	Oracle's database products, applications, business intelligent products, application development tools
Sun Microsystems' India Engineering Centre	Bangalore, 1999	500	Sun's software, including Solaris and Sun one
i2 technologies R&D Centre	Bangalore, Bombay, 1988	1000	Company's global development delivery
IBM's Software Lab India	Bangalore, 1998	Not available	IBM software like Websphere, DB2, Lotus, Tivoli, Rational. Middleware and business intelligence
SAP Labs India	Bangalore, 1998	750 by Sept 2003	Does 10% of SAP's total R&D work here
Philips Innovation Campus	Bangalore, 1996	895 1000 by end of 2003	Develops software for Philips; almost all Philips products with software are developed here
HP Labs	Bangalore, 2002	20	High-level research on futuristic technologies, focus on emerging markets

Source: Singh, 2003.

Patent generation in Bangalore by inventors with permanent addresses in Bangalore was identified from the US Patent and Trademark Office (USPTO) database. USPTO patents in the period from 1980 to 2001 show the largest number of Bangalorean inventors in USPTO to be from Texas Instruments (see Table 6.8). Sporadic patent productivity has been noticed over the two decades with a moderate high in 1997.

Table 6.8   USPTO's ICT patents by Bangalore inventors in Bangalore organizations

Company name/Year	1980	87	89	91	92	93	94	95	96	97	98	99	2000	01	Grand Total
Alcatel USA Sourcing, L.P.								1							1
Amada America, Inc.								1	1				1		3
Amada Company, Ltd.					1	1			1						3
Cypress Semiconductor Corp.							1	2	1	1	1				6
E-Cell Technologies												2			2
GE										1		1			2
Hewlett-Packard Company	1								1	1					3
Honeywell											1				1
IBM				1					1	4	2	2			10
Intel Corporation										1	1				2
ISRO							1								1
Lucent Technologies, Inc.										1					1
Micro Technology, Inc.				2											2
Motorola, Inc.							1	1							2
Multi-Tech Systems, Inc.				1			1		1	1					4
NCR Corporation										1			1		2
Novell, Inc										1					1
NTC Technology											2	1			3
Rebus Technology, Inc.							1								1
S3 Incorporated									2						2
Sequent Computer Systems, Inc.							1								1
Societe Suisse pour l'Industrie Horlogere Management Services S.A.	1														1
Synopsis, Inc.										1					1
Texas Instruments		1				2	6	6	2	6	8	5		4	40
Stanford University	1														1
The Whitaker Corporation			1	1											2
VeriFone, Inc.				1											1
Wipro Limited										1					1
Xerox Corporation					5										5
Grand Total	1	1	2	2	3	9	7	11	7	20	16	14	5	7	105

Table 6.8 shows a gradual drop in patent filings in USPTO after 1997. This trend requires further analysis. An analysis of the number of patents issued will further help in understanding R&D productivity in terms of

patents. For further evidence of home-grown and home-owned inventions, a look at the Indian ICT firms shows promise of patent generation in a work culture that was earlier naïve to patenting.

Indian organizations in the software sector are beginning to show a patent orientation. We see Sasken with the largest number of USPTO patents filed (39 filed), and TCS (35 filed), followed by Ittiam, Vmoksha (with two filed) and Geometric and Vismaya (with one each), (Mahalingam, 2003). Evidence of inventions by Bangalorean ICT professionals is present. This trend will probably increase with more Indian self-funded R&D ICT centers emerging. Such domestic R&D investments will help change India's current image that its ICT business activities are in the low end of the value chain. With the focus of patent generation coming into Indian ICT organizations, the diffusion-innovation cycle is turning adopters into innovators. While patent potential is evident from the kind of R&D done in the Bangalore cluster, what is a bit elusive is innovation in the form of products.

CONCLUSION

The focus in earlier literature on Indian ICT was more on export performances, software services, a lack of innovation and the lack of a development dynamic. A closer study of ICT in India, however, brings in a broad definition of innovation that ICTs bring with them. Adopting ICT innovations from developed countries has the potential to cause diffusion innovations in developing countries. The proliferation of first-stage diffusion innovations into ICT and non-ICT sectors and the initiation of infrastructural innovations to sustain its proliferation have resulted in a knowledge or human capital skill base that is a prerequisite for diffusion innovations of the second stage, namely technological innovation and inventions. Table 6.9 gives a summary of ICT diffusion innovations in India, describing its presence and impact on India.

There is evidence that successful ICT adoption has occurred in India, including the creation of a new industrial sector and market devoted to ICT. When any new technology enters into traditional, populous economies, it may encounter resistance and non-acceptance. In the case of India, however, over the decades the presence of ICT can be seen throughout the country; in the government, industry and primary revenue areas of the GDP such as agriculture, industry and services. The degree of penetration does vary in geographic locations within India. The answer to 'whether ICT in India has diffused into areas beyond software services and outsourcing' is a sure yes.

India shows evidence of both stages of diffusion innovation. Data presented in this study indicate the presence of ICT diffusion innovation.

The experience and learning of the Indian human capital is the prerequisite for ICT innovations and the inventions stage. In foreign markets, software professionals from developing countries experience and develop a learning that is serendipitous, insightful and latent. The tacit transfer of the knowledge gained through this learning is a by-product and has far-reaching implications for a developing country like India. With the learning in the Indian human capital, ICT has the potential to create learning economies, and it has done so in India already. The learning economy is based on the idea that learning and innovation are interactive, partly cumulative, processes, which depends on the existing infrastructure and the willingness to change the institutional set-up of the economy (Johnson, 1992).

Table 6.9   Summary evidence of diffusion innovation in Indian ICT

Type	Status
Diffusion into the country	YES
A new industrial sector	YES
New global markets	YES
Industrialist acceptance and support	YES
Diffusion into non-ICT sectors	YES
Governmental acceptance and support	YES
Diffusion into agriculture, industrialization and services	YES
New work skills in human base	YES
R&D and technical inventions in ICT	YES

The phenomenon of diffusion innovation can create scenarios such as the one in Figure 6.2. A few years hence, it is possible that the list of Indian ICT organizations filing for patents will be much higher, implying that the cycle of diffusion innovation completes itself with the promise of high patent and innovation yield. As shown in Figure 6.2, country B (India in this case) is an early adopter of ICT from original innovators, such as the USA. With successful adoption India is showing promise as a new innovator of ICT. This starts yet another wave of ICT adopting countries (countries C and D in Figure 6.2) – adopting from countries that were once users of ICT (India), now turned innovators.

Thus original innovators of ICT (Country A, for example, the USA) have created value in developing countries by making them secondary innovators. In the third stage countries will buy the technological innovations and inventions from India, becoming adopters who will themselves turn innovators someday if diffusion innovation is successful in all three components of adoption into non-ICT sectors: infrastructural innovations, knowledge build-up and human capital build-up.

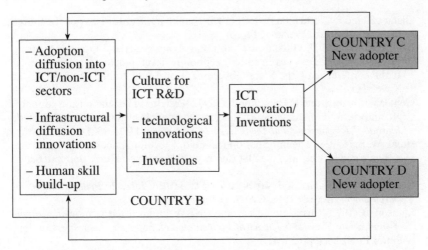

*Figure 6.2   The sequential effect of innovator generation potential of ICT
when adopted from original innovators (country A)*

REFERENCES

Accenture (2001), *Creating a Development Dynamic: Final Report of the Digital Opportunity Initiative*, New York: Markle Foundation and UNDP.

Anderson, H. B. (1998), 'The evolution of technological trajectories 1890–1990', *Structural Change and Economic Dynamics*, **9**, 5–34.

Arora, A., V.S. Arunachalam, J. Asundi and R. Fernandes (2001), 'The Indian software services industry', *Research Policy*, **30**(8), 1267–87.

Chitra, P. (April, 2003), 'Kiosk market comes of age', *Express Computer*, **14**(8) 12–13.

Dahlman, C. J. (1994), 'Technology strategy in East Asian developing countries', *Journal of Asian Economics*, **5**, 541–72.

D'Costa, A. P. (2003), 'Uneven and combined development: understanding India's software exports', *World Development*, **31**(1), 211–26.

Dewar, R. D. and J.E. Dutton (1986), 'The adoption of radical and incremental innovations: an empirical analysis', *Management Science*, **32**, 1422–33.

Drury, D. H. and A. Farhoomand (1999), 'Information technology push/pull reactions', *Journal of Systems and Software*, **47**(1), 3–10.

Ettlie, J. E., W.P. Bridges and R.D. O'Keefe (1984), 'Organization strategy and structural differences for radical versus incremental innovation', *Management Science*, **30**, 682–95.

Fichardo, C. A. (June, 2003), 'Shourie tells IT manufacturers to look inwards for growth', *Express Computer*, 14(15) 2.

Garcia, R. and R. Calantone (2002), 'A critical look at technological innovation typology and innovativeness terminology: a literature review', *Journal of Product Innovation Management*, **19**(2), 110–32.

Glancy, S. and P. Chitra (2003), 'RBI (2002): banking software firms ride the Indian IT wave', *Express Computer*, **14**(20), 15–16.

Goldstein, A. and D. O'Connor (2002), 'Of flying geeks and O-rings: locating software and IT Services in India's economic development', paper presented at the conference of the State Government of Tamil Nadu, Chennai, 11–12 November.

Gopalakrishnan, S. and F. Damanpour (1994), 'Patterns of generation and adoption of innovation in organizations: contingency models of innovation attributes', *Journal of Engineering and Technology Management*, **11**(2), 95–116.

Halal, W. E. (1993), 'The information technology revolution: computer hardware, software and services into the 21st Century', *Technological Forecasting and Social Change*, **44**, 69–86.

Heeks, R. (1996), *India's Software Industry: State Policy, Liberalization and Industrial Development*, Beverly Hills, CA: Sage Publications.

Johnson, B. (1992), 'Institutional learning', in B.A. Lundvall (ed.), *National Systems of Innovation: Towards a Theory of Innovation and Interactive Learning*, London: Pinter Publishers, pp. 23–41.

Koski, H., P. Rouvinen and P. Anttila (2002), 'ICT clusters in Europe: the great central banana and the small Nordic potato', *Information Economics and Policy*, **14**(2), 145–65.

Krugman, P. (1996), *Self-organizing Economy*, Malden, MA: Blackwell.

Leifer, R., C.M. McDermott, G.C. O'Connor, L.S. Peters, M. Rice and R.W. Veryzer (2000), *Radical Innovation: How Mature Companies can Outsmart Upstarts*, Boston, MA: Harvard Business School Press.

Lipsey, R. and C. Bekar (1995), 'A structuralist view of technical change and economic growth', in T.J. Courchene (ed.), *Technology, Information and Public Policy*, Kingston, Canada: Queens University, John Deutsch Institute.

Mahalingam, T.V. (July, 2003), 'Intellectual property: Indian IT wakes up to patents', *Data Quest*, DQ Top 20.

Mishra, P. (2003), 'Karnik: will India Software Inc. get caught in US-Iraq crossfire?', *Express Computer*, **14**(15) (7 April), 1–29.

Nasierowski, W. and F.J. Arcelus (2003), 'On the efficiency of national innovation systems', *Socio-economic Planning Sciences*, **37**(3), 215–34.

NASSCOM (2003), *The IT Industry in India, Strategic Review*, New Delhi: National Association of Software and Service Companies.

Pasha, A. (2003), 'NASSCOM special: telecom software, India Software Inc taps telecom carrier market', *Express Computer*, **13**(50) (February), 12–13.

Phatak D.B. (2003a), 'Vision 2006: a teacher's dream', *Express Computer*, **14**(5) (April), 4–5.

Phatak D.B. (2003b), 'Based on "An Education PC for India" skoch-2000', *Express Computer*, **14**(5) (April), 4.

Quinn, J.B., J.J. Baruch and K.A. Zien (1997), *Innovation Explosion: Using Intellect and Software to Revolutionize Growth Strategies*, New York: The Free Press.

Rogers, E. M. (1983), *Diffusion of Innovations*, (3rd edn), New York: The Free Press.

Schware, R. (1992), 'Software industry entry strategies for developing countries: a "walking on two legs" proposition', *World Development*, **20**(2), 143–64.

Singh, A. (2003), 'MNC R&D centres mushroom in India', *Express Computer*, **14**(14) (June), 15–16.

Smits, R. (2002), 'Innovation studies in the 21st century: questions from a user's perspective', *Technological Forecasting and Social Change*, **69**(9), 861–83.

Srikanth, R. P. (2003), 'Goan IT has a sunny outlook', *Express Computer*, **14**(9) (April), 23–4.

Srikanth, R. P. and S. Glancy (2003), 'Govt, service sector drive smart card growth', *Express Computer*, **14**(16) (June), 14–15.

Swanson, E. B. (1994), 'Information systems innovation among organizations', *Management Science*, **40**, 1069–92.

Tschang, T. (2002), 'China's software industry and its implications for India', paper presented at the Conference of the State Government of Tamil Nadu, Chennai, India, 11–12 November.

Wang, E. H. (1999), 'ICT and economic development in Taiwan: analysis of the evidence', *Telecommunications Policy*, **23**, 235–43.

7. Development through knowledge: capability replication in global innovation communities

Gita Surie*

Micro studies on development and technology transfer to emerging economies suggest that cross-national differences in productivity and performance may be influenced by national systems, institutions, and policies that affect the innovative capabilities and aspirations of firms (Nelson, 1993; Dahlman et al., 1987; Enos and Park, 1988). However, while economists remain interested in cross-national differences at the industry level, the role of the firm in building capabilities is underemphasized. Hence, the processes that shape the development of national capabilities and facilitate innovation are not well understood. This chapter aims to address this lack by developing a framework for capability creation and diffusion in emerging economies such as India, which links firms with industries, the institutional environment, and with global markets.

In the absence of well-developed indigenous markets and the latest developments in manufacturing technologies, firms in emerging economies seek external markets and alternative sources of new technology. This fact is well documented in research on the development of the newly industrialized countries (NICs) and also evidenced by the diffusion of manufacturing technology from the UK to the USA in the early days of industrialization (Licht, 1995). We focus on how cross-border interactions with multinational firms catalyze local learning, adaptation, and innovation; and by inducing competition in the domestic environment, increase specialization, and align domestic firms with the global economy in an evolving international division of labor. Evidence from case studies in the software industry suggests that capability building and learning through knowledge creation is a feasible development strategy for emerging economies with institutional structures that support knowledge-based industries. We suggest that the window of opportunity offered by the low-cost advantage and 'global' identity enjoyed by Indian software firms in international markets can be leveraged to higher-value activities to maintain a position of pre-eminence in knowledge-intensive industries.

The chapter is organized as follows: the first section outlines prior research drawing on theories of learning, knowledge transfer, and diffusion relevant for national performance and development. The second section presents a theoretical framework of knowledge creation, replication, and capability building in firms as social communities linking micro-level learning, problem-solving and innovation to evolution at the industry and national levels. In section three, we document the evolution of Indian participation in knowledge creation via a case study of micro-level learning and innovation in an Indian software firm and its evolution as a participant in local and international markets. In the final section we discuss the implications of this framework for the development of the Indian economy, and for emerging economies in general.

TECHNOLOGY, LEARNING, AND DYNAMIC CAPABILITIES

Theories of development have evolved from the idea that development proceeds in linear stages (Rostow, 1960) to the understanding that structural changes are required for development (Chenery, 1979), followed by political approaches that focus on the dominance–dependence relationship between developed (the center) and developing countries (the periphery), rendering attempts by poor nations to be self-reliant and independent difficult, if not impossible (Baran, 1975; Griffin and Gurley, 1985). In the 1980s and early 1990s, the neoclassical revolution emphasized the beneficial role of free markets, open economies, and the privatization of inefficient public enterprises, attributing development failures to excessive government intervention and regulation (Lal, 1985; Little, 1982; Todaro, 1994). Studies of NICs (Krueger, 1995; Wei, 1995) find support for the position that less government intervention as evidenced by the adoption of liberalization policies in these countries is positively associated with development.

However, government intervention may be necessary to facilitate the operations of markets by investing in physical and social infrastructure, healthcare, and educational facilities, and by providing a suitable climate for private enterprise (Stiglitz, 1998). While theories of endogenous growth recognize problems of incomplete information, externalities in skill creation and learning, economies of scale in production (Todaro, 1994), the focus on the behavior of the economy as a whole (Romer, 1994) has led to a relative neglect of the impact of human capital formation and knowledge creation at the firm level. Moreover, how the development of national systems of science and technology shape institutions that influence participation in knowledge creation must be examined (Nelson, 1996; Cantwell, 1989).

While the rate of technological advance is a central factor associated with cross-national differences in performance, macro studies repress the fact that significant inter-industry differences exist and that research and development (R&D) spending is an important variable in cross-industry analysis (Nelson, 1996). In addition, while dissimilar factor prices can explain international intra-industry differences in productivity and differences in vintage may account for intra-national differences, insufficient attention has been given to differences in internal organization and managerial coordination (Nelson, 1996, p. 25), although these are tacitly acknowledged in studies by Lall (1987), Enos and Park (1988), Dahlman et al. (1987), Bell and Scott-Kemmis (1988). Studies viewing firms as social systems (March and Simon, 1958; Weber, 1947; Perrow, 1979) suggest that the processes by which technologies are selected, and decisions translated into action are far from stable. Thus, the micro processes and mechanisms by which capabilities are built in firms and industries are inadequately emphasized.

The understanding that knowledge underlies technology and is a strategic and competitive resource (Winter, 1987; Winter and Szulanski, 2001; Nonaka, 1994) raises the question of how to determine where knowledge is located and how to transfer and replicate it. A general conclusion derived from various taxonomies of knowledge is that codified knowledge is easier to transfer than tacit knowledge, which is often specific to the context in which it is developed (Winter, 1987; Kogut and Zander, 1993). Hence, while knowledge and capabilities diffuse within countries, cross-border transfers may be difficult (Kogut, 1991). Although the increased use of general and abstract knowledge is argued to make knowledge less context-dependent (Arora et al., 1999), this conclusion overlooks the importance of practice and participation in communities and the role of institutions in shaping the context of transfer. Finally, these studies do not focus on the mechanisms of knowledge creation and capability building or on inter-industry variations in capabilities and performance.

KNOWLEDGE CREATION AND INNOVATION IN GLOBAL COMMUNITIES

We use an evolutionary approach to develop our framework of knowledge creation and capability development. The central task in knowledge creation is the transfer and recombination of tacit and explicit knowledge (Nonaka, 1994) via a craft or industrial system. We focus on knowledge creation via a 'modular assembly' or mass-production system.

In the 'modular assembly' system, a key mechanism is codification, which involves externalizing memory. Codification depends on complex actions such as applying industrial design techniques to draft a scale drawing of a piece of machinery, creating an expert system from formalized rules, to detach knowledge from the individual and render memory and communication capacity independent of human beings. Thus, codification reduces knowledge to information, enabling its reproduction which is almost instantaneous when the learning task is simple. In complex cases, knowledge reproduction occurs through training, practice, and simulation techniques because codification only provides partial assistance (David and Foray, 2002).

Codification thus creates new cognitive potentialities by translating knowledge into symbolic representations. Inscribing through writing, graphics, and so on makes it possible to examine and arrange knowledge in different ways and to isolate, classify, and combine different components, resulting in new knowledge objects such as lists, tables, formulae, and theories. Knowledge arises from a response to a problem; trials, experiments, and solutions to the original problem lead to new problems and theories. Advances in information technology-based recording methods and codification facilitate memorization, communication and learning, and the creation of new knowledge objects (David and Foray, 2002).

Information technologies enhance creative interaction not only among scholars and scientists but, equally among product designers, suppliers, and customers. Virtual objects can be modified ad infinitum, are instantly accessible to all, and serve to facilitate learning. Communities of practice that promote participation and reification (the creation of knowledge objects) are essential for knowledge production (Wenger, 1998). Participation involves renegotiating meaning and creating identity while reification aids problem-solving by externalizing the mental process through the production of artifacts. Innovation and the creation of new products are, thus, a natural consequence of learning and problem-solving within communities.

At a collective level, practice enables the community to reconceive its environment and identity. Innovation and new interpretations emerge from practice and from interactions with other communities that help align competence and identity with other trajectories, thus linking the local with the global.

Establishing effective communities is, therefore, a central task in knowledge creation. Communities are important because tacit elements remain even when knowledge has been codified, necessitating interactions via artifacts. Evidence from research on social capital suggests that communities provide identity and access to resources and knowledge (Coleman, 1988). However, the knowledge production system is becoming more widely distributed across a host of new actors and places (Nelson, 1996;[1] David and Foray, 2002; von Hippel, 1988), a consequence of the rising speed and intensity of innovation as evidenced by the volume of patents requested and approved (OECD, 2002), by the proliferation of new goods and services in the movement towards 'mass customization' (David, 2000), and by the need to innovate for survival in an increasingly competitive and global world (Nelson, 1993; Clark and Fujimoto, 1991). Thus, a key challenge in developing new technologies and innovating, both of which are important for development, is facilitating the creation of knowledge communities across organizational and national boundaries.

FACILITATING KNOWLEDGE PRODUCTION VIA CROSS-BORDER INTERACTIONS

Facilitating knowledge production in global communities involves: (1) fostering relationships and interactions with external communities to ease information sharing and ensuring benchmarking and access to expertise; (2) architecting organizational designs to ease coordination and collaborative knowledge production; and (3) enabling practice, participation, and experimentation to aid problem-solving.

Firms in emerging economies access new knowledge primarily in two ways. First, interactions with buyers in industrialized countries provide information about product specifications and requirements (Enos, 1991; Westphal et al., 1985). Second, domestic firms' interactions with foreign suppliers via technical collaborations, joint ventures, and subsidiaries provide knowledge embodied in documents, machinery, marketing, and manufacturing expertise. In this chapter we focus on the first type of interaction.

In both the above cases, promoting trust is critical to ease the coordination and communication of both tacit and codified knowledge to speed innovation. Trust is widely recognized as contributing to cooperation, information exchange, and enhanced system efficiency (Arrow, 1974; Coleman, 1988). Lack of trust hampers communication, collaboration, and involvement in the supply of training, access to knowledge critical for product development, and the provision of appropriate role modeling. In addition, to adapt products for the foreign market successfully, suppliers from developing countries require access to knowledge about the new institutional context. Moreover, a social community is required for the evolution of a common language to speed the flow of information (Arrow, 1974) and induce the adoption of new benchmarks and aspirations. Second, collaborative knowledge production is speeded by using an organizational design that facilitates concurrent rather than sequential information processing to promote the rapid diffusion of knowledge. This requires effective boundary spanning across internal departments and involving actors in the larger community (such as local suppliers). Organization design is a critical challenge because while specialization increases efficiency (Lawrence and Lorsch, 1969; Thompson, 1967), it impedes knowledge sharing since it fosters different cognitive and emotional orientations (Lawrence and Lorsch, 1969).

Modularity, a strategy for designing complex technical systems and processes efficiently, is a design rule facilitating concurrent information processing (Baldwin and Clark, 2000). Modular systems are composed of independently designed units but function as an integrated whole. Modularity offers design advantages because experimentation and improvement of components can occur within a module without compromising the efficacy of other components and without requiring a change in the system's overall architecture. Modularity provides a way to divide the labor and knowledge of the overall system so that individuals responsible for the system, components, and sub-systems can experiment and make improvements independently. Analogously, organizational structures that encourage interactions between different communities of practice,[2] yet permit modularity, enable speedier problem-solving. The use of geographically dispersed teams is facilitated by the adoption of modular design principles in organization, since each unit is independent.

Third, practice is critical to the development of expertise and knowledge production in firms. When foreign collaborators interact in ways that prevent participation and practice, knowledge acquisition is aborted in local firms (Lave and Wenger, 1991). Inability to experiment, or gain access to the requisite methodologies can make knowledge production costly, difficult, and slow in domestic firms. However, participation in collaborative work diffuses commonly employed concepts and terminological conventions.

The software development process has historically been seen as an art to be performed by those with advanced technical training. Over time, however, the application of industrial engineering concepts helped to systematize and standardize the process. The 'waterfall model' describes this process in six distinct steps (see Table 7.1).

Thus, the evolution of the software industry can be viewed as a movement from a craft-based to a modular system of knowledge production and organization.

Table 7.1 The waterfall systems development model (Kennedy, 2001)

	Systems planning	Technical design	Detailed design	Coding/ testing	Acceptance testing/ implementation	Maintenance
Tasks	Identify software requirements	System architecture ID program needs	Program specifications Write input/ output	Write code Test program Test system requirements	Test with existing systems Install system	Changes Fix bugs New reqmts.
Approx. life cycle costs:	6%	←7%→		←17%→		70%
Able to be completed off-site:						

INDIAN PARTICIPATION IN KNOWLEDGE CREATION

Liberalization of the Indian economy in the wake of India's financial crisis in 1991 led to the abandonment of post-independence economic policies of import substitution and infant industry protection in favor of policies focused on exports and reducing barriers to entry to foreign firms (Jalan, 1991). Competition from multinationals led domestic firms to seek a solution to the problem of how to compete globally and participate in world markets. Cross-border interactions in the context of supplying technology-related services to foreign firms can thus be viewed as experiments in learning situated within an environmental context of transition from a closed to an open economy. Hence, the focus in this chapter is on interactions with global buyers of software services from India.

We examine the evolution of the software industry, and document the development of cross-border communities of practice enabling knowledge creation in a leading software firm. Studying leading firms is important (Teubal, 2003) for encouraging development, particularly since they serve as role models for stimulating entrepreneurial activity (Arora and Athreye, 2002).

THE EVOLUTION OF THE SOFTWARE INDUSTRY

The early days of computing were dominated by public research organizations and the early history of software was linked with the development of the Indian hardware industry (Heeks, 1996). ESSO Standard, the Indian subsidiary of Exxon, installed the first commercial computer in 1961. Thereafter, computers were imported from international suppliers such as IBM, Digital Equipment Corporation, Burroughs, Sperry, and Honeywell. During the 1970s, government and academic computer users relied on imported software bundled with the hardware and also internal software developers. With the increasing use of computers, a domestic market for software emerged as development began to be contracted to outside organizations such as management consultancies. The departure of IBM and other foreign manufacturers in the 1970s prompted the growth of Indian firms to fill the void to offer local companies assistance in importing computers, software development, and low-level data-processing functions, in addition to helping them gain skills in working with UNIX (the first portable, machine-independent, multi-user operating system), the system of choice for personal computers (PCs) and workstations in the 1990s (Saxenian, 2000). As their capabilities grew, the software firms began to look offshore, hoping to leverage their relatively lower labor costs of skilled software programmers.

Advances in infrastructure development, a large English-speaking and low-cost scientific manpower reservoir, and a well-functioning technical education system graduating more than 60 000 technically trained workers each year, catalyzed the emergence of the software industry and a new industrial location, India (see Table 7.2 for productivity measures of selected Indian and US software companies). The Indian information technology (IT) and IT-enabled services industry has grown at a compound annual growth rate (CAGR) of 46 percent in the last four years. Export revenues of India's software services market reached $6.2 billion last year, up from under $500 million in the mid-1990s (Economist, 2003). IT services exports are estimated to grow to $28–30 billion, while IT-enabled services exports are projected to grow to $21–24 billion accounting for more than 30 percent of foreign exchange inflows in 2008 and a major driver of economic growth (NASSCOM, 2002). Also, 80 percent of all Software Engineering Institute Capability Maturity Model (SEI–CMM) level 5 firms are in India.

Table 7.2   Productivity measures, selected Indian and US software companies (US$)

Company	Sales/employee	Operating cost/ employee	Operating profit/ employee
Indian firms			
TCS	35, 310	23,652	11, 658
Infosys	32,014	21,341	10,674
Satyam	27,775	17,364	10,411
Wipro	30, 270	20, 882	9, 388
US firms			
Cambridge Tech			
Partners	166,158	138,837	26,321
Keane Assoc.	93,312	79,204	14,108
Mastech Corp.	80,281	69,218	11,063
Sapient Corp.	134,165	103,826	30,339

Source: 'India Software: a comparison of India's top software exporters', Morgan Stanley Dean Witter, August 7, 1998, cited in P. Ghemawat, 1999, *The Indian Software Industry at the Turn of the Millennium (700-036)* and Robert E. Kennedy, 2001 ('Tata Consultancy Services: high technology in a low-income country', HBS case 9-700-092).

Leading Software Firms

Teubal (2003) suggests that the growth and transformation of a very dynamic sector is triggered by initiatives or pioneering efforts of firms (or individuals) who 'show the way' and that the path subsequently followed by the sector as a whole cannot be understood without reference to those key firms or key agents. Wipro Infotech, one of the leading software companies was established in 1980 and made its entry into the IT area by manufacturing minicomputers to take advantage of restrictions on imports of minicomputers, thereby developing strong skills in hardware design. The company entered the software business in 1989, but failed to develop product software and reoriented its strategy towards software services through the creation of an offshore development center. Later, it began to offer integrated software/hardware services. While there has been some product development activity, it is limited. Wipro's sales in 1998 were $350 million of which $100 million were hardware sales. The next phase for Wipro would involve going up the value chain, via engaging in fixed price transactions for application software development, specialization in vertical segments like finance and retail, and the development of some reusable software components which may represent building blocks for large software projects of clients abroad.

In addition, both Arora and Athreye (2002) and Teubal (2003) suggest that the emergence of 'star' software firms appears to have sparked entrepreneurial activity. Of the 2 500 Indian software exporters, the top five are Tata Consultancy Services, Infosys, Wipro, Satyam, and HCL accounting for about 35 percent of software exports. The main export destinations are the USA (63 percent), Europe (26 percent), while Japan and other countries account for 11 percent (Singh, 2002; see Figures 7.1, 7.2 and 7.3 for sales and export data on three leading software firms).

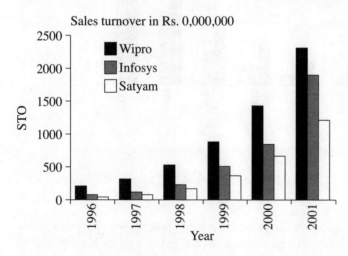

Figure 7.1 Sales turnover of three leading software companies: Wipro, Infosys, and Satyam.

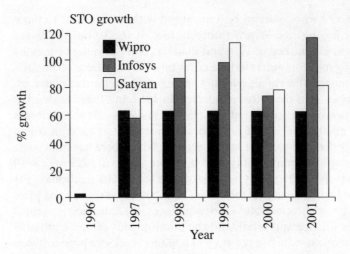

Figure 7.2   Growth of sales turnover: Wipro, Infosys, and Satyam

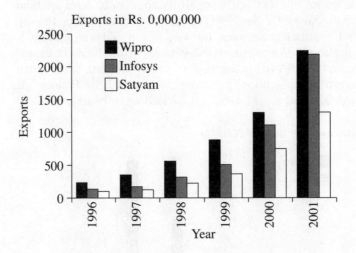

Figure 7.3   Exports of Wipro, Infosys and Satyam

Source   (Figures 7.1, 7.2 and 7.3): Siddharthan and Lall, Institute of Economic Growth, Delhi, 2002

Moreover, methods for generating indigenous global players include encouraging start-up and venture capital firms, and as exemplified by the case of Hughes Software Systems (a subsidiary of Hughes Network Systems, a joint venture of Hughes Electronics and General Motors), by

Table 7.3 Evolution of selected Indian software companies

	1960s	1970s →	Mid-1980s	Late 1980s	1990s	2000 →
Tata Consultancy Services	Founded in 1968. Bureau Services for Tata Group	Formation of alliance with Burroughs. First large US software project secured	Break with Burroughs. Platform Independence. First US Office Development of Migration business	Migration business expanded. Project mgmt./fixed price contracts	Leading provider of customized IT services. Full outsourcing partner. Packaged software products/ programming services. Larger project size and scope. Dedicated development centers. Major exporter ← Move to offshore work →	Focus on globalization. Transformation to a global systems consulting firm
Wipro		Established hardware division, Wipro Infotech in 1979	1984 Wipro began to develop software for IBM clients; and for customers for Wipro hardware. On-site work in US		1998 software/hardware businesses integrated. 1998 – attained level 5 rating on SEI–CMM model. Six Sigma methodologies Software products. Introduction of employee stock option plan ← Move to offshore work →	Software for foreign clients. Focus on US presence & globalizing. NYSE listing
Infosys			Established in 1981. In 1986 it formed an alliance with Kurt Salmon Associates. One major US client. Focus on US and other countries. Employee stock options offered		Move to offshore development centers (ODCs). Level 4 rating on SEI–CMM model. Managed software solutions – fixed time, fixed price projects. Use of global development centers (GDCs). NASDAQ listing. ← Move to offshore work →	Focus on globalizing. Transformation to a global consulting firm with increased US presence

Source: Robert E. Kennedy, 2001 ('Tata Consultancy Services: high technology in a low-income country', HBS Case 9-700-092); Suma Raju, Lynn Sharp Paine, and Carin-Isabel Knoop, 2001 (Wipro Technologies, HBS case 9-301-043); Ashish Nanda and Thomas Delong, 2002 (*Infosys Technologies*, HBS Case 9-801-445).

participating in the India stock market (Teubal, 2003). Consequently, market- and client-related asset spillovers were encouraged in addition to technological spillovers. An analysis of the Infosys case is presented below; the development of other leading software firms followed a similar pattern (see Table 7.3 for an outline of the development pattern of selected Indian companies).

Infosys Technologies: A Case Study

Using our framework of knowledge creation through communities facilitating cross-border interactions, we examine the growth and internationalization of Infosys, a leading software company established by Narayana Murthy in 1981 and based in Bangalore. From its inception, the company focused on the US market given its size and the differential in labor costs of US and Indian software professionals. Growth in the 1980s was slow with only one major US customer until 1986 when Infosys entered a short-lived joint venture with Kurt Salmon Associates to deliver software services. In addition Indian government regulations on setting up foreign offices and restrictions on the entry of Indian programmers into the USA hampered efforts to sell in the USA (Nanda and Delong, 2002).

The program of economic reform initiated by the government in 1991 also intensified competition as multinational companies like IBM began to consider re-entering India to set up development centers. Despite dire predictions that Indian firms would be unable to compete in the war for skilled talent, Infosys adopted practices such as offering employees stock options in line with the compensation packages of multinational companies and improved the work environment: two major reasons for the defection of potential employees to MNCs.

Indian software firms also began moving from body-shopping contracts to off shore development contracts (ODCs) – Indian programmers writing software in India for foreign companies. ODCs offered greater arbitrage opportunities than body-shopping (the average salary for a software professional in India was about $13 000/year compared to $75 000/year for an Indian programmer in the USA). While ODCs lowered the overall costs of development and provided a 24-hour work cycle, they imposed a greater risk on clients. In body-shopping, the client controlled the parameters of the projects and closely monitored the software development process. Companies like Infosys had gained some knowledge of client requirements in the USA through the body-shopping option. In the early 1990s it was one of the leading software companies to pursue ODCs' opportunities. ODCs required the software suppliers to control and monitor software development on behalf of the clients and take charge of knowledge production. To reassure customers, Infosys focused on institutionalizing quality and received ISO 9000 certification, thus further raising quality awareness in the firm (Arora and Asundi, 1999, study ISO certification in Indian software firms and find that ISO certification both enhances quality and has a positive impact on firm growth).

Rapid expansion led to the diversification of the client base which consisted mainly of US clients and geographic locations to gain access to other locations that were rich in engineering and technical colleges. In 1998, Infosys became the first Indian company to receive level 4 certification of the SEI–CMM and was on track to receive level 5 certification in 2000, joining the ranks of the 2 percent of companies worldwide to achieve level 4 or higher certification. Infosys also began to take on an increasing share of the risk involved with software development by offering clients 'managed software solutions' – fixed time, fixed price projects with quality guarantees. In addition, mission-critical software systems were also being developed for clients like Nortel, Reebok, and Nordstrom. For example, beginning in 1992 with simple tool development for Bell Northern Research, a R&D division of Northern Telecom (as Nortel was then called) generating $200 000 in revenues, Infosys' relationship with Nortel developed into an intense collaboration with core R&D engineering groups and even working with Nortel clients generating $8 million in revenues (Nanda and Delong, 2002).

By 1999, Infosys had 114 customers and most of its work focused on writing customized software for installation at client sites. The use of dispersed teams using a modular structure was adopted. First, a typical project required a small team of project leaders to travel to their client's location to ascertain the client's priorities and specifications. Second, the project leaders would return to India and supervise a team. A small group of people usually stayed on site with the client, interacting with the home base via satellite-enabled communications on issues such as changing specifications, obtaining clarity on issues, getting permission for changes, and so on. Once the project was completed, a team would travel to the client's site to install the software, test it, and train the client's staff (Nanda and Delong, 2002).

Infosys established a global identity by using global development centers (GDCs) located in globally optimal destinations in India and abroad, including work at both ODCs and proximity development centers (PDCs) or teams of Infosys employees located close to the customers. Management expected that the GDC model would 'help change the image of Infosys from purely an off-shore development company to an all-purpose global IT based problem solver'.

In its quest to globalize, Infosys tapped the markets in the USA in March 1999, with a $75 million issue of 1.8 million American Depository

Receipts (ADRs) priced at $34 on the NASDAQ stock exchange, becoming the first Indian company to be listed on a US stock exchange. Currently, Infosys faces the challenge of moving up the value chain by executing more complex projects for customers, thus making it a direct competitor of the consulting arms of the Big Five while its cost advantage began to decline. India-based employee costs were rising 25 percent per year and non-India based employee costs at 10 percent per year. Additionally, Infosys plans to become a truly global company by recruiting more locals in the USA and other countries. The company is also considering an investment in the Multimedia Super Corridor, a hi-tech zone in Malaysia due to be completed by 2011 (Knowledge@wharton[3]).

The Infosys case is not unique in the software industry and suggests that economic liberalization intensified competition, leading Indian software firms to seek clients overseas. Interactions with US clients led them to adopt new practices and processes, to improve quality through benchmarking, and to become globally competitive as was the case with Korean firms (Enos, 1991). A virtuous cycle of learning was triggered at each stage, helping the firm to evolve from providing low-level programming services onshore to an offshore developer focused on higher-end projects. The development of new information and technology infrastructure facilitated the use of dispersed teams. A modular project design enabled programmers in an off-shore location to design modules independently while coordination and communication with the client was maintained by onshore teams.

However, an emerging international division of labor between India and the USA in software was apparent, with low-end work programming work done by Infosys in the early stages and the high-end design work being done in the USA However, this division of labor is not static. By the late 1990s, India began to be seen as a global leader in software development, with the trend towards outsourcing projects accelerating and more value-added work being sought by Indian firms like Infosys. However, while in terms of revenue and export performance, the Indian software industry is comparable to Ireland's and Israel's and larger than that of South Korea, earnings of professionals are well below those in Ireland and Israel (OECD, 2000) and its share of world markets remains small.

Since 1999, the IT-enabled services sector has blossomed with firms in India engaged in providing business process outsourcing services to US clients. While the major proportion of the work relates to back-office processing, customer service, and claims processing, there is also a trend towards outsourcing higher-end and time-critical projects such as real estate and financial analysis, market research, and design work (NASSCOM, 2002, pp. 19–29; see Table 7.4 for the projected growth of IT-enabled services).

*Table 7.4   Projected growth of US$ 87 billion for the Indian IT services
and IT-enabled services industry – NASSCOM–McKinsey
report (2002)*

2008	Exports US$ billion	Domestic US$ billion	Total US$ billion
IT services	30	8.5	38.5
ITEs	17	2	19
Software products	10	9.5	19.5
Total	57	20	77

Multinational corporations (MNCs) have been quick to take advantage
of India's competitive environment, by establishing a base to develop and
deliver high-quality software applications to their clients abroad at reduced
operating costs. MNC software export revenues, including those from IT-
enabled services, account for 27 percent of total Indian software export

Table 7.5   Top 20 MNC software exporters

MNC	Employees (as of 31 March, 2002)
1. IBM Global Services	3,100
2. Cognizant Technology Solutions	2,712
3. Oracle India Pvt. Ltd.	2,000
4. Covansys (India) Private Ltd.	1,595
5. Syntel	1,580
6. Hughes Software Systems Ltd.	1,500
7. Hewlett-Packard Software Operations Ltd.	1,489
8. Digital Globalsoft	1,480
9. PwC	1,200
10. OrbiTech Solutions	1,191
11. Siemens Information Systems Ltd.	1,187
12. Xansa (India) Ltd.	892
13. Motorola	800
14. ST Microelectronics	800
15. Texas Instruments India Pvt. Ltd.	741
16. Intel Tech India Pvt. Ltd.	700
17. i2 Technologies	700
18. Cisco	670
19. Robert Bosch	629
20. Huawei	500

revenues of Rs. 36,500 crore in 2001–2002, up from just 15 percent in 2000–2001. One effect of MNC participation in India (this includes companies like IBM Global Services, Accenture, Cognizant Technology Solutions, and EDS) is to intensify competition (Pillai, 2003a, 2003b; see Table 7.5 for the top 10 exporters of software in India). Cantwell (1989) notes that foreign direct investment by multinational firms spurs competition in the new location and initiates innovation and internationalization among domestic firms. Similarly, Dunning (1993) argues that intra-industry spillovers occur through competition-induced increases in productivity of domestic firms.

CONCLUSION

Capability building in the software industry followed an evolutionary path. The ability of software firms to participate more fully in global markets can be attributed to the advantage provided by a technological discontinuity and by the advent of new information technologies that enabled software firms to reach out to global markets from the outset. Software firms were less encumbered than manufacturing firms by administrative heritage. From the 1990s onwards, learning through cross-border interactions and involvement in practice was speeded by the adoption of appropriate technologies and modular organizational design to enable participation across geographically dispersed sites. Successful firms learned, adapted, and innovated through interactions with global customers and the creation of cross-border communities of practice, thus building local capabilities, and confirming evidence from research on international technology transfer that the most vibrant firms in emerging economies are those that build their own capabilities (Lall, 1987).

Software, a new industry, had the opportunity to take advantage of technological changes to start out as a knowledge-based industry. Moreover, government policy played a role in the development of software by encouraging software exports to nurture the indigenous development of the computer industry (Heeks, 1996), and by removing barriers to its growth through reforms in the mid-1980s, early 1990s, and in the mid-1990s, a consequence of the recognition of the growing importance of the software industry and the lobbying efforts of the National Association of Software and Service Companies (NASSCOM). An example is the introduction of the Software Technology Parks Scheme in the early 1990s to ensure adequate infrastructure and administrative support for exporting which facilitated a shift away from on-site to offshore service provision in the 1990s (Saxenian, 2000). Consequently, software rapidly became visible as a global industry.

The rapid and continuing growth of the software industry in the last decade suggests that there is a concomitant growth in the number of members in the community involved in knowledge production. This critical mass of knowledge workers combined with the success of software globally has altered the space of possibilities for Indians leading to the convergence of aspirations and identities with counterparts in the developed world. However, replicating the success of the software industry in other industries and ensuring that the benefits of IT are accessible to the wider population necessitates accompanying changes in the institutional environment. Greater benefits are likely to be reaped from a focus on developing the IT, power and transportation infrastructures to enable all sectors of the economy to use IT to improve productivity and by nurturing a wider range of industries and institutions to support the diffusion of IT.

Moreover, collaboration between public sector research institutions and industry such as the joint participation of the Indian Institute of Science (IISc), and Encore Software, a Bangalore-based software development company, in developing the Simputer, a low-cost mobile PC (priced at approximately US$200) using leading-edge technologies and open-source software must be encouraged along with the formation of a strong local venture capital industry. Such measures may do much to bridge the digital divide and to alleviate institutional bottlenecks that impede wider participation in the domestic and global knowledge economy.

Despite the challenges ahead, evidence from the software industry suggests that developing countries may enjoy a 'late-mover advantage' in industries that take advantage of technological discontinuities to innovate and adopt new organizational forms to exploit opportunities. Thus, cross-border innovation may offer new ways to bridge the gap between poverty and wealth.

NOTES

* The author gratefully acknowledges the support of the National Science Foundation, George Mason University School of Public Policy, the Department of Management Studies, Indian Institute of Science, and the Department of Management at the Wharton School.
1. Nelson (1996) suggests that the distinction between science and technology is blurring with more abstract and basic knowledge being generated at the site of technology development. In addition von Hippel (1988) notes that 'lead users' are often involved in the co-creation of new products and technologies.
2. Such boundary-crossing interactions include buyer–supplier interactions across borders and within each country. Such interactions also include relationships between different groups within the firm such as product design and marketing.
3. I am indebted to insights provided by Basab Pradhan of Infosys at a conference on Competing with Knowledge organized by the Mack Center for Technological Innovation at the Wharton School in November, 2002.

REFERENCES

Arora, Ashish and Jai Asundi (1999), 'Quality certification and the economics of contract software development: a study of the Indian software industry', National Bureau of Economic Research working paper no 7260, Cambridge, MA.

Arora, Ashish, Andrea Fosfuri and Alfonso Gambardella (1999), 'Division of labor and the market for technology: the growth of the chemical industry', paper presented at the Wharton School, University of Pennsylvania, May.

Arora, Ashish and Suma Athreye (2002), 'The software industry and India's economic development', *Information Economics and Policy*, **14** (2), June, 252–273.

Arrow, Kenneth (1974), *The Limits of Organization*, New York: Norton.

Baldwin, Carliss Y. and Kim B. Clark (2000), *Design Rules*, Cambridge, MA: The MIT Press.

Baran, Paul (1975), *The Political Economy of Neo-colonialism*, London: Heinemann.

Bell, Martin and Don Scott-Kemmis (1988), 'Technology import policy: have the problems changed?' in Ashok V. Desai (ed.) (1988), *Technology Absorption in Indian Industry*, New Delhi: Wiley Eastern Limited, pp. 2–70.

Cantwell, John (1989), *Technological Innovations and the Multinational Corporation*, London: Basil Blackwell.

Chenery, Hollis B. (1979), *Structural Change and Development Policy*, Baltimore, MD: Johns Hopkins University Press.

Clark, K.B. and T. Fujimoto (1991), *Product Development Performance*, Boston, MA: Harvard Business School Press.

Coleman, James S. (1988), 'Social capital in the creation of human capital', *American Journal of Sociology*, **94**, supplement S95–S120.

Dahlman, C.J., Bruce Ross-Larson and Larry E. Westphal (1987), 'Managing technological development: lessons from the newly industrializing countries', *World Development*, **15** (6), 759–775.

David, Paul A. (2000), 'Understanding digital technology's evolution and the path of measured productivity growth: present and future in the mirror of the past', in E. Brynjolfsson and B. Kahin (eds) (2000), *Understanding the Digital Economy*, Cambridge, MA: The MIT Press, pp. 49–95.

David, Paul A. and Dominique Foray (2003), 'Economic fundamentals of the knowledge society', *Policy Futures in Education*, 1(1): special issue on 'Education and the Knowledge Economy'.

Dunning, J.H. (1993), *Multinational Enterprises and the Global Economy*, New York: John Wiley and Sons.

Economist (2003), 'Outsourcing: America's pain, India's gain', *The Economist*, 11–17 January.

Enos, J.L. and W.H. Park (1988), *The Adoption and Diffusion of Imported Technology: The Case of Korea*, London: Croom Helm.

Enos, J.L. (1991), *The Creation of Technological Capability in Developing Countries*, New York: Pinter Publishers.

Griffin, Keith and John Gurley (1985), 'Radical analysis of imperialism, the Third World, and the transition to socialism: a survey article', *Journal of Economic Literature*, **23**, September, 1089–143.

Heeks, Richard (1996), *India's Software Industry: State Policy, Liberalization and Industrial Development*, Thousand Oaks, CA: Sage Publications. www.knowledge. wharton.upenn.edu/articles.cfm?catid=2&articleid=364.

Jalan, Bimal (1991), *India's Economic Crisis: the Way Ahead*, New Delhi: Oxford University Press.

Kennedy, Robert E. (2001), 'Tata Consultancy Services: high technology in a low-income country', Harvard Business School (HBS) case no 9-700-092.

Kogut, B. (1991), 'Country capabilities and the permeability of borders', *Strategic Management Journal*, **12**, 33–47.

Kogut, B. and U. Zander (2001), 'Knowledge of the firm and the evolutionary theory of the multinational corporation', *Journal of International Business Studies*, **24** (4), Fourth Quarter, 625–645.

Krueger, Anne O. (1995), 'East Asian experience and endogenous growth theory', in Takatoshi Ito and Anne O. Krueger (eds) (1995), *Growth Theories in the Light of the East Asian Experience*, Chicago, IL: University of Chicago Press, pp. 9–30.

Lal, Deepak (1985), *The Poverty of Development Economics*, Cambridge, MA: Harvard University Press.

Lall, Sanjaya (1987), *Learning to Industrialize: The Acquisition of Technological Capability by India*, Basingstoke: Macmillan Press.

Lave, Jean and Eugene Wenger (1991), *Situated Learning*, Cambridge, MA: Cambridge University Press.

Lawrence, P.R. and Jay Lorsch (1969), *Organization and Environment*, Homewood, IL: Richard D. Irwin.

Licht, Walter (1995), *Industrializing America: The Nineteenth Century*, Baltimore, MD: John Hopkins University Press.

Little, Ian (1982), *Economic Development: Theories, Policies, and International Relations*, New York: Basic Books.

March, James, G. and Herbert A. Simon with the collaboration of Harold Guetzkow (1958), *Organizations*, New York: Wiley.

Nanda, Ashish and Thomas Delong (2002), 'Infosys technologies', Harvard Business School case no 9-801-445.

NASSCOM (2002), 'Strategies to achieve the Indian IT industry's aspiration', in *NASSCOM–McKinsey Report*, pp. 19–29, New Delhi and Mumbai, India: NASSCOM and McKinsey and Company.

Nelson, Richard R. (1996), *The Sources of Economic Growth*, Cambridge, MA: Harvard University Press.

Nelson, Richard R. (ed.) (1993), *National Innovation Systems: a Comparative Analysis*, New York: Oxford University Press.

Nonaka, I. (1994), 'A dynamic theory of knowledge creation', *Organization Science*, **5**, (1), February 14–37.

OECD (2000), *OECD Information Technology Outlook*, Paris: Organization for Economic Co-operation and Development, pp. 131–150.

OECD (2002), *OECD Information Technology Outlook*, accessed at www.oecd.org/EN/document/0,,EN-document-13-nodirectorate-no-1-30897-13,00.html.

Perrow, Charles (1979), *Complex Organizations: a Critical Essay*, New York: Random House.

Pillai, S.K. (2003a), 'Multinational companies are here to use India's cost advantages – and they could pose a threat to Indian software companies', accessed at www.business-standard.com/iceworld/icew216.htm.

Pillai, S.K. (2003b), 'MNC offshore development to gain ground', accessed at www.business-standard.com/today/story.asp?Menu=2&story=8056.

Romer, Paul (1994), 'The origins of endogenous growth', *The Journal of Economic Perspectives*, **8**, 1, Winter, 3–22.

Rostow, Walt W. (1960), *The Stages of Economic Growth*, London: Cambridge University Press.

Saxenian, Annalee (2000), 'Bangalore: the Silicon Valley of Asia', paper presented at the Conference on Indian Economic Prospects: Advancing Policy Reform, Center for Research on Economic Development and Policy Reform, Stanford, CA, May, accessed at www-dcrp.ced.berkeley.edu/Faculty/Anno/Writings/Bangalore%20--%20The%20Silicon%20Valley%20of%20Asia.htm.

Singh, Nirvikar (2002), 'India's information technology sector: what contribution to broader economic development', paper presented at the November 2002 OECD Conference in Chennai, India, accessed at www.oecd.org/oecd/pages/document/displaywithoutnav/0,3376,EN-document-notheme-1-no-no-36687-0,00.html.

Stiglitz, Joseph (1998), 'Towards a new paradigm for development: strategies, policies, and processes', Prebisch Lecture at UNCTAD, Geneva, October, accessed at www.worldbank.org/html/extdr/extme/jssp101998.htm.

Teubal, Morris (2002), 'Observations on the Indian software industry from an Israeli perspective: a microeconomic and policy analysis', *Science, Technology and Society Journal* (New Delhi), **7** (1), 151–86.

Thompson, J.D. (1967), *Organizations in Action*, New York: McGraw-Hill.

Todaro, Michael (1994), *Economic Development*, New York: Longman.

Von Hippel, Eric (1998), *The Sources of Innovation*, New York: Oxford University Press.

Weber, Max (1947), *Essays in Sociology*, translated, edited and with an introduction by H.H. Gerth and C. Wright Mills, London: Kegan Paul, Trench, Trubner.

Wei, Shang-Jin (1995), 'The open door policy and China's rapid growth: evidence from city-level data', in Takatoshi Ito and Anne O. Krueger (eds) (1995), *Growth Theories in the Light of the East Asian Experience*, Chicago, IL: University of Chicago Press, pp. 73–104.

Wenger, Etienne (1998), *Communities of Practice: Learning, Meaning, and Identity*, New York: Cambridge University Press.

Westphal, Larry E., Linsu Kim and Carl J. Dahlman (1985), 'Reflections on the Republic of Korea's acquisition of technological capability', in Nathan Rosenberg and Claudio Frischtak (eds) (1985), *International Technology Transfer: Concepts, Measures and Comparisons*, New York: Praeger.

Winter, Sidney G. (1987), 'Knowledge and competence as strategic assets', in David J. Teece (ed.) (1987), *The Competitive Challenge: Strategies for Industrial Innovation and Renewal*, New York: Harper & Row.

Winter, S. and G. Szulanski (2001), 'Replication as strategy', *Organization Science*, **12** (6), Nov–Dec, 730–743.

8. Inimitability of network resources in the research and development services domain of the Indian information technology industry

Nagarajan Dayasindhu[*]

INTRODUCTION

A pilot case study reveals that inimitable resources like the ability of the employees to comprehend relevant technologies and specific design/programming capabilities lead to sustained competitive advantage in the research and development (R&D) services domain of the Indian information technology (IT) industry. Semiconductor Company (SC), a global leader in the manufacture of integrated signal processing chips, is a part of a network of organizations in the R&D services domain of the Indian IT industry. This network of organizations designs hardware and software systems based on SC's chips. SC believes that resources are spread across a network of organizations. It appears that competitors of SC have tried but failed in their attempts to create a similar network of organizations. This observation is consistent with the research on networks of organizations (Gulati et al., 2000).

LITERATURE REVIEW AND RESEARCH QUESTIONS

Relevant research literature on the resource-based view (RBV), inimitability of resources, networks of organizations, and network resources are discussed in this section. Resources are the assets, capabilities, organizational processes, organizational attributes, and knowledge, that are used by organizations to implement strategies to improve effectiveness and efficiency (Barney, 1991). Networks of organizations are composed of a select, persistent, and structured set of autonomous organizations engaged in creating products or services based on implicit and open-ended contracts to adapt

127

to environmental contingencies and to coordinate and safeguard exchanges (Jones et al., 1997). Network resources are those resources that extend beyond the boundaries of the organization and reside within a network of organizations (Gulati, 1999). Research literature reveals that resources and network resources can be a source of achieving sustained competitive advantage. An organization is said to possess competitive advantage when its current or potential competitors can neither simultaneously implement nor duplicate the benefits of its value creating strategy (Barney, 1991). The competitive advantage is sustained only if it continues to exist after the efforts to duplicate the advantage by competitors have ceased (Barney, 1991). In essence, RBV posits that valuable, rare, inimitable, and non-substitutable resources provide sustainable competitive advantage for an organization. Among these characteristics of resources, it appears that inimitability of resources is central to sustained competitive advantage. Inimitability of resources is dependent on unique historical conditions, social complexity, characteristic causal ambiguity, time compression diseconomies, asset mass efficiencies, interconnectedness of asset stocks, and asset erosion.

There are empirical research studies in the RBV that successfully explain sustained competitive advantage. Miller and Shamsie (1996) applied the RBV to organizations in the US film studio industry between 1936 and 1965 and identified that property-based and knowledge-based resources led to competitive advantage under stable industry structure while knowledge-based resources led to competitive advantage under moderately dynamic industry structure. Jarvenpaa and Leidner (1998) applied the RBV in a developing country context to an organization in Mexico that pioneered the information industry in that country. Case study methodology was used to unravel the resources of strategic foresight and flexibility, coupled with trustworthiness that is critical in achieving a sustained competitive advantage. Eisenhardt and Martin (2000) argue that the RBV reaches a limiting case in a high-velocity industry characterized by ambiguous industry structure, blurred boundaries between organizations, fluid business models, shifting players and unpredictable non-linear changes.

According to Barney (1991) an organization's resources can be inimitable due to one or a combination of three reasons such as unique historical conditions, social complexity, and causal ambiguity. However, King and Zeithaml (2001) posit that it is the characteristic causal ambiguity about not knowing what in the resources (and not the causal ambiguity regarding the link between resources and sustained competitive advantage) that makes them inimitable. Reed and DeFillippi (1990) investigated three characteristics of causal ambiguity, that is tacitness, complexity, and specificity that make it a source of resource inimitability. Deirickx and Cool (1989) argue that inimitability of resources depends on time compression diseconomies, asset mass efficiencies, interconnectedness of asset stocks, asset erosion, and causal ambiguity. Assets in this context refer to the bundles of resources.

Networks of organizations have been described in different ways in research literature (Gulati et al., 2000; Powell, 1990). A description that is specific and relevant to this research views networks of organizations as composed of a select, persistent, and structured set of autonomous organizations engaged in creating products or services based on implicit and open-ended contracts to adapt to environmental contingencies and to coordinate and safeguard exchanges (Jones et al., 1997). Gulati (1999) refers to network resources as those that reside not so much within the organization but in the inter-organization network in which the organization is placed. Gulati et al. (2000) identify four network resources, that is network membership, network structure, tie modality, and network management that need to be inimitable to serve as a source of sustainable competitive advantage for an organization that is a part of a network. Though reasons for inimitability have been well researched for resources that exist within organizations, network resources that exist within a network of organizations are not explored well (Gulati et al., 2000).

The central question that motivates this research is: *Why do network resources become inimitable for an organization that is a part of a network of organizations?* The answer to this question is essential to unravel how an organization that is a part of a network can achieve sustained competitive advantage.

Since the theoretical framework of the study lies in RBV, all premises and assumptions of the RBV hold for this theoretical framework too. The central premise of the RBV is that resources are heterogeneous and immobile (Barney, 1991). It is complementary to the Competitive Forces paradigm and does not compete with it (Foss, 1996). This implies that inimitable network resources need to be aligned to provide sustained competitive advantage in the context of the prevalent industry structure. Eisenhardt and Martin (2000) argue that the RBV can be applied without any modification in a moderately dynamic industry but reaches a limiting condition in a high-velocity industry context.

RESEARCH METHODOLOGY

The exploratory nature of the research question, its contemporary nature, and researcher's lack of control over the events makes case studies an appropriate research methodology (Yin, 1994, 6). The review of research literature and a pilot case study of the R&D services domain of the Indian IT industry reveal that the inimitability of resources and network resources is a source of sustained competitive advantage for organizations in the R&D services domain of the Indian IT industry. A set of ten interviews with middle and senior management in eight organizations that contribute to more than 80 percent of revenues in the R&D service domain on the Indian IT industry (that constitute the pilot case study) indicated pointers to a unique network of organizations that had been created by SC. The data from these interviews suggested that SC's model in establishing Design Group (DG) was unique in the industry and SC's competitors are not successful in creating such a network. For organizations that are not a part of a network, the inimitability of resources like comprehending technologies and design/programming skills is a source of achieving sustained competitive advantage. In the case of SC that is a part of a network of organizations, it is the inimitability of network resources like building and managing a network of organizations (apart from resources like comprehending technologies and design skills) that is a source of achieving sustained competitive advantage.

The pilot case study led to the current research that uses a holistic case design and the unit of analysis in this research is the DG of SC. This is appropriate since DG is the point of contact for SC and the network of organizations. The important sources of data for the case study were interviews with employees of DG and organizations that were a part of the network, and direct observations of DG at work. The case study is first described as a 'story' of the global semiconductor and Digital Signal Processing (DSP) industry, the R&D services domain of the Indian IT industry, and the strategies of SC and DG. Based on the case descriptions and the theoretical framework, a cognitive map of the view of the product managers of DG on the reasons for inimitability of network resources is generated (Miles and Huberman, 1994: 134–7). References to secondary sources of data for the case study are not revealed in order to camouflage the identity of SC. The process of inducting theory using case studies in management research has been argued to be appropriate in emerging domains (Eisenhardt, 1989). Dyer and Wilkins (1991) argue that a single case is more suitable for the researcher to understand the context to the extent of generating a theory.

Twenty-two in-depth protocol-based semi-structured interviews lasting for one-and-a-half to two hours provided data. Multiple interviews with employees of DG and an organization that is part of the network were conducted over a period of eight months. The head of DG in India is responsible for nurturing the network of third-party organizations and is also involved in managing some projects with the network. The product managers of DG focus on specific customer domains, that is audio, video, and so on. These product managers who report to the Head of DG in India are responsible for hardware and software systems designs in a particular domain, and managing projects and relationships with third-party organizations. Two direct observations of DG's product managers at work with their counterparts in the third-party organizations also provided data. This involved an observation of a couple of conference calls that were coordinated from DG that gave an understanding of how the network actually works in practice.

CASE STUDY

The Global DSP Industry

SC is an important constituent of the global semiconductor and DSP industry. The rapid growth of the IT, telecommunications, and consumer electronics industry can be attributed to the advances in the semiconductor industry. In 2000, the global semiconductor market had revenues of over US$ 200 billion. The semiconductor industry consists of several market segments that operate under their own unique competitive environments. Table 8.1 represents the size and growth rates of these market segments based on estimates by the investment bank SG Cowen and World Semiconductor Trade Statistics in 2001 (Xu et al., 2001).

Table 8.1   The global semiconductor industry

	Size in 2000 (US$ billion)	Growth rate in 2000 (%)
Discretes	17.5	30.6
Optoelectronics	9.7	67.2
Analog Circuitry	30.6	38.5
Microprocessors	30.2	11.0
Microcontrollers	12.5	28.9
DSPs	6.5	47.7
Microperipherals	11.3	8.7
Custom Logic	31.1	48.1
Memory	51.0	60.0
Bipolar Digital	1.1	6.4
Total	201.5	36.9

There are four major players in the global DSP industry including SC. In addition to these four major players there are also a few niche players. The DSP industry is characterized by strong buyer bargaining power. Under the just-in-time manufacturing model, buyers purchase DSPs only when demand for their products exists and this gives them a stronger position on price negotiation *vis-à-vis* the manufacturers of DSPs. In a market that is characterized by strong buyer bargaining power, SC has tried to differentiate itself from its competitors by providing value-added design services for its customers. SC has adopted a differentiation strategy by taking on a part of the R&D and new product development efforts of its customers by providing them with a system solution-based on their DSP. For providing this value-added service to their customers, SC has become a part of the R&D services domain of the Indian IT industry. SC has formed a network of organizations in the R&D services domain of the Indian IT industry that have the skills to design systems based on its DSPs.

R&D Services Domain of the Indian IT Industry

The R&D services domain in the Indian IT industry refers to both Indian and multinational organizations located in India whose revenue is derived from the R&D and/or new product development budgets of their customers. The annual export revenue of the R&D services domain of the Indian IT industry is estimated to be in the region of US$ 800 million to $1 billion during 2000–01 and at an optimistic compound annual growth rate (CAGR) of 40 percent is expected to touch US$ 4 billion by 2004–05 (Mihalka, 2001). The pilot case study reveals that customers chose India for R&D activities for its world-class and low-cost human resources. These customers are constantly under pressure to obtain more R&D per dollar spent and accelerate product development. The offshore billing rates in the R&D services domain varies between US$ 30 per man/hour to US$ 120 per man/hour (Mihalka, 2001). Organizations in the R&D services domain believe that inimitability of resources like the ability of the employees to comprehend relevant technologies and specific design/programming capabilities are the reasons for their sustained competitive advantage. The R&D services domain of the Indian IT is moderately dynamic, which is characterized by a relatively stable industry structure with defined boundaries and identifiable organizations, clear business models, and linear change (Mihalka, 2001). The R&D services domain of the Indian IT industry is dominated by a few organizations that are also a part of the software services domain. In addition, the R&D services domain consists of the Indian subsidiaries of the global customers. These global customers are semiconductor and electronics equipment manufacturers. There are also a few small Indian organizations that offer their services to specific niches in the R&D services domain.

SC and its competitors have realized the importance of the R&D services domain of the Indian IT industry. All these organizations have fully owned Indian subsidiaries that design DSPs. In fact, a couple of them have also outsourced a part of DSPs design to large Indian organizations in the R&D services domain of the Indian IT industry. SC has outsourced the design of hardware and software systems based on its DSPs to other organizations (that SC calls third-party organizations) in the R&D services domain of the Indian IT industry. SC manages this outsourcing of hardware and software systems through a dedicated division, DG. The subsequent sections describe how SC through DG has created a network of organizations in the R&D services domain of the Indian IT industry and how DG manages the network.

Semiconductor Company and Design Group

SC is an organization headquartered in the USA having a multi-billion dollar revenue in 2000. It is among the global leaders in integrated semiconductor chips for signal processing applications and DSP and was founded in the mid-1960s. The Chairman of SC had this to say about the business of SC in an interview with a leading business magazine in 2001:

> SC itself started with a single product line, shifted to functional circuits, then we shifted from simple parts to integrated circuits, subsequently from signal processing to digital processing. Now we also offer complete design solutions.

A division of SC, DG, established in the mid-1990s, is operating in the R&D services domain of the Indian IT industry to build and manage a network of third-party organizations. Most of the product managers of DG are based in India although other product managers are in facilities of SC in the USA. DG was established to leverage and manage Indian skills in the R&D services domain that resides with the third-party organizations. Unlike other organizations in the R&D services domain, DG is not an integrated design shop but is a part of a horizontal network of organizations that supply DG with specialized hardware and software design capabilities. DG provides complete solutions (that include R&D services) based on SC's chips to customers with the assistance of third-party organizations in the network. An illustration of the network in operation follows.

DG identifies a potential customer say a mobile handset manufacturer. It markets a complete solution including design services to win an order to design the circuits for a handset that displays video and is compatible with industry standards. DG works on a high-level design for the circuits and draws up specifications for hardware and software design that are developed by other organizations in the network. DG gives the organizations in the network a design specification and the contract to design the hardware or software. Over a period of time DG has identified the domain, and hardware and software design capabilities of the various third-party organizations in the network. At present, there are about a dozen third-party organizations in the network and over three hundred hardware and software design professionals working for DG in these third-party organizations. The third-party organizations vary in size in terms of total number of employees and revenue. The network of third-party organizations nurtured by DG is a select set of organizations out of which more than 50 organizations constitute the bulk of the R&D services domain of the Indian IT industry. The network is composed of autonomous organizations that operate like a single entity when it works to produce a reference design for a customer of DG/SC. Figure 8.1 is a representative part of the network of organizations.

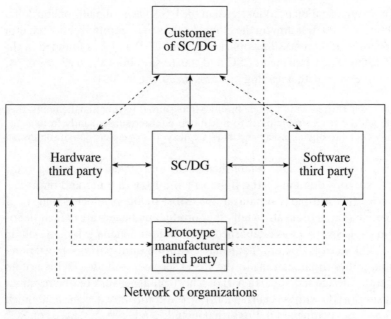

Key
Legend:
◄────► Indicates a strong link between the two organizations.
◄----► Indicates a weak link between the two organizations.

Figure 8.1   A representative part of the network of organizations, its customers, and third party organizations

DG's objective is to get entrenched in the customer market and thwart cost-based competition for SC's chips by providing a value-added service, that is the reference design to customers based on SC's chips. Thus DG takes on a part of the R&D and product development work of the customer. The customer may pay a non-recurring engineering cost and a software (designed by a third-party organization) licensing cost. This is a mutually beneficial situation for SC and the customer because the customer gets the non-core design work outsourced to SC (which in turn outsource it to the third-party organizations in India) and if the customer accepts the SC's reference design, it leads to increased sales of SC's chips. The central feature of this strategy is that it relies on the strengths of SC, its customers, and the third-party organizations. Apart from focusing on semiconductor chips, SC also has the responsibility to build and manage a network of third-party organizations. According to the Head of DG in India the philosophy that drives the network of third party organization can be articulated as:

> The third parties are an extension of my organization. And there is a fundamental give and take to create a win-win culture based on relationships.

The main motivating factors that has led SC to develop a network of organizations in the R&D services in the mid-1990s are a need to differentiate from competitors to increase global market share and be well positioned in specific high-growth market segments. The rationale for choosing the R&D services domain of the Indian IT industry are the availability of world-class design talent at costs that are lesser by about 50 percent than developed countries like the USA. Moreover, using a network of third-party organizations to provide reference designs assists customers of DG to lower new product development cost by about 30 percent and to reduce time to market from one year to about seven to eight months. Relationship building and communicating have been the foundation of SC's strategy that has nurtured a network of third-party organizations in the R&D services domain of the Indian IT industry.

The Chairman of SC believes that India has the potential to become a world leader in IT design since there are world-class software and hardware professionals in India who have accumulated rich experience. In an interview in 2001 the Chairman of SC states:

> I foresee that India will be the design house of the world. Not in manufacturing, but definitely in design. However, a few important measures have to be taken. Indian engineers would have to stay on in the country, work from here, bring in success stories and highlight sustainable models.

The Chairman of SC has made sure that his organization is the preferred partner for the third-party organizations in India. An interesting point to note is SC established DG a couple of years before its India Chip Development Subsidiary (ICDS) was established. In the case of a competitor of SC, its equivalent of ICDS was established in the mid-1980s and the concept of creating a network of third-party organizations seems to have garnered momentum only in 2000 after false and disinterested starts in the past.

Strategy of Design Group

DG's strategy has two components. The first component is initiating organizations to become members of the third-party network and establishing relationships with them. The second component is managing the relationships with the network of third-party organizations. This strategy of DG results in enhancing two capabilities, namely building a network of third-party organizations and managing the network of third-party organizations. The two capabilities are spread across the network of organizations and not with DG alone since they are non-existent without the support and commitment of the third-party organizations. The subsequent subsections describe how DG's strategy enhances the two capabilities.

Initiating and establishing relationships, and building the network

The first wave of liberalization of the Indian economy in 1991 paved the way for some IT professionals to start their own entrepreneurial ventures. The 1990s seems to be the era when Indian IT professionals realized that their hardware and software design services are world-class and can cater to the global market. SC was a supplier to most of the Government organizations from the late 1970s and the marketing head of SC in India (who has been head of DG in India since its inception) had already built relationships with most of the DSP teams working in these organizations. SC counted on some of these professionals who joined private organizations or started entrepreneurial ventures in the R&D services domain of the Indian IT industry post-1991 to support DG's proposed network of third-party organizations. Many of the third-party organizations have been working with DG ever since it was established in the mid-1990s. Some of the newer organizations in the network are offshoots of organizations that were already a part of the network.

Third-party organizations that are a part of the network are those who have been identified by DG as having excellent technical capabilities. In some cases it was DG that encouraged individuals and teams from organizations who shared a common vision as that of DG to start third-party organizations. Product manager 2 of DG believes that it takes time and effort to get an organization to become a member of the network. He says:

> It is difficult to imitate this kind of membership since most organizations with good talent in the domain of signal processing have been spotted and nurtured

by SC for more than ten years in certain cases. The third parties are attracted not only by financial rewards but also value the relationships with the team in DG and SC. There are not many quality organizations in the R&D services domain of the Indian IT industry that have expertise in signal processing technology that are not already a part of the network with DG.

It appears that developing a pattern of relationships between organizations in the third-party network may actually take a much longer time than the five years that is quoted. This is evident from the fact that the head of DG in the USA and the head of DG in India have over the last two decades built relationships with those who are today the top management of the third-party organizations that are a part of the network.

The chief executive officer (CEO) of third-party A feels:

One of our Director's association with SC for more than a decade is the foundation on which our pattern of relationships with DG is built on.

Initiating and establishing relationships, and managing the network

The relationships between the top management of the third-party organizations and SC often date back to a decade. Quite a few of the top management executives of the third-party organizations were working for the customers of SC in the past. These executives remained in contact with the head of DG and the relationships between DG and the third-party organizations are largely based on norms that evolved over these years.

Interestingly the norms that govern relationships in this network seem to be influenced by the fact that SC is much bigger than the third-party organizations. SC's revenue for 2001 is more than twice that of the total revenues of the R&D services domain of the Indian IT industry. Since SC is a global leader in designing chips for signal processing, the third-party organizations seem to be proud of being associated with it. It appears that the norms that govern the relationships between DG and the third-party organizations evolve over a period of at least five years or more. According to the CEO of third-party A:

It is a privilege to have a long standing working relationship with SC. They are big guys but still act like partners.

While the Head of DG is also of the opinion:

Our network management is always influenced by the learnings from our past experiences of working with the third party. There is no substitute for learning by doing in managing third parties.

SC was the first among its competitors to realize and acknowledge the world-class system design capabilities in India even though its competitors were using India as a base for designing their chips. This discovery of SC was instrumental in setting up DG in the mid-1990s.

Managing relationships and building the network
There appears to be little tacit knowledge or characteristic causal ambiguity associated with making network membership inimitable. According to product manager 3 of DG,

> It does not require any special knowledge to keep the third party organizations in the network. If the third party organizations perform well then DG ensures that they are in the network and assigns them more projects to create a win-win situation. It is thus easy to maintain network membership of existing third party organizations once they have proven their worth and to attract new organizations that will need to prove their worth before being accepted as a part of the network.

DG and a majority of the third-party organizations are based in Bangalore; there are also third-party organizations that are based in Chennai, Taiwan, and even in Belgium. Network membership depends on how well SC and DG know the third-party organization and its top management executives. However, this relationship is important only after the third-party organization has exhibited its superior technical expertise. The CEO of third party A states:

> Third Party A is a member of the network by virtue of having world-class digital signal processing and telecom expertise. Our membership is recognition of our expertise by SC. This is probably the primary reason why we have a good relationship with SC and DG. We did not become members based only on our good social relationship with SC and DG.

The role of complex social relations is not evident. Network membership is not dependent on the pattern of relationships in the network and complex social relationships or how the relationships are managed. In fact, the pattern of relationships and how the relationships are managed depend on membership.

Once an organization becomes a third party it implies that it is committed to the network. The initial commitment of DG and the third-party organizations maintains membership. There is no ambiguity in the pattern of relationships between DG and third-party organizations since the domain expertise of these organizations is known to DG.

Managing relationships and managing the network
There is a great degree of tacitness involved in nurturing norms that governs DG's relationships with the third-party organizations. Identifying third-

party organizations and building norms that define relationships to help manage projects is something that is learnt by doing. The head of DG in India believes that success of the norms that govern relationships with third-party organizations is human resource specific and with an inherent tacitness in what has made the norms of relationships with third parties work when he says:

> The mentoring of the third party organizations by DG reflects its Indian mindset while the contractual rules on fixed cost pricing reflect its American style of functioning. This may be a result of the fact that half the employees of DG are Indian while SC is an American organization. Moreover, the fact that SC uses only local managers and not expatriate managers in countries they operate in must play an important role in maintaining the network of third party organizations in India.

Every project done with a third-party organization is a learning experience for DG to refine the norms that govern the relationships between DG and the third-party organizations in the network. This learning is essential to optimize the performance of the network that will accrue the best rewards to all the organizations. Product manager 2 of DG believes that constant interaction with the third parties is required to sustain and modify the norms of relationships. He states:

> DG knows that third party C can be trusted to stick to deadlines and does not expect weekly reports while the same does not hold good with third party E in spite it being a SEI-CMM Level 5 [Software Engineering Institute-Capability Maturity Model Level 5] organization.

The head of DG spends about 25 percent of his working hours every week to network management. He spends this time talking with the top management of the third-party organizations and visiting them. These meetings help in fostering camaraderie, and are an exchange of technology and market-related information. Specific project-related issues are also discussed in the meetings.

The following section contains analytical explanations on the reasons for inimitability of network resources based on the data obtained from interviews with employees of DG and third-party organizations, and direct observations of the working of DG.

Analysis of the Case Study on SC and DG

The strategies of SC and DG, and the theoretical framework described earlier, provide for analytical explanations to generate hypotheses on why network resources become inimitable. The analysis is based on the cognitive map that represents the view of product managers of DG on the inimitability of network resources. Figure 8.2 represents the cognitive map.

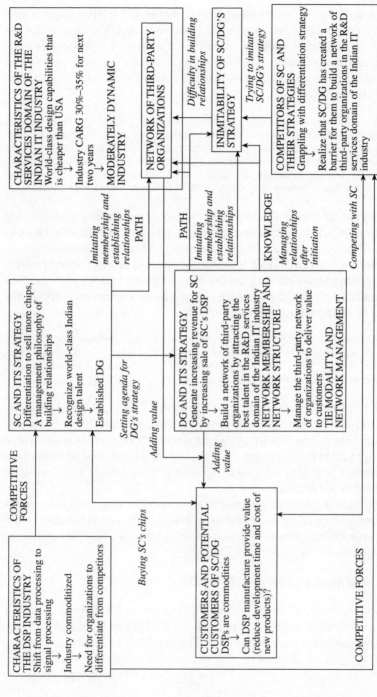

Figure 8.2   View of product managers of DG on the inimitability of network resources

The strategy that DG employs, which is inimitable for its competitors, to achieve SC's objectives is initiating membership and establishing relationships with third-party organizations, and managing those relationships. The theoretical framework reveals that the main reasons for inimitability of resources are unique historical conditions, time compression, diseconomies, resource mass efficiencies, characteristic causal ambiguity, social complexity, interconnectedness of resource stocks, and resource erosion (Deirickx and Cool, 1989; Barney, 1991).

A commonality between unique historical conditions, time compression diseconomies, and resource mass efficiencies is that they are all in some manner related to how SC's marketing division in India identified world-class Indian design talent to help in its differentiation strategy from the 1980s. SC established DG in the mid-1990s to facilitate initiating membership and establishing relationships with third-party organizations in the R&D services domain of the Indian IT industry, and managing relationships with them. The SC's Indian connection, which dates back to over two decades, has set the path for initiating organizations to become a part of the third-party network and establishing relationships with these organizations. The circumstances, location, and organization culture that determine accumulation of inimitable resources are dependent on the path of the evolution of the organization (Arthur, 1983). Time compression diseconomies imply that an organization needs a particular amount of time to acquire resources. This process cannot be compressed in time and is path-dependent. Studies on R&D in organizations show that crash R&D programs that have higher financial outlays for a short time are less effective than R&D programs where the yearly financial outlays are lower but spread over a longer period (Scherer, 1967; Mansfield, 1968). Resource mass efficiencies are also path-dependent since it is easier for an organization to acquire a certain resource if it already possesses high levels of that resource. Thus it is appropriate to categorize unique historical conditions, time compression diseconomies, and resource mass efficiencies that represent initiating membership of organizations in the network and establishing relationships with these organizations as the *path dimension of inimitability*.

The commonality between characteristic causal ambiguity, social complexity, interconnectedness of resource stocks, and resource erosion seems to be the fact that they are related to the manner in which DG uses the knowledge of working with them to define and redefine norms that govern relationships and using this knowledge to manage the relationships. This is evident from how DG has gone about convincing the third-party organizations in the network to accept a fixed cost pricing or how it monitors progress of a project with a third-party organization. One of the features of causal ambiguity is that it is tacit, that is the organization knows what it is but cannot explain what it means. Social complexity is the unique organization culture and relationships that result from the organization culture that are not easily imitable. Though many organizations can possess the same physical resources, only a few know to use socially complex resources like interpersonal relations, organization culture, and so on to exploit the physical resources in a manner inimitable by competitors (Wilkins, 1989). Knowing how other resources influence certain resources is referred to as 'interconnectedness of resource stocks'. It is difficult to imitate resources that are interconnected, as it would involve knowing and imitating all resources to which they are interconnected. Von Hippel (1978) posits that effective new product development is related to the extensive service networks of organizations that are receptive to customers. Resource erosion explains whether an organization knows how to indulge in punitive behavior that maintains the resources and makes them inimitable. Thus it is appropriate to categorize characteristic causal ambiguity, social complexity, interconnectedness of resource stocks, and resource erosion that represents managing relationships with organizations that are part of a network as the *knowledge dimension of inimitability*.

The following section analyzes two components of DG's strategy with respect to building a network of third-party organizations and managing the network, and links them with the theoretical framework to generate hypotheses on the reasons for inimitability of network resources.

Path Dimension of Inimitability and Building the Network

The pattern of DG's relationships with the third-party organizations depends on circumstances and situations that were encountered while working with them in the past. If a competitor has not worked with a third-party organization in the past it is unlikely that the competitor will be able to organize the network with an optimal pattern of relationships. The product managers of DG believe that the relationships that have been built for over a decade with the top management of the third-party organizations have resulted in these organizations becoming members of the network. These relationships are difficult to be replicated in a shorter timeframe by competitors. Once DG got a few third-party organizations into a network, it was easy to convince other similar organizations to join the network. The relationships that were developed when SC was selling its chips to those who became the top management of the third-party organizations were the foundation on which stronger relationships were built upon. It will be difficult for SC's competitors to attract SC's third-party organizations and build a pattern of relationships since they have not done this in the past.

Path Dimension of Inimitability and Managing the Network

The norms that are the basis of relationships between DG and third-party organizations have evolved over the past decade when SC was marketing its chips to the top management executives of the third-party organizations. Network management evolved and is still evolving based on the circumstances that defined the success of certain projects and failures of certain others. A competitor of SC will not know how to manage the network unless it has had a history of working with the third-party organizations in the network. The competitors of SC have set up fully owned subsidiaries to design their chips but have not realized or been slow to realize the potential of a network of a third-party organizations to design systems based on their chips. The competitors of SC are thus less experienced than DG to manage a network. DG has built long-standing relationship with third-party organizations governed by certain norms and it is easier to build on those norms to enhance the relationship. DG can be more accommodative in certain cases or convince third parties to accept its point of view in certain other cases. Competitors of SC who have not yet built a network of third-party organizations will first have to establish a set of norms that define their relationships with the third-party organizations. Only then can they convince the third-party organizations to accept changes in the management of the network. It appears that DG has a lead of a decade over its competitors with respect to managing a network of third-party organizations.

Knowledge Dimension of Inimitability and Building the Network

There appears to be little tacit knowledge or characteristic causal ambiguity associated with making network membership inimitable. Network membership is a result of the relations that have been established by the senior mangers of SC and the senior employees of the third-party organizations. If the third-party organizations perform well then DG ensures that they are in the network by providing them with more projects. There is no ambiguity with respect to the pattern of relationships with the third-party organizations. Network membership is not guaranteed based only on a good social relationship between the third-party organizations and DG. There do not seem to be any significant social complexities involved in building a network of third-party organizations and building a network is dependent only on the path DG has taken. Being a member of the network of third-party organizations is not dependent on other resources like managing the network. It appears that the competitors of SC cannot imitate the network of third-party organizations unless they take a similar path. The initial commitment of DG and the third-party organizations maintains membership. There are no membership contracts between DG and the third-party organizations that need to be renewed annually. There seems to be no special effort required by DG apart from the working relationships that seem to have a bearing on the membership of and pattern of relationships with third-party organizations.

Knowledge Dimension of Inimitability and Managing the Network

Norms that govern the relationship between DG and the third-party organization is largely tacit. For example the mentoring of the third-party organizations by DG reflects its Indian mindset while the contractual rules on fixed cost pricing reflect its US style of functioning. A lot depends on managing the relationships well. The ambiguity and the tacit nature of managing the network make it difficult for a competitor of SC to imitate unless the competitor has learnt by doing something similar. And none of SC's competitors have yet done something similar to what DG has done in creating a network of third-party organizations in the R&D services domain of the Indian IT industry. The product managers of DG have developed a rapport with their counterparts in the third-party organizations and are good friends with one another. Managing the network of third-party organizations is complex since DG has to work with the teams in third parties to define appropriate technologies to focus and develop reference designs in those technologies that current and potential customers of SC will be interested in. DG also needs to check with customers on what they think about the reference designs in development and communicate the customers' feedback to the third-party organizations. The complexity can be managed only by learning through doing. Every project is a new experience that assists DG in learning what needs to be factored in the next project they assign to the third-party organizations. Every project done with a third-party organization is a learning experience of DG to refine the norms that govern its relationship with that organization. This learning is essential to optimize the performance of the network that will accrue the best rewards to all the organizations. The top management of DG and the third-party organizations spend a significant portion of their time on updating each other on issues of common interest.

CONCLUSION

A framework for inimitability of network resources appears to emerge from this research. Network membership and structure are nurtured and made inimitable by the path dimension. Similarly, tie modality and network management are also nurtured and made inimitable by the path dimension. The knowledge dimension that is derived from the experiences while working with other organizations in the network also make tie modality and network management inimitable. The results of this research imply that an organization that is a part of a network and also its hub like SC needs to evolve along a path that nurtures network resources and makes them inimitable to gain sustained competitive advantage. The path dimension of inimitability appears to be important for all network resources. If an organization has achieved sustained competitive advantage by possessing inimitable network resources, it may be difficult for competitors to catch up. Competitors have tried imitating SC's strategy of nurturing a network of organizations for designing hardware and software systems based on their chips but have not been successful.

NOTE

* I thank Professor Tojo Thatchenkery (George Mason University), the organizer of the US National Science Foundation workshop on 'Learning from The Indian Development Experience' for inviting me to present this paper. This paper is based on my doctoral dissertation at the Indian Institute of Management Bangalore (IIMB). I acknowledge the contributions of Prof. Srinivas Prakhya (IIMB), Prof. S. Krishna (IIMB), Prof. Kalyani Gandhi (IIMB), and Prof. V Srivatsan (New York University) who were my dissertation committee. I also acknowledge the comments of Prof. Balaji Parthasarathy (Indian Institute of Information Technology Bangalore), Prof. Ganesh Prabhu (IIMB), and Prof. Rishikesha T. Krishnan (IIMB).

REFERENCES

Arthur, W.B. (1983), 'Competing technologies and lock-in by historical small events: the dynamics of allocation under increasing returns', unpublished manuscript, Center for Economic Policy Research, Stanford University.
Barney, J.B. (1991), 'Firm resources and sustained competitive advantage', *Journal of Management*, **17**, 99–120.
Deirickx, I. and K. Cool (1989), 'Asset stock accumulation and sustainability of competitive advantage', *Management Science*, **35**, 1504–11.
Dyer, W.G. and A.L. Wilkins (1991), 'Better stories and not better constructs, to generate better theory: a rejoinder to Eisenhardt', *Academy of Management Review*, **16**, 613–19.
Eisenhardt, K.M. (1989), 'Building theories from case study research', *Academy of Management Review*, **14**, 532–53.
Eisenhardt, K.M. and J.A. Martin (2000), 'Dynamic capabilities: what are they?', *Strategic Management Journal*, **21**, 1105–121.
Foss, N. (1996), 'Strategy, economics and Michael Porter', *Journal of Management Studies*, **33**, 1–24.

Gulati, R. (1999), 'Network location and learning: the influence of network resources and firm capabilities on alliance formation', *Strategic Management Journal*, **20**, 397–420.

Gulati, R., N. Nohria and A. Zaheer (2000), 'Strategic networks', *Strategic Management Journal*, **21**, 203–15.

Jarvenpaa, S.L. and D.E. Leidner (1998), 'An information company in Mexico: Extending the resource-based view of the firm to a developing country context', *Information Systems Research*, **9**, 342–61.

Jones, C., W.S. Hersterly and S.P. Borgatti (1997), 'A general theory of network governance: exchange conditions and social mechanisms', *Academy of Management Review*, **22**, 911–45.

King, A. W. and C.P. Zeithaml (2001), 'Competencies and firm performance: examining the causal ambiguity paradox', *Strategic Management Journal*, **22**, 75–99.

Mansfield, E. (1968), *The Economics of Technological Change*, New York: W.W. Norton and Company.

Mihalka, M. (2001), *India IT Services: Hardware Meets Software*, Hong Kong: Merrill Lynch.

Miles, M.B. and A.M. Huberman (1994), *Qualitative Data Analysis: An Extended Source Book*. 2nd edn, Thousand Oaks, CA: Sage Publications.

Miller, D. and J. Shamsie (1996), 'The resource-based view of the firm in two environments: the Hollywood film studios from 1936 to 1965', *Academy of Management Journal*, **39**, 519–43.

Powell, W.W. (1990), 'Neither market nor hierarchy: network forms of organization', in B. Staw and L.L. Cummings (eds), *Research in Organizational Behavior*, Greenwich, CT: JAI Press, pp. 295–336.

Reed, R. and R.J. DeFillippi (1990), 'Causal ambiguity, barriers to imitation and sustainable competitive advantage', *Academy of Management Review*, **15**, 88–102.

Scherer, F. (1967), 'Research and development resource allocation under rivalry', *Quarterly Journal of Economics*, **81**, 359–94.

Von Hippel, E. (1978), 'Successful industrial products from customer ideas', *Journal of Marketing*, **1**, 39–49.

Wilkins, A. (1989), *Developing Corporate Character*, San Francisco: Jossey-Bass.

Xu, D., L.C. Zong, T. Dunn, S. Ghosh, S. Sinha, S. Solanki and B. Yee (2001), 'Opportunities for competitor Y in the digital signal processing market', unpublished project report, University of California, Berkeley.

Yin, R.K. (1994), *Case Study Research, Design and Methods*, 2nd edn, Thousand Oaks, CA: Sage Publications.

PART III

Industry issues and patterns

9. Creating information technology industrial clusters: learning from strategies of early and late movers

Kavil Ramachandran and Sougata Ray

INTRODUCTION

Interest in industrial clusters as a means to accelerate regional development has attracted renewed attention in recent years, particularly after the boom in the information technology (IT) industry in Silicon Valley (Sturgeon, 2003). At the same time, efforts by several states and countries to recreate Silicon Valley-type regions have had mixed results. Why does it happen so? Our enquiries through case studies of two Indian states produce four sets of factors central to the successful formation of IT clusters. While the role of industry attractiveness and factor conditions are well known, the role of the local entrepreneurship pool is less well discussed. Our findings suggest that the role of state as an entrepreneur in attracting and encouraging entrepreneurship is important in the creation of IT clusters.

Indian IT Industry

Technological revolutions sometimes bring unexpected opportunities for countries. India, a laggard among developing countries in terms of economic growth, is demonstrating a high degree of competitiveness in knowledge-intensive software development and IT-enabled services and is a favoured location for investment. The Indian IT industry has experienced a major boom over the last decade and has emerged as a major player in the Indian economy. The software industry in India grossed an annual revenue of US$ 12 billion during 2002–03, up from US$ 10.1 billion in 2001–02, registering an overall growth of 18.8 percent in dollar terms. More than 8 000 firms, located in cities like Bangalore, Chennai, Hyderabad, Kolkata, New Delhi and Pune have been providing a range of software services, mostly targeted at foreign customers (NASSCOM, 2003).

The Indian IT industry grew out of the pioneering efforts of companies like Tata Consultancy Services (TCS) (Kapur and Ramamurti, 2001). These firms undertook small projects overseas for multinational firms, and slowly climbed up the value chain as their reputations evolved. By the beginning of the new millennium, almost two out of every five Fortune 500 companies began outsourcing their software requirement to India. It is believed that India has been able to create a valuable position in the global IT industry due to the impeccable quality consciousness of its software developers and its huge cost advantage when compared to the Western world (Bhatnagar, 1997; Arora et al., 2000).

Indian companies are making rapid progress on quality standards. As many as 15 out of 23 companies in the world that have acquired the Software Engineering Institute (SEI) Capability Maturity Model (CMM Level 5, the highest quality standard for software practices) are located in India. However, they are gradually losing the cost advantage (Chakraborty and Dutta, 2002). However, it still has a number of advantages including the availability of a large number of English-speaking people. There is an acute need to broaden the base of the industry with the creation of more and more IT firms with specialized skills and domain expertise to capitalize on future stages of IT evolution. There are a number of small firms trying to establish themselves in the product category, compared to most others that are focusing on the services space. This is not easy. However, individual IT firms alone cannot overcome these challenges, as has been noted in many other newly industrialized countries (NICs) in Asia. A combined and coordinated effort by the central and state Governments, industry associations and IT and related companies is needed to sustain the advantage of the Indian IT industry.

The Indian IT industry has generated considerable interest among scholars in the past few years. Unfortunately, research that systematically explores why a large number of Indian IT firms have emerged globally competitive in a large spectrum of IT products and services is limited. The analysis that is available recognizes the role and importance of IT clusters in shaping the evolution of the industry.

Industrial Clusters and Indian IT Industry

The growth of the Indian IT industry has been in distinct phases. Though Indians own a majority of the IT companies in India, multinational corporations (MNCs) have also played a major role in developing the industry. The history of the industry suggests a close link between software and hardware in its earliest days. The IT industry has responded to the various markets that have grown at different times and tried catering to those (for example, software services, software exports and software products). The software capabilities were initially developed as import substitutes and with a fullly-fledged orientation to the domestic IT market. Gradually software exports were started and became the buzz of the industry in the past decade.

As the software industry has been growing rapidly in recent years, there are centres of excellence emerging in India. The share of southern India in software exports increased from 25 percent in 1991–92 to more than 40 percent in 2001–02. Though Chennai in the south had emerged as a software centre early on, it was soon overtaken by Bangalore with Hyderabad emerging as a recent challenger. The Bangalore cluster is the largest in terms of sales though not in terms of the number of companies. Compared to Bangalore's software exports of approximately US$ 2.75 billion in 2002–03, Hyderabad's exports amounted to US$ 822 million. However, the number of firms in both cities was about the same (*Business Standard*, 2003). To promote rapid growth of the IT industry, central and many state governments have created software technology parks in which both economic and social infrastructure are readily available. These parks have played an important role in enabling clusters to develop.

The dynamism and economic success of numerous clusters operating in countries such as Italy, Germany and Japan in diverse industries such as automobile, leather, textile, jewellery and optical frames has been well documented. Despite some inter-firm variability, the firms in a cluster show striking similarities in the way they are structured, behave and perform as they are more or less governed by the same policy, competitive technology, institutional and socioeconomic environment (Porter, 1990). The constellation of these forces together creates an environment that becomes the source of constraints, contingencies, problems and opportunities, which affect the terms on which a firm transacts business and derives and sustains competitiveness. It is, however, obvious that mere concentration of IT enterprises is no guarantee of successful cluster formation, since advantages associated with clustering do not always emerge automatically and spontaneously. Firms should feel the benefits of living and growing together through sharing a number of value links.

It is important to understand why successful IT clusters have been formed in some cities such as Bangalore and what needs to be done to sustain and replicate the success. Though many scholars have tried to explain why India could emerge as an IT super power, little has been said on how these IT clusters emerge and what role the entrepreneurial leadership[1] of government can play in IT cluster formation in a country like India. In the following part of the chapter, the formation of the IT cluster in Bangalore and the factors that have shaped this are discussed. Further, this assessment is based on an assumption that IT clusters in a few states have helped the emergence of a globally competitive IT industry in India. The significant contribution made by state-level governments in shaping the formation of IT clusters is illustrated by presenting case studies of two major states in south India, Karnataka and Andhra Pradesh. Bangalore, which has emerged as the 'Silicon Valley' of India, is the capital of Karnataka. Hyderabad in the neighbouring Andhra Pradesh is fast catching up, and is expected to be the next 'Silicon Valley' of India (Zwingle, 2002).

Formation of the IT Cluster in Bangalore

Bangalore houses the most prominent IT cluster in India. From a mere 13 software firms in 1991–92, the city now has over 1100 software firms working in areas such as computer chip design, systems software and communication software. The industry employs more than 80 000 IT professionals in the city. Compared to other locations in India, there is also high-end technology/industry concentration such as very large system integrators (VLSI) and telecom services and higher degrees of MNC concentration with over 200 foreign firms. It is ranked fourth as a global hub of technological innovation, behind San Francisco and Austin in the USA, and the Taiwanese capital Taipei. But why and how did Bangalore emerge as the leading hub of the Indian IT industry?

Early factor advantage

Bangalore had the presence of both economic and non-economic factors that made it a place of preferred choice for locating business and attracting investment (Ramachandran, 1986).

Among the advanced factors, highly skilled labour plays a very important role in the development of any industry (Hanna, 1994; Porter, 1990). As software makes intensive use of human capital, availability of highly skilled technical and managerial manpower becomes the key location factor. Bangalore has a large, highly skilled IT talent pool available at a relatively low cost, due to the city's large educational, research and industrial infrastructure. The city benefited from the location of science- and technology-related research and training institutions, as it was considered ideal in terms of climate and infrastructure to conduct research in sensitive areas like defence, aerospace and electronics. The seed was sown with the establishment of the Indian Institute of Science, several space and defence research organizations and a number of public sector enterprises in fields such as electronics and aeronautics. These institutions created a good pool of technical know-how, and skilled labour.

A large and sophisticated network of educational institutions supplies the human capital required by the software industry. Of the 66 engineering colleges in Karnataka, 26 are located in and around Bangalore, including many specializing in IT. Many of the graduates who migrated to the USA for higher education and jobs form part of the social network that nurtures the local software industry. Investments made by government and other public institutions for specialized infrastructure such as technological and management institutions have contributed to the development. Bangalore's high-quality social infrastructure and moderate climate make it an ideal place to live.

Multinational firms drive growth of local entrepreneurship
Texas Instrument's choice of Bangalore as the location for a 100 percent export-oriented unit in 1984 was a turning point in the development of the IT industry in Bangalore. Many more blue chip multinationals like Digital Equipment, Hewlett-Packard and IBM followed suit leading to a cumulative investment of US$ 1.3 billion by 2001. Since then, Bangalore has remained the most favored location for a number of multinationals. During January 2001–May 2002 Bangalore attracted about 40 percent of the 112 foreign direct investment (FDI) ventures established in India. Further, the emergence of entrepreneurial and managerial *Brahmins* who are better suited to the knowledge-intensive industries such as software and IT-enabled services is an important socio-cultural and ethnic factor explaining the formation of this industry in India and particularly in Bangalore (Taeube, 2002). Over the years, Bangalore has become one of the most important locations for most Indian IT graduates too. Local firms such as Infosys and Wipro, and others such as TCS and Satyam that are headquartered elsewhere also set up operations. Infosys and Wipro are two of the three largest IT firms in India; while the founder of the former hails from Karnataka, the founder of the latter obtained technology for computer manufacturing from the Indian Institute of Science in Bangalore and decided to make it his home from the beginning.

Attractive industry: tapping the export market
Although many Indian software firms cut their teeth in the domestic market after IBM left India, their success today comes from serving foreign customers, especially in the USA (Kapur and Ramamurti, 2001). The US accounts for nearly 60 percent of Indian software exports, followed by Europe with 23.5 percent, and Japan just 3.5 percent. Given the small size of the domestic market, Indian firms had to be export-oriented and were dependent on the growth of the export market (Chakraborty and Dutta, 2002), with Bangalore-based firms being no exception.

The IT industry has some peculiarities of its own which helped Indian firms grow without domestic demand. Since the 1970s, outsourcing of software development activity by firms in developed economies became a trend due to huge increases in software costs, increased demand for complex information systems applications, rapid obsolescence rates of the information technology infrastructure and inadequate supply of IT personnel. As a result, IT work is now distributed globally on the basis of cost, location of customer sites and expertise, largely independent of the IT company's country of origin (Salzman, 2000). Following such outsourcing, many firms in the USA were able to use their own personnel on more valuable and creative projects (Arora et al., 2000). Differences in time zones allow work to be carried out by Indian teams at times that enables a 24-hour production context, thus shortening cycle times and improving productivity and service quality. The social network, connecting people of Indian origin in the USA often working in IT cluster areas with engineers and managers in India, has also played an important role in exploiting this advantage (Kapur and Ramamurti, 2001).

Bangalore remained the most favoured destination for Indians who started ventures based in India and working for the Indian subsidiaries of foreign multinationals (Heeks, 1999; Taeube, 2002). In 2000, 71 of the 75 multinationals located in Bangalore had executives of Indian origin returning from overseas assignments as heads (Ghemwat, 2000). Overseas Indians started or invested in new companies that fuelled new venture formation. Also, US companies opened software centres in India to strengthen local interaction or to carry out development work in wholly owned research and development (R&D) subsidiaries. By 2001, that list included Cisco, Hewlett-Packard, IBM, Lucent, Motorola, Oracle and Sun Microsystems.

Benefiting from the cluster advantage

A cluster of independent and informally linked software firms and institutions located in the same city has definitely allowed firms to exploit advantages in efficiency, effectiveness and flexibility (Porter, 1998, 2000). A close relationship between local industry and the major research institutions/ universities in the area; reasonably active venture capital; some degree of inter-firm cooperation; a tolerance for spin-offs; and nurturing of the firms largely outside the purview of large, ponderous, bureaucratic firms and financial institutions could be observed in Bangalore. The Bangalore cluster has influenced the development of software firms in three broad ways as argued by Porter (1998). First, by increasing the productivity of companies based in the area; second, by driving the direction and pace of innovation, which underpins future productivity growth; and third, by stimulating the formation of new businesses, that expands and strengthens the cluster itself. Being part of a cluster has allowed companies to operate more productively in sourcing hardware, software and people; accessing information, technology and local institutions; coordinating with related companies, and measuring and motivating improvement. Software firms have been able to tap into an ever-growing pool of high-quality people, thereby lowering their search and transaction costs in recruiting. It has become easier to attract talented people from other locations because the cluster of firms signaled opportunity and reduced the risk of relocation for employees. However, there is not enough evidence to suggest that formal inter-firm Keiretsu-type linkages (Tyrini, 1994) exist among IT firms in Bangalore, whereby they gain from reintegration in the value chain and use of efficient networks of market transactions as argued by some scholars (for example, Scott, 1988; Storper, 1997).

Local firms have easy and preferred access to the accumulated extensive market, technical and competitive information available within the cluster. In addition, personal and professional relationships, and old boys' networks have fostered trust and facilitated the flow of information. The cluster has also developed an unmatched reputation for Bangalore as an industrial location, which in turn has benefited firms located in the city in dealing with global buyers and suppliers. Beyond reputation, the city-based firms have often profited from a variety of joint marketing mechanisms, such as company referrals, trade fairs, trade magazines and marketing delegations.

Such clustering as discussed has made things more attractive and easier for foreign customers as well to meet many potential vendors in a single trip, allowing them to multi-source or switch vendors. This has led to a high degree of healthy local rivalry generating a rapid increase in the number of IT companies in Bangalore.

Foreign firms in India follow two contrasting strategies to maintain their technological edge. Firms such as Hewlett-Packard, Oracle and Motorola opt for fully controlled affiliates, closely integrated into their corporate networks, but subcontract product development to local software firms. Others such as Nortel and Cisco opt for collaboration and joint ventures with local firms. In the latter case, the establishment of joint ventures and collaboration agreements have been facilitated by expatriate Indian managers.

The diffusion of technology, facilitated by the entry of multinational firms from the USA has helped firms move up the value curve. At the same time, Indian software firms like Infosys and Wipro have opened offices in the USA, or are acquired US companies, to serve better their clients on high-end projects and to have listening posts in Silicon Valley. Thus, physical distance has been bridged by the strengthening of cross-national, intra-firm networks and by inter-firm social networks among Indians and overseas Indians.

Clustering in Bangalore has played a vital role in innovation and value upgrading in the same manner as envisaged by Porter (1998). As most sophisticated buyers in the world were part of this cluster, local firms usually had a better window on the market than isolated competitors did. Small and medium-sized companies continued to get opportunities to grow as the bigger companies moved into larger projects vacating space for the smaller ones. The ongoing relationships with other entities within the cluster have also helped companies to learn early about evolving technology, hardware and software availability, service and marketing concepts, and so on.

Cluster formation in Bangalore has greatly facilitated new business formation. The environment in Bangalore has provided the context for local IT firms to take birth, be nurtured during their infancy, organize resources including manpower, acquire capabilities and compete in the foreign markets. Professionals working within the cluster have easily perceived gaps in products or services around which they could build new businesses. Given that barriers to entry are lower in the IT sector, and needed skills, technology and staff, are often readily available at the cluster location, many entrepreneurs have surfaced.

Take the case of MindTree Consulting, a high-value-adding software consulting firm promoted by ten IT professionals with top management experience in global firms such as Wipro Technologies, Cambridge Technology Partners, Lucent Technologies and KPMG. The founders brought not only experience and expertise in IT and management developed over a long period, but also their rich network. This helped them to raise capital, attract talent and strike strategic alliances helping the business grow rapidly.

Local government – indifference to intermittent active facilitation
The role of the state and the local governments, albeit small, was also important in developing the industry. Some areas in and around Bangalore benefited from a package of incentives, announced for their industrialization, when they were classified as backward in 1971. In 1997, Karnataka became the first state to announce a specific policy for the promotion of IT, and to provide significant tax concessions and other benefits to attract IT ventures.

In recent years, like most first movers, Bangalore started facing the pinch on two counts. First, the rapid growth of population impaired the liveability in Bangalore with dramatically escalated real-estate prices, congestion, poor road conditions and other overloads on the local infrastructure. Second, many other state governments started aggressively promoting IT with better infrastructure and policy support to attract investments. This provided alternative location choices for software firms in India. In the absence of government initiatives, firms such as Infosys had to initially invest heavily to overcome the bottlenecks in physical infrastructure because of demand supply imbalance on several fronts: water, power, road and public transport (Ghemwat, 2000). Recently, some Bangalore-based firms moved to these new locations while implementing their expansion plans. With the rapid erosion in the relative factor advantage, the role of local government has increasingly become critical to sustain the prominence of Bangalore-based IT cluster. The recent initiatives by the state government have, however, started paying dividends again with several new IT-based investments flowing in.

Proactive policies to attract multinational firms to exploit the human resources, technology leverage by local firms, emergence of a new class of entrepreneurs and their linkages with the epicentre of IT in Silicon Valley and other IT centres, and the facilitating role of the state Government have played a crucial part in the emergence of the Bangalore cluster. This cluster, the first of its kind in India, has enjoyed the benefits and suffered the pangs of a typical first mover in a highly dynamic industry.

FORMATION OF CLUSTER AS A LATE MOVER – THE CASE OF HYDERABAD

Since the establishment of the Software Technology Park of India (STPI) in 1991–92, Hyderabad has grown rapidly to harbour 1 154 firms with exports of US$ 822 million in 2002–03 (Business Standard, 2003). The industry has grown rapidly in the last three years. More than 500 firms registered with STPI in Hyderabad are in the process of starting operations. The firms will help with the formation of IT clusters and the city will get a major boost. Recently the state government has been able to attract a number of leading firms from India and abroad to set up operations in Hyderabad by providing better infrastructure, concessions, hidden subsidies and local demand through e-governance projects of the state government. About one-third of the registered units are foreign companies contributing about 40 percent of the total investment of US$ 622 million at the end of 2002–03 (*Business Standard*, 2003). It has simultaneously backed local firms such as Satyam Computers and InfoTech Enterprises to grow and flourish. As a result, Satyam has emerged as the largest exporter from the city.

Entrepreneurial Leadership of the State

The Andhra Pradesh (AP) state government led by chief minister Chandrababu Naidu (1993–2004) has been able to make giant strides in shaping an IT cluster in and around Hyderabad. The entrepreneurial vision and strategic clarity are evident in the number of initiatives the chief minister has taken to position Hyderabad as a knowledge hub of India. This includes campaigning and facilitating the setting-up of a number of pioneering international quality institutions in the area of IT, biotechnology, life sciences, business management and insurance, all emerging growth areas. The creation of a finance district to house a number of institutions and agencies is expected to lead to a cluster of financial organizations in Hyderabad. The entrepreneurial leadership is as much reflected in these initiatives as in brand building around them. The chief minister has taken a personal interest in negotiating with a number of multinational firms. All these form the building blocks of a grand strategy to catch up with the development process, which is knowledge-driven in the emerging context. These steps are far superior to anything happening in Bangalore and Chennai. In fact, the local governments in Bangalore and Chennai have adopted many of the entrepreneurial steps taken in Hyderabad.

The entrepreneurial leadership of the state is reflected in a number of ways. For instance, the AP was one of the first states in India to formulate an IT policy in 1999. Recognizing the emerging global opportunity in the IT-enabled services sector (ITES), the AP formulated a separate ITES policy in 2002. The chief minister demonstrated superior entrepreneurial leadership compared to counterparts in other states. He would personally make PowerPoint presentations, greet delegates and get clearances on priority basis much faster and better than other states. In short, he was a tireless champion.

Hyderabad now has a number of high-quality private schools for primary and secondary education. Some of the other initiatives include creation of a number of parks, botanical gardens and other eco-tourism centres, a major urban afforestation programme all over the city, promotion of tourism in a big and concerted way and building the image of Hyderabad as the first choice to live. All these are elements of a grand strategy design based on emerging industrial location factors. There is a definite and conscious effort to make Hyderabad and surroundings and the state as a whole attractive for the knowledge- and service-driven industries to grow. It is such qualities of entrepreneurial leadership that provide the necessary fuel to push the state to a more robust production function and to enter a new and higher economic paradigm, as explained by Schumpeter (1949).

The initiatives have started paying off as can be seen from a recent survey conducted by NASSCOM (2002) on city competitiveness. Hyderabad is ranked 1 ahead of Chennai (rank 3) and Bangalore (rank 6). The competitiveness assessment was based on three parameters, availability and quality of infrastructure, availability and cost-effectiveness of manpower and policy support (see Table 9.1).

*Table 9.1   Relative attractiveness of cities**

Parameters	Bangalore	Chennai	Hyderabad
Telecom Infra	8	4	5
Power	7	2	3
Real estate	6	5	3
Manpower	6	5	2
City perception	1	3	2
Entrepreneurship history	1	4	5
Policy initiatives	6	4	1
Power			
Real estate rent (US$/sq ft/month)	0.659	0.548	0.521
Manpower rates (US$/hr)	0.519	0.470	0.432
Overall competitiveness			
Scores	5.31	3.91	2.93

Notes: * Based on a NASSCOM survey of IT-enabled services companies in India in 2002.
The survey covered nine cities. The lower the score, the greater the competitiveness (Nasscom,
2002 – *The ITES: BPO Super 9*).

DISCUSSION

The detailed analysis of how Bangalore, an early entrant, and Hyderabad, a late entrant, created IT clusters show some interesting patterns. As noted in Figure 9.1, competitiveness of a location for cluster formation depends on a number of variables.

Indeed, industry attractiveness is a critical factor that creates the necessary customer pull and momentum for any firm to flourish, and consequently any location to create wealth. Industry structure determines the relative bargaining power of the forces operating on a player in an industry. This logic applies to both industrial firms and clusters (Porter 1980, 1990, 1998). In a growing industry such as IT, attractive demand conditions often facilitate the entry of new players, when entry barriers are not very strong. It would not have been possible for a late entrant like Hyderabad to make itself IT attractive had the IT industry shown signs of maturity.

The availability of relevant factors, primarily driven by economic infrastructure and manpower of high quality are necessary for a cluster to emerge and evolve at a location. Knowledge-based industries are influenced by a different set of location factors compared to traditional manufacturing-based industries (Saxenian, 2000; Ramachandran, 1986). Regional development indeed depends on the development of economic

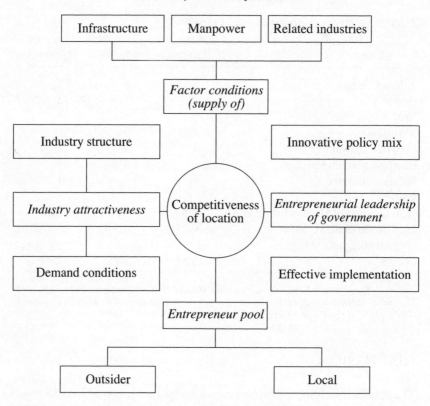

Figure 9.1   Dynamics of formation of industry cluster

activities and income generated in the region. Ramachandran (1986, 1989) has shown a shift in the mix of location factors from economic to social as a region develops its economic infrastructure, in line with the Maslowian (1954) hierarchy of needs argument. According to Ramachandran (1986), as the supply of physical infrastructure reaches a 'reasonable' level, the need of entrepreneurs and managers to have fairly high-quality social infrastructure goes up. This is particularly so in knowledge-driven industries, where employees, the key source of value addition, are highly mobile. The kind of economic infrastructure such as for communication would not be the same for manufacturing and non-manufacturing industries. Entrepreneurs and managers look for a combination of factors while choosing their location. As noticed by Ramachandran (1986), the role of non-economic, social factors in tilting the location choice to a place, which is better to live, is also found to be very high. Hyderabad's recent efforts in creating an attractive social infrastructure must be viewed from this perspective.

The role of the state as an entrepreneur and strategist has also become apparent. A late entrant must have a clear innovative approach to build competitiveness as argued in relevant literature in entrepreneurship and strategic management. Every link in the value chain offers scope for innovation. The spirit of entrepreneurship should flow through the whole administrative system to become competitive. Hyderabad had such a very clear strategic intent (Hamel and Prahalad, 1989).

States, as organizations striving to build competitiveness, need to have the qualities of market competitive firms to build and sustain competitive advantage. This is particularly so in a fast-changing environment. It is under such situations that high-quality entrepreneurial leaders are needed, who can envision the future growth trajectory and build resources not only in terms of infrastructure, but also in terms of creating an attractive, confidence-boosting environment through brand (image) building. Time is one of the most crucial variables and is traded at a very high premium for a latecomer intending to develop an IT cluster. Besides, IT firms have a rapid decision cycle on most strategic decisions including the choice of investment destinations. Therefore fast response, short lead time, quick decisions and single window clearances by the government provide a region with a decisive edge over other locations. It is here that the role of the entrepreneurial leader such as the chief minister of the AP and the deftness of the team become all the more crucial. The continuity of entrepreneurial policies and leadership over a sufficiently long period is yet another dimension.

The need for a local pool of entrepreneurs is very important, both at the early stages to kick-start the growth of the cluster and at a later stage to sustain momentum. For entrepreneurs, 'home proximity' is the most important location factor (Ramachandran, 1986), particularly in societies such as India with strong cultural bonding among family and community members. In case the relative factor advantage of the cluster goes down temporarily, a capital flight is bound to happen. However, local entrepreneurs are more likely to continue and work for the revival of the cluster advantage because of their greater stickiness to the location.

IMPLICATIONS AND CONCLUSIONS

Development is achieved through a long-term cyclical process. It is observed that impetus for change has to come from somewhere to push a nation from a slow to a high growth trajectory. The industrial revolution in Europe in the late seventeenth and early eighteenth century was initiated by the social and religious institutions that had created conditions for technological inventions, founding the base for the subsequent development of the national environments of many European nations (Weber, 1978). In the case of the USA, it was private entrepreneurship that led to a large number of technological innovations and commercialization of inventions made in Europe.

The developmental approaches adopted by Europe or the USA are that of pioneering industrial nations. The game changes substantially for nations that are in a catch-up mode (Abramovitz, 1986). Many studies (for example, Tyson, 1988; Vogel, 1988) on successful NICs such as South Korea and Taiwan argue that this initiation was made by the government by either directly or indirectly influencing the supply of human resources, capital, technology and information to foster technological innovation and its diffusion (Mathews, 1999). Experiences of NICs have led to the emergence of a new paradigm of industrialization built on the premise of policies that are market-augmenting, that is, directly controlled and monitored by the state rather than market-conforming, that is, liberalized from direct state intervention and control (Amsden, 1989; Lall, 1990). This paradigm is radically different from that propounded by Porter (1990) and other neoclassical economists who have given government only a supporting role. However, this paradigm of development is now well accepted and finds increasing application in states that are in the catch-up mode. The vehicles for technology leverage have varied from country to country, *Keiretsus* in Japan (Tyson, 1988), industrial *chaebols* in Korea (Amsden, 1989; Kim, 1997), public sector R&D institutions and their spun-off firms in Taiwan (Mathews, 1997), and more recently multinational firms in Singapore (Mathews, 1999).

Though discounted in the purest capitalist sense, the role of government in leading the development process, particularly in poor countries, is very high (Meir and Stiglitz, 2001). The purpose of government intervention is to move the economy from lower (lethargic equilibrium) to a higher-level (prospects) equilibrium. It is when the government is led by entrepreneurial leaders that such a paradigm shift takes place on the lines with the innovation arguments of Schumpeter (1949). One of the key means of pushing rapid development is by the creation of physical infrastructure (Rosenstein-Roden, 1943). Adelman (2001) has argued for a hyperactive government to accelerate the process of development, which will prevent special interest groups from hijacking market-oriented reforms. In short, rapid development often assumes the presence of the state as an entrepreneur, envisioning the strategy for growth and providing facilities to attract investments both from within and outside, as has happened with many successful NICs.

At least three local level critical factors – relative factor conditions, entrepreneurial leadership of the state government and a pool of entrepreneurs – are needed for the successful evolution of a location into an IT cluster as a late mover. For an early mover like Bangalore, these factors evolved over a long period, on most occasions not by design, but by chance. Therefore, the role that the Karnataka government has been playing is to maintain the supremacy of the Bangalore cluster. This role is qualitatively different from that of other state governments, which must take a more direct role in shaping the formation of IT clusters as late movers. This is evident in the development model followed by some NICs mentioned above.

While industry attractiveness and factor conditions make a location attractive for investment, it is the quality of entrepreneurial leadership that determines the possibilities of a late entrant location becoming a leader. We believe that a detailed study of the strategic growth followed by Bangalore and Hyderabad provide valuable lessons for other locations trying to develop a number of knowledge-intensive industries. For any other IT cluster to emerge in India as a late mover, the cluster formation process can be better planned and expedited. Any state government in India trying to emulate the IT cluster in Bangalore has to use catch-up and leap-frog models by choosing any combination of vehicles of technology leverage. It has to play a crucial role in shaping the cluster by developing and promoting educational and research institutions, attracting investment in high-technology areas by providing better factor conditions and creating local demand, and simultaneously promoting local level entrepreneurship to capitalize on the initial investment by larger Indian and foreign firms. Therefore entrepreneurial leadership of the state becomes the key variable in shaping the formation of an IT cluster starting late with relative factor disadvantage.

NOTES

1. Entrepreneurial leadership has two basic components. The first is entrepreneurship, which is defined in terms of innovations based on market opportunities. The other is leadership, which is reflected in terms of the ability to motivate the team and carry it along to accomplish the innovation objectives, with the help of appropriate people, systems and processes. The crux of entrepreneurship is innovation, which may be related to product, inputs, process or market (Schumpeter, 1949). Manimala (1999) extended the scope of innovations to cover systems, processes and other inputs. In a turbulent environment, the need to innovate on a number of fronts is constantly inevitable to build competitive advantage. To succeed, the innovator's imagination must be keen, though tempered with business judgement. Some of the qualities required to do so are steady persistence to overcome obstacles, fear and possible disaster (Maclaurin, 1953).

   In an organizational context, whether it is a firm or a government, building and sustaining competitive advantage revolves around the quality of leadership it has. As mentioned above, the leader must possess entrepreneurial qualities. For innovations to occur, that too in a tradition-bound, bureaucratic, mature organization such as a government in this context, the leadership must possess additional qualities. Not only must the leader create a work climate for innovative practices to flourish, but also to orchestrate seeking and realizing opportunities to expand the business (McGrath and MacMillan, 2000). The leader must support and encourage hands on practices that involve problem solving with people at work.

McGrath and MacMillan (2000) have argued that these three qualities are important for creating an entrepreneurial mindset in the organization. Besides, an entrepreneurial leader must also allocate resources, attention and talent *disproportionately* (emphasis added), and build counter-pressure to fight inertial forces. Similarly concepts of planning, control and learning, which are appropriate for mature organizations, may be inappropriate and destructive to new initiatives (Block and MacMillan, 1985; Kanter 1989).

For an entrepreneurial leader to be successful, a rich team with an entrepreneurial mindset is important, which McGrath et al. (1995) defined as 'Deftness'. The team should share a common vision to build competitive advantage through innovations. Possibilities of sustaining competitive advantage are greater when the entrepreneurial initiatives are based on a strategic intent (Burgelman, 1983; Hamel and Prahalad, 1989; McGrath et al. 1995).

REFERENCES

Abramovitz, M. (1986), 'Catching-up, forging ahead and falling behind', *Journal of Economic History,* **46**(2), 385–406.

Adelman, I. (2001), 'Fallacies in development theory and their implications for policy', in G.M. Meier and J.E. Stiglitz (eds), *Frontiers of Development Economics: The Future in Perspective*, pp. 103–34.

Amsden, Alice H. (1989), *Asia's Next Giant: South Korea and Late Industrialization*, New York: Oxford University Press.

Arora, A., V.S. Arunachalam, J.M. Asundi and R.J. Fernandes (2000), 'The globalization of software: the case of the Indian software industry', final report submitted to the Sloan Foundation, New York, www2.heinz.cmu.edu/project/india/.

Bhatnagar, S.C. and S. Madon (1997), 'The Indian software industry: moving towards maturity', *Journal of Information Technology*, **12**, 277–88.

Block, Z. and I.C. MacMillan (1985), 'Milestones for successful venture planning', *Harvard Business Review,* **63**(5), 4–8.

Burgelman, R.A. (1983), 'A process model of internal corporate venturing in the diversified major firm', *Administrative Science Quarterly*, **28**, 223–244.

Business Standard (2003), 'Andhra Mouse catches up fast in Infotech', 26 November, p. 1.

Chakraborty, C. and D. Dutta (2002), 'Indian software industry: growth patterns, constraints and government initiatives', working paper, Sydney University, School of Economics and Political Science, www.econ.usyd.edu.au/publication/2915. ECON2002-1, notes: 1 86487 488 0.

Ghemwat, P. (2000), 'The Indian software industry at the millennium', HBS Case No. 9-700-036.

Hamel, G. and C.K. Prahalad (1989), 'Strategic intent: to revitalize corporate performance, we need a whole new model of strategy', *Harvard Business Review*, May–June, 63–84.

Hanna, N. (1994), *Exploiting information Technology for Development: A Case Study of India*, Washington, DC: World Bank.

Heeks, R. (1999), 'Software strategies in developing countries', *Communications of the ACM,* **42**(6), 15–20.

Kanter, R.M. (1989), *When Giants Learn to Dance,* New York: Simon & Schuster.

Kapur, D. and R. Ramamurti (2001), 'India's emerging competitive advantage in services', *Academy of Management Executive*, **15**(2), 20–33.

Kim, L.S. (1997), *Imitation to Innovation: The Dynamics of Korea's Technological Learning*, Boston, MA: Harvard Business School Press.

Lall, S. (1990), *Building Industrial Competitiveness in Developing Countries*, Paris: OECD.

Maclaurin, W.R. (1953), 'The sequence from invention to innovation and its relation to economic growth', *The Quarterly Journal of Economics*, **67**(1), 97–111.

Manimala, M. (1999). *Entrepreneurial Policies and Strategies: The Innovator's Choice*, New Delhi: SAGE Publications.

Maslow, A.H. (1954), *Motivation and Personality*, New York: Harper & Row.

Mathews, J.A. (1997), 'A Silicon Valley of the East: creating Taiwan's semiconductor industry', *California Management Review*, **39**(4), 26–54.

Mathews, J.A. (1999), 'A Silicon Island of the east: creating a semiconductor industry in Singapore', *California Management Review*, **41**(2), 55–78.

McGrath, R.G. and I.C. MacMillan, (2000), *The Entrepreneurial Mindset: Strategies for Continuously Creating Opportunity in an Age of Uncertainty*, Boston, MA: Harvard Business School Press.

McGrath, R.G., I.C. MacMillan and S. Venkatraman (1995), 'Defining and developing competence: a strategic process paradigm', *Strategic Management Journal*, **16**(3), 251–75.

Meir G.M. and J.E. Stiglitz (eds) (2001), *Frontiers of Development Economics: The Future in Perspective*, New York: Oxford University Press.

NASSCOM (2002), *The ITES: BPO Super 9*, New Delhi: National Association of Software and Service Companies.

NASSCOM (2003), *The Software Industry in India: A Strategic Review*, New Delhi: National Association of Software and Service Companies.

Porter, M.E. (1980), *Competitive Strategy*, New York: Free Press.

Porter, M.E. (1990), *The Competitive Advantage of Nations*, New York: Free Press.

Porter, M.E. (1998), 'Clusters and the new economics of competition', *Harvard Business Review*, November–December, 77–90.

Porter, M.E. (2000), 'Location, competition and economic development: local clusters in global economy', *Economic Development Quarterly*, **14**(1), 15–34.

Ramachandran, K. (1986), 'Appropriateness of incentives for small scale enterprise location in less developed areas: the experiences, United Kingdom, Japan and India', unpublished PhD thesis, Cranfield Institute of Technology, UK.

Ramachandran, K. (1989), 'Small enterprise promotion: role of incentives', *Entrepreneurship and Regional Development*, **1**(4) (October–December), 381–93.

Rosenstein-Roden, P.N. (1943), 'Problems of industrialisation of eastern and south-eastern Europe', *Economic Journal*, **53**, 202–11.

Salzman. H. (2000), 'The information technology industries and workforces: work organization and human resource issues', www.uml.edu/centers/CIC/pdf/salzman/nas-it-indiait-execsummary.pdf, National Academy of Sciences Committee on Workforce Needs in Information Technology.

Saxenian, A. (2000), 'The origins and dynamics of production networks in Silicon Valley', in M. Kenny (ed.), *Understanding Silicon Valley*, Stanford, CA: Stanford University Press, pp. 141–64.

Schumpeter, J.A. (1949), *The Theory of Economic Development*, Cambridge, MA: Harvard University Press.

Scott, A.J. (1988), *New Industrial Spaces*, London: Pion.

Storper, M. (1997), *The Regional World: Territorial Development in a Global Economy*, New York: Guilford Press.

Sturgeon, T.J. (2003), 'What really goes on in Silicon Valley? Spatial clustering and dispersal in production networks', *Journal of Economic Geography*, **3**, 199-225.

Taeube, F.A. (2002), 'Structural change and economic development in India: the impact of culture on the Indian software industry', *Development by Design, ThinkCycle*, Bangalore, India.

Tyrna, I. (1994), 'The Japanese management structure as a competitive strategy', in Helmut Schitte (ed.), *The Global Competitiveness of the Asian Firms*, New York: St. Martin's Press, pp. 35–48.

Tyson, Laura D. (1988), 'Making policy for national competitiveness in a changing world', in A. Furino (ed.), *Cooperation and Competition in the Global Economy*, Cambridge, MA: Ballinger Publishing Company, pp. 95–120.

Vogel E.F. (1988), 'Competition and cooperation: learning from Japan', in A. Furino (ed.) *Cooperation and Competition in the Global Economy*, Cambridge, MA: Ballinger Publishing Company.

Weber, M. (1978), *Economy and Society*, vol 2, Berkeley, CA: University of California Press, pp. 179–201.

Zwingle, Erla (2002), 'Mega cities', *National Geographic*, **202**(5), 70–99.

10. Managerial synergies and related diversification: software services and the business process outsourcing sector in India

Suma Athreye and Vasanthi Srinivasan

INTRODUCTION

Until 1995 most of the work done by Indian software companies was on site, with teams of programmers traveling to the client site in order to write software and implement the systems that were written. With the proliferation of software technology parks, high-speed data communication services and visa restrictions in the USA and European countries, the offshore model proved to be a cost-effective option. In the offshore model of software delivery, most of the programming work was done in India with firms' managing the development of software to client specifications. The proportion of offshore revenues in software exports climbed steeply as Figure 10.1 shows. They now account for a little less than 60 per cent of all revenues.

The significance of this development in the evolution of the Indian software industry is that from trading in skilled labor in the late 1980s, Indian firms built up the capability and reputation of being able to deliver a subcontracted service at a low cost with adequate quality and on-time delivery. In the process, generic organizational capabilities were developed in managing large-scale labor resources, their training and deployment and being able to maintain the processes required for delivering outsourced services.

The offshore model of software delivery is an example of the generic outsourced service model. The existence of an information technology (IT) link connects the service provider with clients. Since 1998 outsourcing of business processes has been on the rise and increased from Rs. 565 million in 1999 to Rs. 2400 million in 2003, reflecting an annual average rate of growth of revenues of about 45 percent per annum. Table 10.1 provides

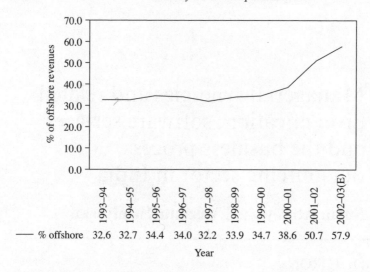

	1993–94	1994–95	1995–96	1996–97	1997–98	1998–99	1999–00	2000–01	2001–02	2002–03(E)
—— % offshore	32.6	32.7	34.4	34.0	32.2	33.9	34.7	38.6	50.7	57.9

Year

Figure 10.1   Percentage of offshore revenues in software exports (1993–2003)

Source: Computations are based on figures from NASSCOM 2001. The IT software and services industry in India: strategic review and NASSCOM website data from www.nasscom. org/ArtDisplay.asp?Cat_id=314&Page_id=1&live=0#Delivery, accessed on 10 May, 2005.

a breakdown by type of business process outsourcing (BPO) activity. In terms of type of activity, the content development and customer interaction segment have seen the sharpest rates of growth.

The BPO services could be provided by captive subsidiaries of multinational firms or by third-party firms. Several multinational companies have established captive BPO subsidiaries in India such as Accenture, American Express, GE Capital and HSBC. Third-party outsourcers have been of three types: business house subsidiaries that have entered the BPO domain (for example Hinduja TMT), diversifying firms from the software services sector (for example Wipro's Spectramind, Progeon) and completely new firms (for example Daksh e-services, 24/7 Customer). In recent months some of these completely new firms have been bought by multinationals (for example Daksh e-services by IBM).

In this chapter we study the related diversification of software firms into the BPO sector. In particular, we examine whether software services firms were particularly advantaged by being able to leverage their generic organizational and managerial capabilities in the BPO area. Offsetting such an advantage would be the knowledge of particular domains or clients that might help outsourcing firms tailor their management practices better to

Table 10.1 Growth of IT-enabled services

Type	1999–2000 Employment	(Rs. crore) Revenues	2000–01 Employment	(Rs. crore) Revenues	2001–02 Employment	(Rs. crore) Revenues	Growth revenues (%)
Customer interaction services	8 600	400	16 000	850	33 000	1 650	94
Back-office operations	15 000	950	19 000	1 350	35 000	2 850	111
Transcription services	5 000	120	6 000	160	5 200	150	–6
Content development	15 000	820	27 000	1 600	30 000	2 100	31
Other remote services	1 400	110	2 000	140	3 000	210	50
Total	45 000	2 400	70 000	4 100	106 200	6 960	70

client needs, or a general reputation for good management that would help in securing contracts.

The remainder of the chapter is organized in the following way: Section 2 outlines the synergies between software and BPO services. Section 3 discusses some factors that may limit the value of such synergies. Section 4 outlines our main hypotheses and describes the data and methods used in the empirical analysis. Section 5 discusses the results of the empirical investigation and Section 6 draws a conclusion to the study.

SYNERGIES BETWEEN SOFTWARE AND BPO SECTORS

The conceptual similarity of the underlying business model in offshore software delivery and BPO delivery certainly suggests that important synergies may exist for software firms that diversify into IT. Both are produced remotely, rely on satellite links to deliver the service, and are human capital-intensive. The competitive strengths that make one a good offshore software provider might also be helpful in being a good BPO provider. These include an understanding of customer requirements, planning and scheduling the work in a way that the clients' expectations are met, ability to scale up operations in a limited period of time, project management and dynamically creating an in-house ability to manage the project.

Can organizational processes and practices (including human resource (HR) management) learnt in one line of activity (for example software) confer gains in other areas of production (for example BPO)? The literature from business strategy makes a strong argument for such synergies in the related diversification strategies of firms. A related diversification strategy involves adding businesses whose value chains possess competitively valuable 'strategic fits' with the value chain of the firm's present businesses. Strategic fit exists whenever one or more activities comprising the value chains of different businesses are sufficiently similar as to present opportunities for transferring competitively valuable expertise or technological know-how or capabilities from one business to another (Porter, 1985).

Why do we believe that such synergies exist between software and BPO? The synergies are most obviously apparent for infrastructure investments and management. One set of advantages for software firms operating in the BPO sector comes from the existence of economies due to some shared costs – for example investments in communications infrastructure and the administrative costs of support functions like finance, HR, and so on. The effects of these advantages are likely to be brought down by costs of entry for software firms into BPO. It also puts them in a better competitive position *vis-à-vis* completely new start-ups though not against larger entrants such as multinational corporation (MNC) subsidiaries and conglomerate arms who may be able to absorb such costs more easily. These advantages also allow firms to bid for 'STAT jobs' (short turn around time jobs). For example, a medical transcriptionist allotted a job with turn around time is as low as two hours. Other things being the same, it is the infrastructure that makes the difference. A company with dedicated connectivity will have an edge over other companies here.

However, apart from shared infrastructure costs, there are also specific managerial competencies. An understanding of remote work is a generic competency. Remote working requires a different approach to management. The experience of working with a variety of customers across geographical locations provides Indian software companies with the capability to handle work in cross-cultural contexts. Understanding customer needs, being able to draw up specifications that the company can meet and being able to satisfy the demands are key project management skills. Similarly the development of managerial and leadership capability to manage multi-domain multi-location projects is also a generic competency. Managing large-scale operations requires demonstration of managerial and leadership competencies at the workplace by individuals.

At an aggregate level, there is certain evidence that parts of the services sector have been favorably affected by software growth. Arora and Athreye (2002) have argued that this shows the leverage from experience of software, even though the skill set being used in IT services is rather different from that being used in software development. The software and BPO sectors have similar sources of comparative advantage. A survey by Merrill-Lynch quoted in a NASSCOM–McKinsey strategy document revealed that cost-cutting was a key criterion for outsourcing services to India, with cost savings being viewed as India's topmost competitive advantage. Considering that labor costs represent 20–30 per cent of a typical client's business, India's low-cost skills were attractive. The salary of a database manager in India could be as low as a fifth of an equivalent post in the USA. This is of course very similar to the way software exports started.

Casual empirical evidence does back up this claim. First, there is the timing of the rapid growth of the informal IT sector studied by Kumar (2000a, 2000b). This spans the provision of IT maintenance services to firms, data entry firms and customization services for domestic users – services that were virtually nonexistent about a decade ago. Estimates by NASSCOM–McKinsey (2002), reported in Table 10.1, show a rapid growth of the IT-enabled services in India, in the last four years, *after* the offshore model became popular and understood. According to the NASSCOM projections, the offshore economics of BPO is as good as those of IT services or even better.

At the micro level, the evidence that is most suggestive of synergies between the two sectors comes from noting that many of the large software services companies have entered this segment by either acquiring equity in an existing third-party facility or by setting up their own unit. Thus, Wipro acquired Spectramind, IBM acquired Daksh eServices, while Infosys and Satyam have set up their own subsidiaries, Progeon and Nipuna, respectively, to deliver BPO. TCS has entered into an agreement with US-based Household International to provide it with BPO services. It appears that they benefit from the brand identity and reputation created in the software services to provide BPO services as part of a suite of services to their clients.

This trend is not however restricted to the large firms in software. While analyzing the NASSCOM (2001) register of IT services firms in 2001, we were able to find many more examples of software companies that were engaged in BPO delivery. We report this in Table 10.2. The table shows that some 63 percent of IT services firms and about 58 percent of firms in software products reported some BPO work as well. The average size of such firms when measured by average sales figures was smaller and their average size as measured by employment was usually higher than that for the software services and software products group. Productivity figures for software and BPO firms are thus correspondingly lower. In turn, this could mean either that the inherent productivity of such mixed activities is low because it displays a lack of market focus or that smaller and medium firms with lower productivity diversified into BPO as the recession hit these companies.

Table 10.2   NASSCOM firms by type of activity, 1999–2000

	Number of firms	Average revenue size (Rs. million)	Average employment size (in numbers)
All firms	628	539.2	298.4
Software services firms	492	636.9	330.2
Software product firms	447	620.3	313.2
Software services and BPO	314	552.7	414.9
Software products and BPO	259	493.2	372.7

Source: Authors' computations from NASSCOM (2001).

There may of course be many reasons why medium to large software companies have a presence in the BPO sector. They might get into the BPO sector as a way of offering more value-added services in software in the future, offering prospective clients the full suite of product and support services they need. If so, the motivation for entry into the BPO sector is a value-added integrating strategy whose effect may be seen in the value of projects bid for in the future rather than a strategy based upon leveraging common organizational strengths, which would increase current revenues per person. Second, their presence in the BPO sector may emerge out of a strategy, which is aimed at derisking their portfolio, and ensuring stable revenues and revenue per person rather than higher revenue per person. BPO ensures a continuous stream of revenue, which is a value proposition for many of these large companies. However, given that the profile of the employees in the IT services and the BPO sectors are different in terms of skills and competencies required, it may be possible to provide alternate human capital deployment strategies if they are seen as independent businesses.

SIMILARITIES, BUT ALSO DIFFERENCES: LIMITS TO THE SYNERGIES

Similarities in the macro features and the underlying business model coexist with specific differences as the two sectors differ from the other in important ways. Table 10.3 summarizes some important differences in the business economics of software service firms and BPO firms. While the average entry costs seem similar between the two sectors, it takes much longer to acquire a BPO client, possibly because of the strategic nature of some BPO operations. Billing rates vary over a narrower range for BPO firms with the high-end billing rates resembling the lower-end billing rates for software firms, suggesting that software firms at the lower end of the software sector may find the economics of BPO attractive. However, the service contracts are of a vastly larger size and longer tenure for the BPO sector than they are in software and this also makes for higher profit margins in this sector, which is attractive for firms diversifying from almost any area of business in India.

Non-price attributes have become important for competition relatively early in certain parts of the BPO sector. Thus, for example, BPOs compete on price but also on the possibility of multiple locations, which derisk the customers' outsourcing, on a better understanding of the customized product, which results in quicker and more reliable technical support at better service levels. The existence of these non-prices' attributes favors firms with reputation, vertical integration and multinational operations.

Table 10.3 Differences in business economics: software and BPO sectors in India

Parameter	Software firms	BPO firms
Entry capex ($/seat)	8–10,000	4–10,000
Time to obtain client	3–6 months	9–12 months
Billing rates: low end ($/hour)	20	6
Billing rates: high end ($/hour)	150	22
Service contract: size ($ million)	1–10	15–30
Service contract: tenure	6–12 months	3–7 years
Human resources: qualifications	Engineering/MCA	Graduates
Human resources: training	3–6 months	1–9 months
Human resources: attrition	8–10%	15–30%

Source: I-Sec Research, Industry and Ministry of Human Resources, as cited in ICICI (2002).

There are also larger costs of training in the BPO sector compared to the software sector where the evolution of standards and training institutions in the private sector has probably taken the weight of such training off the private firms. Though the BPO sector draws on a larger labor pool, the high cost of training ensures that it is also a sector with a higher rate of attrition. In the last year several firms have come together to make a voluntary restraint agreement against the poaching of staff from each other.

The value of reputation and the costs of training in turn raise the sunk costs in the industry and may be expected to influence the market structure. One striking difference is in the market structure in the Indian BPO industry, which is very different from that in Indian software. The software industry remained price competitive for a fairly long period and stayed unconcentrated. Even now the largest five firms account for about a quarter of all sales and the top ten firms for about a third of all sales. An advantage of this is that the productivity improvements (due to learning by incumbent firms) were transmitted due to the pressure of market competition entirely to client firms. Indeed billing rates for software have fallen over time even as productivity in the sector has increased. This may not be the case in the BPO sector, though it is too early yet to tell. The larger sunk costs may deter future entrants to the sector and also cause smaller entrants to leave quickly, ultimately producing a relatively more concentrated structure in the BPO industry. Estimates based on the NASSCOM (2001b) Directory suggest that the largest five firms account for a little less than two-thirds of output, while the largest ten firms account for about three-fourths of all output. This is quite different from software even in the early days of the industry in the late 1980s.

Table 10.4   Differences in factors accounting for success in IT services and BPO sectors

Dimensions	IT services	BPO business
People	Ability to stay abreast with new technologies Upgrade skills a critical success factor Needs engineers, technical skills as well as strong analytical skills	Strong operations' capabilities Ability to deliver throughput on an everyday basis
Processes	Ability to understand business requirements on site, develop and test a solution offshore, and then implement it onshore Ongoing maintenance could be a combination of onshore and offshore	Ability to map business requirements, migrate them offshore and deliver on a daily basis from offshore Ongoing onshore presence will be minimal and is unimportant
Technology	Knowledge of multiple technology platforms to be able to handle and test diverse requirements Need to constantly upgrade to newer platforms and technologies	Relatively standard technology platforms – often driven by client preferences Uptime of communications infrastructure absolutely critical to the business

Source: Adapted from Gurbaxani (2002).

The different economics facing the firms in the two sectors may ultimately limit the value of synergies between software services and the BPO sector. Related to the different economics, Gurbaxani (2002) points out several important differences in success factors between the IT services and the BPO segment delivery models as shown in Table 10.4. Based on the factors he enumerates as being crucial to success in the two sectors, one might even argue that there is no unique capability that has been acquired by Indian organizations engaged in the software services, which can be leveraged valuably in the BPO business. The NASSCOM–McKinsey Strategy Report (2002) also appears to recognize these differences. They argue that if India needs to grow in the BPO services, Indian organizations will need to acquire diverse skills. They would require a better understanding of the legal and regulatory issues in customer markets; acquire domain expertise in specific areas like healthcare and energy, for example, where the business processes are industry-specific and develop an understanding of cross-cultural contexts.

To manage themselves better, many of the BPO companies have begun to invest in building their own processes as they learn from their experience. For example, an e-publishing company doing typesetting and copy-editing work for the journals and books brought out by publishers in the UK has created an automated workflow system, through which various jobs are automatically routed to different proof-readers once they are downloaded. The workflow system helps in better control of the work processes since it is online and the current status of each and every job is visible to the supervisors. Most internal communication is predominantly through emails. This new workflow system gives a 20 per cent savings on time and hence cost.

In another example, the head of a medical transcription company has developed a tracking system, which will allow the chief executive officer (CEO) and the chief operating officer (COO) to see at any time the status of every job that has come into the system. The customized software that enables them to do this was built after a number of years of looking at work patterns. Thus, despite the overall similarity in the business models, and even in the presence of some shared costs, there are important differences in the specifics of the two sectors that may outweigh any gains due to the presence of an externality. Furthermore, while BPO requires knowledge of the use of software, it does not need to know how software is written. To the extent that a number of organizational procedures and processes are specific to the outcome that is delivered, there will be differences in the specific organizational requirements of BPO, which cannot be gained from the production of IT services.

HYPOTHESIS, DATA, AND METHODOLOGY

We summarize the discussion so far in the following two propositions and the corresponding empirical hypothesis:

Proposition 1: Synergies do exist between software and BPO sectors.

Hypothesis 1: Such synergies predict a relatively larger presence of software firms relative to other firms as entrants to the BPO sector.

Proposition 2: The value of the synergies between software and BPO may be outweighed by other factors as suggested in Section 3 and Table 10.4. One way to assess the value of synergies is to look at a performance measure and ask how far it is affected by the origin of the firm, that is coming into BPO from the software services sector as opposed to being a new entrant.

Hypothesis 2: The previous software experience of the entrant does not matter much, but sector-specific dummies should be important to the explanation of productivity.

To test these propositions we use data drawn from the BPO directory published by NASSCOM (2001b). There are two noteworthy features of the data. First is the heterogeneous nature of outsourcing activities that are involved in the catch-all phrase of BPO. While customer interaction services like the call centers have received a lot of media attention, there are a number of high-end business processes getting outsourced in the areas of financial services, corporate support functions (for example finance, accounts, HR), engineering and design services (including analytics, content development and R&D services). Second, the missing value problem is a severe one and may bias our reported results. In particular, multinational firms and conglomerates are pretty poorly represented in revenue and employment figures. IT firms are in contrast overrepresented.

We assess Proposition 1 by looking at the share of entrants that have diversified from IT services in the total numbers of firms, revenues and employment. In order to assess Proposition 2, we assess the impact on performance of being an entrant diversifying from the IT services sector, while controlling for other factors such as age, certification and type of BPO activity, through a regression analysis of the data. Table 10.5 summarizes the variables used in the regression analysis.

The *dependent variables* in our statistical model are revenue per employee (AVPROD) of a firm, or the size of the firm as expressed by the logarithm of revenues (LNREV). Better measures of performance would have been value added and the survival of the firm, but the BPO directory does not have such data.

We explain the differences in AVPROD as arising from the following factors:

1. The entrant type of the firm which, in turn, will consist of four dummy variables corresponding to the types in Table 10.5.
2. The age of the firm that signals reputation rather than learning given the recent emergence of the industry.
3. Whether the firm has obtained certification or not.

Table 10.5　BPO firms by entrant type, 1999–2000

	Number of firms	Average revenue size (Rs. million)	Average employment size (in numbers)	Number of firms with certification
All firms	204	217.81 (91)	245.22 (186)	37 (201)
Conglomerates	38	133.80 (14)	228.26 (34)	4 (38)
Multinational subsidiaries	23	313.65 (8)	622.32 (19)	8 (23)
IT service firms	67	305.68 (42)	222.12 (65)	19 (67)
New firms	73	96.29 (27)	170.41 (68)	6 (73)

Notes:
1. We classified firms into entrant types by utilizing information on firm web sites.
   Companies that have business interests ranging across diverse industries are called conglomerates. New firm is any company that has entered the BPO sector with no prior experience in a similar sector.
2. There were problems with missing data for revenue estimates and the numbers in parentheses indicate the number of firms that had valid data.

4. Size of the firm as measured by the logarithm of employment in the previous year.
5. Dummies to control for particular sectors of BPO, namely transcription, call centers, business office processing, R&D and engineering services and content management.

The use of dummies in the regression means that one group has to be omitted to avoid multicollinearity. We omitted the group NEW from entrant types and TRANSC from BPO sectors. In turn these omissions also mean that the coefficients on the dummies have to be interpreted as group mean relative to the omitted dummy. A negative sign on the dummy variable thus indicates a group mean that is below the average of the omitted group.

DISCUSSION OF RESULTS

Analyzing the 210 companies listed in the Directory provides a somewhat different picture from what we presented in Table 10.3. As shown in Table 10.6 below, there are four different types of entrants among BPO firms. About 20 per cent of them are independent organizations set up by large

Table 10.6 Distribution of firms across BPO categories

	Call centers	Back-office processes	Content management	R&D and engineering services	Transcription services	Total by type of firm
Conglomerates	10	8	7	3	10	38
MNE subsidiaries	4	7	3	4	5	23
IT services	10	14	26	8	9	67
New firms	24	23	10	8	8	73
Total by type of BPO	48	52	46	23	32	201

Source: Authors' computations on NASSCOM (2001b) directory.

conglomerates that are in related/unrelated-diversified businesses. Many of these conglomerates are also engaged in the software services sector. Another 10 percent consist of dedicated centers/subsidiaries of large multinational corporations. Another 30 percent are IT services and IT training organizations that have entered into this segment and about 30 percent are completely new players in the segment.

These tables lend limited support for the first proposition. In terms of numbers, IT services' companies and training firms account for less than a third of all entries. A factor that stands out clearly is the difference in scale, which is much larger for multinationals, especially when measured by employment size. For some kinds of BPO activity such as call centers this is clearly an advantage. Looking at sectors of BPO activity, as in Table 10.7 however, we could not find any strong patterns in this regard. MNE firms seem to have a higher share of firms in call centers and transcription services while many IT firms are in the area of content management. New firms are dominant in terms of numbers of firms in call centers, and back-office operations.

Table 10.7   Description of variables used in econometric estimations

Name of variable	Description
Dependent variables	All variables are for the 1999–2000 period
AVPROD	Revenue per man of a firm: computed as Sales Revenue (in Rs. Million) divided by the total employment of the firm
LNREV	Size of the firm: computed as the logarithm of its sales revenue
Independent variables	
CERT	Certification obtained by a firm: CERT=1 if yes, CERT=0 if no.
AGE	2000 – year of establishment
CONG	Dummy variable, CONG=1 if a firm is an arm of a conglomerate
MNES	Dummy variable, MNES=1 if a firm is a subsidiary of a MNE
ITS	Dummy variable, ITS=1 if a firm diversified into BPO from IT services
NEW	Dummy variable, NEW=1 if a firm is a new firm into BPO
LNEMPL	Logarithm of employment: used as a control for size
Sector dummies	CALLC=1 for call centers; BOP=1 for back-office processing; RDENGG=1 for R&D services and engineering; CONTMGM=1 for content management and TRANSC=1 for transcription services

The econometric results are presented in Table 10.8. Each column reports a different specification.

Table 10.8   Results of the econometric estimations

Dependent variable/	AVPROD		LNREV	
independent variables	(1)	(2)	(3)	(4)
CONSTANT	0.289	0.37	11.126	11.392
CONGO	−0.21	−0.24	−0.436	−0.57
MNES	−0.69	−0.60	0.351	0.27
ITS	−0.15	−0.21	0.610	0.57
CERT	0.32	0.359	0.543	0.58
AGE	0.04	0.05*	0.12**	0.12***
CALLC	0.38		1.49	
BOP	−0.13		−0.08	
CONTMGM	0.04		0.42	
R&DENGG	0.46		0.67	
LNEMPL			0.90	0.91
Diagnostics				
Residual sum	47.813	50.485	120.748	132.466
of squares (d.f.)	(49)	(53)	(47)	(51)
F-statistic	1.031	1.340	7.56	11.704
Prob (F)	0.43	0.262	0.00	0.00
R square	0.159	0.112	0.62	0.76
Adj R square	0.005	0.028	0.54	0.57

Notes:
1. Omitted dummies are NEW for new firms and TRANSC for transcription services.
2. *** denotes 1% level of significance, ** denotes 5% level of significance and * denotes 10% level of significance.

AVPROD appears to be the highest for new firms (the value of the constant term), when controlling for other factors such as certification, age and area of activity. Among other firms, MNC subsidiaries appear to have the lowest revenues per person relative to new firms. The productivity of software firms and conglomerates is broadly similar and not significantly different from that of new firms; though from the size of the coefficient, their average productivity seems marginally lower than that for new firms.

None of the sector dummies are significant though the signs indicate that R&D and engineering services have a higher revenue per person. Specification tests (that is F tests for (1) versus (2) and (3) versus (4)) indicate that (2) and (4) are preferred as it is not possible to reject the hypothesis that the sector dummies' coefficients are zero. The only factor that appears to have a positive and significant effect on productivity is the age of the firm.

The second performance measure we use is the size of the firm as measured by LNREV. Controlling for age and certification, the type of entrant is not significantly different from each other in average size. Older firms tend to have a larger size and AGE once again has a positive and significant sign. In fact columns (3) and (4) report an unrestricted estimate of productivity since LNREV–LNEMPL is in fact LNPRODY. The coefficient on LNEMPL is close to 1 and this also shows that near constant returns to labor obtain in the BPO sector.

These results do not confirm the idea of synergies that favor related diversification from software firms. Rather it seems more likely that diversifying firms from software were probably a mixed group of firms that wanted to leverage their abilities and others who wanted to avoid fading margins in software. This would accord well with the data in Table 10.3 and would account for the higher standard error in the results. What does exert a positive impact on performance is the age of the firm, which we interpret as signaling the importance of reputation rather than experience in outsourcing or learning.

CONCLUSION

We began with the hypothesis that learning in software outsourcing held lessons for successful outsourcing in BPO. We also saw that a number of software firms had diversified into the BPO sector. However, analysis of the data show very little evidence of organizational externalities that causes IT services diversifiers into BPO to do better than other types of firms. A somewhat surprising suggestion from our examination is that new firms have a higher average revenue per person than any of the other types of firms we considered, even though this is not a statistically significant difference.

Sector specificities do not seem to matter much in explaining the differences in productivity and size. The only clear result we have is that older firms tend to do better. One interpretation that could be given to this result is that BPO outsourcing is a relatively new area of business, and the older firms using BPO perhaps have learnt more about the business. Both of these conclusions need more investigation with improved data.

REFERENCES

Arora, A. and S.S. Athreye (2002) 'The software industry and India's economic development', *Information Economics and Policy*, **14** (2), 253–73.

Athreye, S.S. (2005) 'The Indian software industry and its evolving service capability', *Industrial and Corporate Change*, **14** (3), 1–26.

Gurbuxani, P. (2002) 'Strategies for marketing software services in a turbulent global environment', a paper presented at the Marketing of Technology Product Conference held at the Indian Institute for Management, Bangalore, 27 December.

ICICI (2002) 'Industry report: business process outsourcing, next frontier', ICICI Securities, Mumbai, India.

Kumar, N. (2000a), 'New technology-based small service enterprises and employment: the case of software and related service industry in India', version 2.3, mimeo, International Centre for Development Research and Cooperation, New Delhi.

Kumar, N. (2000b) 'Developing countries in the international division of labour in software and service industry: lessons from Indian experience', version 2.1, mimeo, Research and Information System for Developing Countries.

Porter, M.E. (1985) *Competitive Advantage*, New York: Free Press.

NASSCOM (2001) *The IT Software and Services Industry in India: A Strategic Review*, New Delhi: NASSCOM.

NASSCOM–McKinsey (2002) *Indian IT Strategies*, New Delhi: NASSCOM.

11. Intellectual property in the Indian software industry: past role and future need

Stanley Nollen[*]

INTRODUCTION

In clusters of modern low- and high-rise office buildings set amid acres of lush greenery here, thousands of engineers are hard at work, writing software for the latest telephones, designing next-generation microprocessors, and developing wireless broadband technology.

The work of these engineers is generating significant amounts of intellectual property (IP) for US companies like Cisco Systems, General Electric, IBM, Intel, Motorola, and Texas Instruments – whose various Indian units have filed more than 1 000 patent applications with the US Patent and Trademark Office. Some applications, with patents already granted, date to the early 1990s. But most applications from India have been filed in the last two years and still await decisions by the patent examiners in Washington, DC.

New York Times, December 15, 2003

As shown in the news story, there is a growing interest among US companies to locate some of their software development activities in India. According to a *Dataquest* report, multinational development centers in India filed 845 patents in the fiscal year 2003 and 1 216 in fiscal 2004. In contrast, Indian companies filed an unusually small number of 104 patents applications (*Dataquest*, July 15, 2004, p. 150).

Three questions are discussed in this chapter.

- How much IP has been created by the Indian software industry in the past and how much do we expect to be created in the near future?
- How well protected is software IP in India?
- What role has IP played in the growth and development of the Indian software industry in the past and how will that role change in the future?

DEFINITION AND DESCRIPTION OF THE INDIAN SOFTWARE INDUSTRY

Software is one component of the broader information and communication technology (ICT) sector that also includes computer hardware, telecom equipment and services, and electronic components used in ICT products. Some companies, especially big companies, are both software and computer hardware producers (such as Wipro and HCL), and some companies are also engaged in telecom businesses (such as Tata and Hughes). In this study we do not refer to any computer hardware business or to its components or peripherals (laptops, desktops, workstations, servers, disk drives, semiconductors, microprocessors, printers, scanners, modems, switches, hubs, routers, or other networking equipment). We do not refer in this study to any telecommunication products (such as handsets, personal digital assistants, fiber optic cables, or VSATs), or telecommunication services (such as mobile telephony or local, long distance, or international fixed-line telephony).

Software Services and Products

Indian software was a $16 billion industry in 2003–04, and it employed 813 500 professionals. In contrast, the Indian computer hardware industry was $3.7 to $4.6 billion in the same year (the range of figures in this and the following data reflect differences in sources, which are NASSCOM and *Dataquest*; the figures do not include telecom equipment or services). The software industry in India can be described in terms of what it produces which are software services (also called software development), software products (packaged), and IT-enabled services (also called business process outsourcing (BPO)).

IT-enabled services refer to a range of business services that require software in order to be delivered to the customer – software is a critical input, not the output. These services include inbound call centers (also called 'customer care'), web-based sales transactions, employee payroll and benefits administration, credit and debit card and other billing and accounting services, insurance claims processing, database marketing, medical transcription services, and engineering services.

Software Applications and Activities

In this chapter we focus on software services and products, and therefore we describe these businesses more fully. We divide both services and products into the types of applications or functions they perform. For example, software services are used for enterprise resource planning, e-commerce, and migration of data, to choose just three applications among many. Software services are usually customized (unique to each customer in part), while software products are standardized. Software products range from commonplace word processing and spreadsheet packages to computer-assisted design packages and industry-specific applications such as bank accounting operations.

We break down software services into activities or service lines performed by the software vendor based on a combination of technical labor skills and management skills required and value addition achieved, in order from low to high.

Hierarchy of software services

- Data entry; maintenance of existing systems
- Custom applications development and applications outsourcing; Production, programming (writing lines of code)
- Design; engineering (existing or new software)
- Systems integration; information systems outsourcing, turnkey projects; project management, education and training
- Network infrastructure management
- Consulting; end-to-end solutions

The first two sets of activities are likely to be performed mostly on site ('body-shopping' in which the Indian software engineer moves temporarily to the customer's place of business). These activities have in the past accounted for a large majority of all revenue earned. The latter activities are likely to be performed mostly offshore in India, and they have been smaller in revenue earned. Consulting activity, for example, was estimated to account for about 20 percent of all software services revenue in 2003–04 (*Dataquest*, 2004). However, software export revenue from billings for offshore work exceeded revenue from on-site billings for the first time in 2002–03.

THE CREATION OF IP IN THE PAST

IP played a small role in the growth and development of the Indian software industry in the 1990s. It was not part of management decision making and did not matter to company strategy. How can we explain this apparently counter-intuitive outcome?

In the past, Indian software companies did not create very much intellectual property that was especially valuable. Most of the Indian software activity was at the entry level of the global industry's business. Programming at a client's workplace with on-site delivery required technically educated people, but it did not result in the creation of very much new knowledge. It was not advanced software development. The basis for competing was low-wage skilled workers who produced software services at a lower cost and equal or better quality than US firms did.

Although we cannot measure IP directly, we can use several indicators, each one of which is incomplete by itself, to begin to assess the amount of IP creation in the Indian software industry.

- Input indicators: Research and development (R&D) spending
                         Payments made abroad for technology
- Output indicators: Patents
                         Copyrights
                         Technology income earned abroad

In principle, we believe that firms produce new knowledge from their existing stock of knowledge, their current R&D expenditure, and knowledge acquired from other sources, such as payments for technology from foreign sources – these are inputs.

Experience tells us that R&D spending is roughly proportional to patents – one of the outputs of IP creation – although the ratio varies by industry and is higher for small firms than big firms. To get a rough idea of knowledge creation from patents, we can simply count them. But to reflect better the technological and commercial value of patents, we can include data on the number of citations that patents receive from subsequent patent awards (Jaffe and Trajtenberg, 2002).[1] Copyrights are an output that applies especially to software. Firms may not seek patents or register copyrights for a variety of reasons. However, firms still own IP, the amount and value of which might be reflected in income earned from it abroad.

Data for India and the software industry lead us to several findings about IP creation (summarized below and in Table 11.1; sources are cited at the foot of the table).

Inputs for Intellectual Property

R&D spending in the Indian software industry to create new technology has occurred infrequently and has been small in magnitude

The Indian environment has not been conducive to large scale IP-related work (*Dataquest*, July 15, 2002, p. 193).

In the Indian software industry as a whole, less than 1 percent of revenue is spent on R&D. Among listed Indian software companies in particular,

4.3 percent had expenses for laboratory or R&D equipment in recent years, amounting to 0.3 percent of their sales revenue at the median. (Listed companies are traded on any Indian stock exchange and are subject to information disclosure requirements; many foreign-owned companies are not listed.) Among IT companies operating in India, both Indian and foreign (these include hardware, software, telecom equipment and services, and industrial electronics companies), 63 percent reported R&D activity; however, only 9.6 percent of these IT firms reported innovative rather than adaptive R&D (innovative R&D intends to create new products or processes whereas adaptive R&D seeks to adapt foreign product or processes to Indian production or market conditions).

For the USA as a whole, R&D expenditure is 3.7 percent of gross domestic product (GDP). Large US firms such as IBM spend billions of dollars on R&D (more than 5 percent of their sales revenue). There are exceptions among companies in India. For example, Hughes Software Systems, a US company operating in India, spends 12 percent of its revenue on R&D, and Tata Consultancy Services, an Indian company, is another substantial R&D investor.

The payment for technology from abroad through the external market by Indian software firms has been small

In recent years, 6.5 percent of listed Indian software companies, or 18 firms, paid for technology in this way, and the median size of the payment was 0.4 percent of sales revenue. From another data source, 34 percent of Indian and foreign IT firms (including hardware, telecom, and industrial electronics) made lump-sum or recurring royalty payments abroad.

Firms might make technology payments abroad in order to make or sell existing products domestically, whether they are made in India or imported into India – without IP implications – rather than create new products or processes. Not all technology payments abroad necessarily are associated with IP creation, and we cannot distinguish between these two motives.

Technology from abroad that is used to create new and valuable IP can also be obtained by non-equity strategic alliances that firms have with foreign firms where no market transaction in technology exchange takes place. Among a sample of Indian and foreign-owned IT firms, 15 percent had international technology alliances in 1999–2000.

Outputs of IP: Patents

Indian software firms have had less US patenting activity than foreign firms operating in India. The distribution of patenting activity has been very uneven
Indian software firms have fewer US software patents than foreign-owned software firms that create software innovations in India (at least in part).

Only 4 percent of the biggest Indian software firms had any US software patents awarded from 1996 to 2003 whereas 33 percent of the foreign-owned software firms had patents awarded based on work done in India. The three Indian software firms with software patents were awarded five in this time period; the leading company was Sasken Communication Technologies. The nine foreign-owed software firms with patents were awarded 167 (although not all of them were software patents); the leading company was IBM, which has a major research laboratory in India (although other US software companies also have substantial software development centers in India).

Indian software firms filed three software patent applications in the USA in the 2001–2003 period whereas foreign-owned firms filed 93 applications.

Software patenting has been underrepresented in India compared to the rest of the world

Software patenting activity, both patents awarded and applied for, has been relatively small in India. About 1.7 percent of all US software patents from all countries worldwide were invented in India in the 2001–03 time period – including both Indian firms and foreign firms operating in India – whereas the Indian software industry accounted for about 3.5 percent of worldwide information technology spending (NASSCOM 2003). In terms of US software patent applications filed but not yet awarded, India was further underrepresented, with less than 1 percent of the applications filed worldwide in the USA. (These conclusions depend on different methods of data analysis and the numerical results may not be strictly comparable.)

Software patents by Indian firms and foreign-owned firms operating in India appear so far to be less valuable than average patents in advanced fields

Among US patents awarded to software firms in India in the 1996–2000 period, the average number of citations per patent cumulated over the five years was 5.6. In comparison, US patents in advanced fields averaged 29.3 citations per patent cumulated over a five-year period beginning three years after the patent award. (Citations received by patents in a year in advanced fields increase with the patent's age up to roughly 10–12 years of age; nevertheless the data we present are comparable between software firms in India and advanced fields worldwide.)

Software patenting is increasing dramatically

Software patenting activity in the USA has increased substantially in the most recent three-year period compared to the previous five-year period. Worldwide, the number of software patents awarded in the USA increased at a rate exceeding 40 percent per year in the most recent three years. The increase was even more dramatic among companies in India, for both Indian firms and foreign firms operating in India, where the number of patents awarded to software firms increased from 10 per year in the 1996–2000 period to 40 per year in the 2001–03 period.

Outputs of IP: Copyrights

More Indian software firms have registered copyrights in the USA than have US patents
Over the same 1996–2003 time period, 18 percent of the biggest Indian software firms had registered copyrights in the USA, and the total number of copyrights for which they were the authors were 128, of which 116 were actual software copyrights.

Copyrighting activity in the USA by Indian software firms has been much less than for foreign-owned software firms
Fifty-nine percent of foreign-owned software firms that had operations in India were authors of US copyrights over the long 1978–2003 time period, and they had a total of 110 914 copyrights (however, some of these copyrights were not for software, and, unlike the case of patents, we do not know how much of the copyrightable material production by foreign firms took place in India versus other countries including the home country). In the same time period, Indian software companies had 208 copyrights (the same companies that had copyrights in the later 1996–2003 period.).

Copyright registrations for software in India appear to exceed those in the USA
In recent years, about 500 software copyrights (excluding copyrights for printed materials) were registered in India by all firms, including Indian and foreign-owned firms, and large and small firms. (This figure is tentative due to the difficulty of accessing Indian copyright data.)

The distribution of US copyrights by Indian software firms has been very uneven, and that of foreign firms has been concentrated in one firm only
Of 116 US software copyrights registered by 14 Indian firms as authors during the 1996–2003 time period, over half were accounted for by one firm (HCL Technologies) and three-quarters were accounted for by two firms (adding Network Solutions to the list).

Among the 16 foreign-owned large software firms with operations in India that have registered copyrights as authors in the USA during the 1978–2003 time period, one firm accounts for 97 percent (IBM). The second firm has 1 percent of the copyrights (Microsoft).

Outputs of IP: Fees

Some Indian firms have earned income from fees received for their technology even if they don't have patents, but the number of them that do so has been small and their earnings have been small

While only a few Indian software companies have sought patents in the USA to date, some companies have earned income from their technology without owning any patents. About 10 percent of all listed Indian software firms, or 27 firms, earned income from technology fees or royalties paid to them from abroad in recent years. The median technology income figure as a percent of sales revenue was 1.5 percent for those firms that had technology income.

More listed Indian software firms earned income abroad from technology via fees or royalties than paid for technology abroad in this way.

Ownership and Value of IP to Indian Software Developers

To the extent that Indian companies did create IP that contained new knowledge, it was in the past typically created as part of a customized software development contract with a foreign client. It was a one-off engagement to meet the particular needs of the client. This had two implications for the Indian software supplier.

First, the software that the Indian company created was the property of the client for whom it was created and who paid for it. It did not belong to the Indian vendor, and in principal could not be used again without consideration being given to the original client. Therefore the software services, even if valuable to the client, were not of much future business value to the Indian company.

Second, the customized software was unique to the business application for which it was created and therefore did not have much, if any, value in other business applications. It did not have value for other clients and therefore it was not of much future business value to the Indian software supplier.

IP PROTECTION FOR SOFTWARE

Innovation in software products can be protected as IP, usually either through the use of copyrights or patents. Both patents and copyrights are devices that are intended to protect a firm's or an individual's innovation from misuse by others, although they are quite different devices for doing so.

Copyrights, generally, protect the *expression* of an idea. That is, copyright protection extends to a specific work, but cannot be applied to the ideas

Table 11.1   Indicators of IP creation by Indian and foreign-owned software companies in India

Measure	Value
Inputs	
Laboratory or R&D equipment expense	• 12 firms or 4.3% of all publicly listed software firms in India had lab or R&D equipment expense. • The median expense for firms with this expense was 0.4% of sales revenue; the average was 3.8%.
R&D expense	• Less than 1% of the revenue generated by the Indian software industry is spent on R&D. • 63% of Indian and foreign IT firms (computer hardware and software, telecom equipment and services, industrial electronics) operating in India reported R&D expense in 1999/2000 but only 9.6% of these firms reported innovative rather than adaptive R&D.
Technology fee & royalty expense	• 18 firms or 6.5% of all publicly listed software firms had technology fee and royalty expense. • The median expense for firms with this expense was 0.3% of sales revenue; the average was 2.0%. • 34% of all Indian and foreign IT firms made lump-sum or recurring royalty payments abroad.
Outputs	
Patents	*Indian software firms* • 3 of the 78 biggest Indian software firms or 4% had US software patents awarded from 1996 to 2003. • 5 US software patents were awarded to these firms in this time period. • In the 2001–2003 period, the biggest Indian software firms filed 3 software patent applications. *Foreign-owned software firms in India* • 9 of the 27 biggest foreign-owned software firms operating in India or 33% had US software patents awarded from 1996 to 2003. • These foreign-owned firms had a total of 167 patents over these years; all of these patents were created in India, but not all were for software. • In the 2001–2003 period, the biggest foreign-owned software firms operating in India filed 93 software patent applications in the USA. *Patent growth* • The pace of software patenting accelerated from 10 software patents per year in the 1996–2000 period to 40 per year in the 2001–2003 period for software created in India by Indian and foreign-owned software companies. *Patent value* • Among patents that were awarded 3–8 years ago to Indian and foreign software firms operating in India, there were 5.6 citations per patent on average.

Copyrights	*Indian software firms*
	• 14 of the 78 biggest Indian software firms or 18% were authors of copyrights registered in the USA from 1996 to 2003.
	• These Indian software firms had a total of 128 copyrights over these years, and 116 of them were software copyrights.
	• Of the 116 US software copyrights registered to Indian firms, 70 were registered in the 2001–2003 period and 46 were registered in the 1996–2000 period.
	Foreign-owned software firms in India
	• 16 of the 27 biggest foreign software firms operating in India or 59% were authors of copyrights registered in the USA over the long 1978–2003 time period.
	• These foreign firms had a total of 110,914 copyrights over this long time span, created in all of their locations worldwide including their home country; not all of these copyrights were for software. The equivalent figure for Indian software firms was 208 copyrights.
	Indian copyrights by all software firms
	• About 500 copyrights per year for software alone have been registered recently in India by all firms (Indian and foreign, large and small).
Technology fee and royalty income	• 27 firms or 9.7% of all listed software firms in India had technology fee and royalty income.
	• Median income for firms with this income was 0.7% of sales revenue; the average was 1.5%.

Note: *Dataquest* (July 2004) reports higher numbers of patents filed and granted for both Indian and foreign firms than the figures shown in this table, whose main source is the US Patent and Trademark Office (USPTO), in part because the figures refer to US software patents rather than all IT patents worldwide from these firms, and the *Dataquest* figures are estimates.

Source: Capital Markets, Capital Line database of financial statement data from listed companies in India. Tabulations by N.S. Siddharthan and Qi Lei; *Dataquest* (July 2003, July 2004); US Patent and Trademark Office website, www.uspto.gov. Tabulations by Niranjan Rao and Stanley Nollen; US Library of Congress, Copyright Office website, www.copyright. gov. Tabulations by Niranjan Rao and Stanley Nollen; Survey data from unpublished research conducted by Confederation of Indian Industry and Georgetown University, 1999/2000. Tabulations by Stanley Nollen and Aradhna Aggarwal.

contained in such work. The application of copyright protection for software products was firmly established internationally via the World Trade Organization's (WTO) agreement on trade-related aspects of intellectual property rights (TRIPs). Under Article 10 of the TRIPs agreement, WTO members are required to treat computer programs, whether in object or in source code, as literary works as defined in the Berne Convention. Copyright protection thus extends automatically to software code once the code has been written and recorded in a medium (that is, the hard drive of a computer). A copyright holder may use his or her right to prevent others from using, making, selling or distributing unauthorized copies of the work.

Unlike copyright protection, the TRIPs agreement does not explicitly extend patent protection to software. Instead, patent protection for software has been a policy choice made by individual governments. Generally, patents are granted to new inventions provided they meet the minimum threshold requirements of novelty, utility and nonobviousness (otherwise known as 'inventive step' in some countries). Like copyright, a patent holder may use his or her right to prevent others from using, making, selling or distributing unauthorized copies of the protection invention.

The protection offered by patents is broader than that of copyrights because copyright protection extends only to a specific work whereas patent protection covers the specific invention and all inventions deemed similar (under the US Doctrine of Equivalents). For this reason, patents are seen as more valuable if they can be obtained. However, patent protection tends to be more expensive to obtain than copyright protection, because patents require a formal application process in every country where protection is desired. This application process often involves not only application fees, but attorney and translation fees as well.

The extent to which software may be patented varies by country, depending on the requirements and limitations placed on software patenting by the country. In the USA, the 1981 *Diehr* decision had set the standard for software patentability until recently. In *Diehr*, the Supreme Court recognized that software was essentially a mathematical formula or algorithm, and, in the abstract, was unpatentable. However, the Court went on to hold that a patent 'containing a mathematical formula [that] implements or applies that formula in a structure or process ... is performing a function which the patent laws were designed to protect (for example, transforming or reducing an article to a different state or thing)'. While this decision meant that software embedded in a device could be protected along with the device, it was unclear whether software that did not produce a physical transformation could be patented.

The 1998 *State Street* (State Street Bank and Trust Co. vs Signature Financial Group) and 1999 *AT&T* (AT&T Corp. vs. Excel Communications Inc.) decisions by the Federal Circuit have since clarified this once murky question of software patentability. Under the revised interpretation of the patent law, the Federal Circuit held in these cases that software might be patented if applied to produce 'a useful concrete and tangible result.' Further, the Federal Circuit held that a physical transformation is unnecessary, and that a transformation of data in one form to another will serve to establish the requisite tangible result. Both the European Union (through the European Patent Office) and Japan allow patenting of software, but the protection is extended essentially to the same extent it was in the USA under the *Diehr* decision.

Protection of IP in India

The protection of IP was of little interest to Indian software companies in the past. In part this lack of interest is explained by the small 'new knowledge' content of Indian software services – there was not much IP to protect. Indian companies did not own the customized IP they might have created since their work product fell under work-for-hire standards or ownership was explicitly transferred to the hiring company. But even if Indian companies created software services that had new knowledge value, they did not seriously take steps to protect it.

The chief IP protection available for software in India is copyright protection. India's copyright law conforms to the requirements set out by the TRIPs agreement and thus software is protected as a literary work in India. However, the effectiveness of copyright protection depends not only on standards established by laws, but also on enforcement of the standards by the judicial system.

India has had a bad reputation among foreign business people for IP protection (Mansfield 1994), but that has not come from software services that account for most of India's software industry. Instead it has come from the piracy of packaged software products.

- India was one of 11 countries on the US Trade Representative's (USTR) 'Priority Watch List' for 2003 for unfair trade in IP under Special 301 provisions of US trade law. Three other countries (including China) are in still more serious USTR categories.
- India was reckoned to be the fifth worst offender in terms of dollar losses due to piracy of business software (installation without a license) amounting to $343 million in 2002.
- India had the eleventh highest rate of software piracy in 2002: 70 percent of all software used was pirated.

The piracy rate for China was 92 percent and in the USA it was 23 percent. The worldwide average business software piracy rate was 39 percent in 2002 (Business Software Alliance 2003; International Intellectual Property Alliance 2003) (see Table 11.2).

Indian Views of Patents for Software[2]

India has not granted product patents and as such patent protection was not available for packaged software. It is doubtful that software products will be patentable once India fully conforms with TRIPs standards in 2005. Under Indian law, computer programs are seen as embodying a pure mental

Table 11.2   Business software piracy rates and revenue losses in India and other countries

Country	Piracy rate (%)		Revenue lost ($ millions)	
	1997	2002	1997	2002
India	**69**	**70**	**185**	**343**
China	96	92	1,449	2,408
USA	27	23	2,780	1,961
World	40	39	11,440	13,075

Source: Business Software Alliance (2003).

act because they are seen as essentially the application of mathematical algorithms. Thus, computer programs themselves are unpatentable in India.

However, India does grant patents for software that is part of a physical system and is the means to achieve a particular outcome, or that has a 'technical effect'. These patents may be more aptly thought of as hardware rather than software patents. The rise in importance of embedded software (in which software is fixed within hardware and cannot be reprogrammed) may blur the distinction between software and hardware patents, or may make software more frequently patentable as part of a larger product. This view of patents also prevailed in the USA until the late 1990s when the *State Street* and *AT&T* decisions did away with such limitations. A similar change in thinking in India is possible, and depends on the outcome of the usual competing arguments about the value of patent protection.

The fact that software patenting is becoming more important worldwide is not lost on Indian policy makers, and its wisdom is a much debated policy option. Whether software should be patentable in India, or whether copyrights are the more suitable form of protection, depends on several arguments. Doubts about software patenting, with rejoinders, appear below.

1. Software tends to evolve incrementally over time, and it tends to model reality rather than invent new techniques; many competent programmers might be able to invent or reinvent software routines so that *the non-obvious criterion ought to be difficult to demonstrate*.

   This is an argument against the wrongful award of software patents, not their availability. Indeed, many inventions in other fields for which patents are available cannot meet the non-obvious requirement and thus should not be granted patent protection.

2. *The software industry is technologically dynamic and rapidly makes existing software obsolete* so that the concept of 20-year protection is at odds with the conduct of the industry; in fact, some software becomes obsolete before a patent application can be decided.

   A patent holder has the choice to continue patent protection for the full 20-year term, or to discontinue paying the patent maintenance fees if the software becomes obsolete and thus release the invention from patent protection. There is no reason to deny patent protection for software to those who want it for the full 20-year term just because some software patent holders would discontinue protection before the term expired.

3. Whether by affecting the interoperability between different software platforms or by blocking types of user interfaces, patents could reduce consumer choice and *negatively affect the overall social benefit of software products.*

   A practical example of this concern is the case of the Eolas patent in the USA, where the threat of enforcing a broadly crafted patent claim affecting 'plug-in' technology sent ripples of concern across scores of software producers and internet businesses. Many claimed that enforcement of the patent would hinder further development of the internet. The USPTO re-examined the patent and has since rejected it. This case demonstrates that there is much left to be desired in patent examinations for software, and it shows that a patent system can be flexible enough to avoid enforcement of software patents that can harm the social benefit provided by software.

4. Since copyright is already available for software, patent protection is not necessary as long as copyrights are enforced.

   Because copyrights protect only a single expression of an idea, competitors can circumvent copyright protection and relatively easily make use of an innovative idea conceived by another company. Indian software company managers express this view. Patent protection provides a broader level of protection, and if applied to software, can encourage innovation in the field more than copyright does.

Indian Views of Copyrights for Software

Copyrights protect the expression embodied in software and prevent its literal reproduction. While copyrights are conferred automatically, they can be officially registered to facilitate legal enforcement (for example, to give more police powers to conduct raids to investigate allegations of infringement). Copyrights do not protect ideas (such as the logic, algorithms, or methods in a software program), which are the domain of patents, or layouts, which are the domain of trademarks. Nevertheless, 'a copyright is a hugely strong weapon,' according to Pravin Anand (interview, October 30, 2003), and underutilized.

Standards
Indian protection of copyrights for software is strong in some respects and weak in others. A basis for comparison is provided by the World Intellectual Property Organization (WIPO) Copyright Treaty that came into effect in March 2002, to which there were 42 signatories in 2003; India is not a signatory.

- India protects reproduction in all forms including temporary reproduction (such as that which occurs in the transmission via the internet) by virtue of its membership in the Berne Convention.
- India provides 'make available' protection (the copyright owner has the right to control distribution of copies; you are responsible if you unknowingly make available to others software that you have legally purchased or licensed), which is part of the WIPO Copyright Treaty even though India has not signed this treaty.
- India does not guard against 'circumvention of technological measures' that copyright holders use to protect otherwise easily copied software (for example, registration of software to prevent its use on multiple computers). This is a key part of the WIPO Copyright Treaty and India is expected to provide this protection soon.

The Indian copyright law that was regarded as very strong was weakened by amendments in 2001 that made room for exceptions to copyrights. The effect of the main weakening was that India now allows making copies of software for noncommercial personal use (for example, using software purchased for business at home).

Other exceptions apparently permit some decompiling of programs and reproduction to observe functionality, which will facilitate 'intelligent' copying that is difficult to enforce.

However, a high-level task force is preparing recommendations for revisions in the Indian copyright law, with prospects for full WIPO and TRIPs compliance in the future.

Enforcement
The enforcement of copyright standards achieved by a country can be assessed by its compliance with the TRIPs agreement of WTO, which entails both standards and enforcement. Enforcement is the more likely area of non-compliance. Adequate enforcement means effective action against infringements, expeditious remedies that constitute a deterrent, fair and

equitable application, reasonably simple and inexpensive procedures, and timely decisions.

> the framework to implement (copyright laws) is abysmally lacking ... there are not enough copyright lawyers. The copyright office does not have a database of copyrights in electronic format. *Dataquest* (July 2002, p. 195)

The enforcement of Indian copyright law is strong in one respect – it provides for injunctions to 'stop the wrong' so that a copyright holder gets immediate relief. However, enforcement is deficient in two important respects, and these weaknesses outweigh the sole strength.

Weak infringement
It is difficult to prove that damages should be awarded, fines are too small, mandatory prison terms specified in the law have never been invoked, and the consequence is that the infringer is scarcely penalized and can move on to copying someone else's software.

Low conviction rates
First, magistrates are not technically trained nor experienced in IP or software issues and must handle a wide variety of cases. The tendency is to give the benefit of doubt to the accused. Second, there are too few judges to hear cases, and long delays occur before the judicial process is concluded – 10–15 years is typical. Of nearly 100 cases filed since 1996, two judgments have been rendered as of 2003 (both convictions). Third, prosecution is taken up by government lawyers in cases that involve police action rather than private law firms. Finally, there are too few police officials dedicated to economic offenses, and enforcement is variable state-by-state.

The time required to complete enforcement actions is much too long, and this surely is out of compliance with TRIPS expectations.

Weak enforcement of IPR in India might be explained either by the relatively low level of government engagement in the industry, or the fairly low level of innovative activity in the industry at least through the 1990s (Jayakar, 2003). Improvement may be forthcoming. It is likely that a high-level task force now at work will recommend the establishment of special intellectual property courts to be staffed by fully qualified judges.

Effects of No Patents and Weak Software Copyright Enforcement

The lack of patent protection for software in India and inadequate enforcement of software copyrights have not been impediments to the creation of intellectual property by Indian software companies up to the present time. We identify four reasons for the lack of impact up to now.

The unimportance of patents

For several reasons, patents have not been important for Indian software companies. First, Indian software companies that wanted to protect their IP in software would seek patents in the USA if at all, but not in India (which does not grant software patents), mainly because their largest market by far was the USA, which is where a company wanted to exploit and defend its IP. In small markets, such as the Indian domestic market, the cost of obtaining and defending patents was not worth the benefit.

Second, if sophisticated software services were performed, and if new tools or methodologies were created in doing so, they were created for the client's particular purposes. Customized software was not useful to others. If it did not have value to other firms, there was no issue about protecting it.

Third, the benefit/cost ratio for patents in the USA for Indian software firms typically was unfavorable. For most of these companies, the likely benefit to be gained from obtaining a patent was small and the cost was relatively high. An average cost for a software patent through its life cycle is $35 000 (*Dataquest*, 2004). The filing fee is a small part of the cost; most of the cost arises from payments to lawyers (US law firms or Indian law firms with offices in the USA) to conduct patent searches, and to keep the patent active if granted. For small Indian firms, and most Indian software firms are small, this cost is too high.

If a patent is obtained in the USA, it is not valid in a second country market, such as a European country, so that if the firm's IP is to be protected in a second market, a second patent is required. If patents were universal or honored by multiple countries, the benefit/cost ratios would be more favorable. Patents, once obtained, are only as good as the firm's ability to defend them. Violations of a firm's patent need to be detected and then prosecuted. Lack of detection reduces the expected benefit, or prosecution of violations raises the expected cost, either of which reduces the Indian software firm's reckoning of the patent's benefit/cost ratio.

A special feature of software services and products is that technology changes rapidly – today's new technology obsolesces in a short time, maybe in less than a year, but typically within three years. Accordingly the value of a patent is typically smaller in this industry than elsewhere simply because the length of its useful life is short.

The value of patents in software is further diminished if the knowledge that it represents is incompletely useful to potential competitors. If the patented idea is commercially valuable only in conjunction with complementary inputs, competitors must have those inputs to be threats to the firm that created the technology. For example, proprietary software is likely to require both hardware and customer service as part of a package that is valuable to buyers of the software. Customer service is likely to depend in part on tacit knowledge. Competing software vendors might not be able to match this package offered by the innovating software firm, and therefore the innovator's proprietary software does not need patent protection. If the technology contains a substantial tacit knowledge component, even if it is not part of a complementary package, potential competitors might not be able to provide the service to customers as well as the innovator company even if the explicit component that was not patented or copyrighted was known to them.

To obtain a patent compels public disclosure of the codified idea for which the patent is sought. Disclosure, coupled with the high costs of obtaining patents and the frequently dubious value they confer to the firm, leads to alternatives to patenting. The obvious first alternative is to attempt to keep the new technology secret (unless it is necessarily revealed when used), or to prevent its use by unauthorized persons by means of locks.

The need for patents or copyrights to protect intellectual property might be avoided when the marketplace contains only a few buyers and sellers of the technology. A small number of managers on either side of the transaction might be able to informally agree on the terms and conditions for the use of IP without resort to licensing contracts against patents or copyrights (Siddharthan, 2000).

Low value of copyrights

Copyrights are available in India and all countries for software, although the strength of copyright law and its enforcement are not equal in India to that of the USA. Even if enforcement were vigorous, copyrights have usually not been a part of Indian software protection. There are two reasons, apart from weak enforcement: It is hard to know if or when a copyright is being violated, and it is easy for a copyright to be evaded. Indian software company managers express their reservations, below:

> Copyrights offer little protection. They are not so useful because it is easy to get around them. If I copyright software written in the English language, someone else can produce the same software in the Hindi language, which is a different expression. We do register copyrights, but only for written materials such as manuals, not for software.

> Copyrights aren't worth much. How do you know when your copyright is being infringed? We do not register copyrights either in the US or India.

> We have filed for 15 patents in the US, but they are all for software products, not services. Copyrights are of little value for software services.

Earning returns to IP

Indian software company managers who are conscious of their firm's IP usually have not sought to earn a monetary return to it directly. Usually no recurring royalty nor lump-sum payment is charged for a client's use of the firm's proprietary technology. Instead the Indian software firm typically includes the value of its IP in the contract price it negotiates with the client, but not separately specified. The value of new software technology is difficult to determine if a market price has not been established for it, so to fix a royalty rate could be an unsatisfactory negotiation. Of course, if the IP is not patented or copyrighted – and most software is not – then to price it explicitly to a client is all the more difficult to do. The lack of separate pricing or earnings returns directly from IP diminishes its apparent value.

Software piracy

Despite the past irrelevance of IPR protection for Indian software companies that developed software services, the widespread piracy of software packaged products in India was important to the Indian software industry's development in one simple but indirect way: the availability illegally of pirated software products spread the use of computers and computing much more widely in the population than could otherwise have occurred.

That widespread piracy occurred can be understood from both economic and cultural standpoints. Packaged software product prices were high for people in low-income countries like India. It was not possible for software products companies to charge two prices in two markets, a low price in the low-income countries and a high price in the high-income countries, even if the two markets had different price elasticities that would make it profitable to do so, because arbitrage across markets was easy, transportation costs were near zero, and the product was long-lasting and durable (not perishable). Culturally, the extent to which software piracy occurred depended on the national regard for IP. Rather than viewing the copying of software (and some other creative works) as unethical, some Indians thought it was necessary and justified because it was essential and priced out of reach, and because of a cultural view that stressed common interest rather than private interest.

THE CHANGING BASIS FOR COMPETITIVENESS IN INDIAN SOFTWARE

Despite the record of the past, the creation and protection of IP is becoming important for Indian software companies. As an industry grows and develops, the basis for competing changes. Firms' competitive advantage might change from cost to quality, and from product quality to service quality. Production technology might change from labor-intensive to capital-intensive or from unskilled labor-using to skilled labor-using. New competitors from other countries might arise if they acquire the critical factors of production or access to foreign markets, or if their governments succeed in promoting the industry.

The Indian software services industry, which was the first among outsourcing locations for software services sought by multinational enterprises in North America, faces an industry evolution. By the end of the 1990s, perhaps marked by the end of Y2K work, the Indian first-mover advantage was over. Competitive advantage was shifting. Other countries have some of the same inputs that India has, or were developing them.

The move toward offshore outsourcing work introduced client communication as an additional requirement for business success, and it coincided with the introduction of software design and engineering work into the client relationship. It marked the first small contribution that new knowledge could make to the Indian software company's client engagement.

> The low-cost, high-tech delivery model, followed so far by most players in the industry, will no longer ensure success. ... players need to fundamentally rethink their business models and develop new sets of capabilities to emerge successful in the long run (Kirin Karnik, President of NASSCOM, in *NASSCOM-McKinsey Report (2002)*).

As some of the bases for competitive advantage in Indian software diminish – especially low labor cost and government support for industry – other countries are becoming stronger threats. The countries that Indian software managers mention most often are the Philippines, Israel, Ireland, Russia, and China. A recent McKinsey study identified China and Philippines as India's potential competitors in the short run (NASSCOM–McKinsey, 2002). Indian software companies are changing their business strategies by changing their business segments in two ways. First, they are seeking to move away from programming on site, and instead moving toward higher value-added and more sophisticated and complex offshore software services such as systems integration and consulting.

Second, they are seeking to develop packaged software products. Software products are normally more risky than customized software services because they might not succeed in the marketplace. Both of these shifts in business segments call for new and different capabilities compared to lower-end software services. Most important, they both require more creative and business-centered relationships with clients, with more insight into customers' needs and more global marketing knowledge.

Table 11.3 Importance of various competitive factors for the success of the software industry: H = high, M = medium, L = low

Basis for competing	Software services				Software products	IT-enabled services; business process outsourcing
	Programming	Design, engineering	Systems integration	Consulting		
Inputs						
Labor cost	H	M	L	L	L	H
Labor qualifications	M	M	M	H	H	L
Management capability	L	M	H	H	H	M
Domain knowledge	L	M	H	H	H	M
Technology						
Technology level, R&D	L	M	M	M	H	L
Foreign technology	M	M	M	H	H	M
Clustering	L	M	M	M	M	L
Infrastructure						
Financial institutions	L	L	L	M	M	M
Legal – IP rights	L	M	M	M	H	L
Physical infrastructure	L	M	M	L	L	M
Government						
Government incentives	H	H	H	H	H	H
Trade policy	H	H	L	L	H	H
FDI policy	M	M	M	L	M	M

204

Market competitiveness						
Ease of entry, exit	H	H	M	L	L	H
Foreign competitors	L	L	M	H	H	L
Suppliers, distributors	L	L	H	L	M	L
National culture						
Individualism	L	M	M	L	H	L
Openness	M	M	H	H	H	L
Non-resident Indians	L	M	M	H	H	M
English language	H	M	H	H	M	H
Time zones	H	L	L	L	L	H

Notes:

Labor cost depends on labor productivity (output per hour) and labor wages.

Labor qualifications: type and level of formal education as a measure of labor skill.

Management capability: general management coordination and control, and marketing management.

Domain knowledge: how well the needs of the customer are known, both industry and country domains.

Technology level: how advanced the technology is, implying R&D for more advanced.

Foreign technology: use of imported scientific tools and payment of technical fees abroad.

Clustering or agglomeration: nearby geographical location of software firms; for example, Bangalore financial institutions: banks, capital markets.

Legal infrastructure: IPR means protection of intellectual property.

Physical infrastructure: roads, rails, ports, power, water, telecom.

Government incentives: tax relief, subsidies.

Trade policy: import tariffs, currency convertibility.

FDI (foreign direct investment) policy: ease of setting up foreign operations.

Ease of entry, exit: easier entry means the market is more competitive.

Foreign competitors: more, stronger foreign competitors means the market is more competitive.

Suppliers, distributors: more good suppliers means the market is more competitive.

Openness: free exchange of ideas, abundant interaction.

Non-resident Indians: people of Indian origin who live and work outside India.

Source: Responses of five Indian software company managers and author's judgments.

205

Competitive Basis for Software Business Segments

A closer and more detailed look at the bases for competing in each of the several segments of the software industry shows the change in capabilities that will be required of Indian software firms if they are to shift toward higher value-added software services and packaged products (Table 11.3).

Low labor cost, the result of low wages and high productivity, is critically important for competitive success in entry-level software services such as programming, but much less so in high-end software services such as systems integration and consulting, for which labor qualifications are more important. Management and marketing capabilities exhibit the opposite pattern as labor cost: they are low in importance for programming and high in importance for systems integration and consulting. Domain knowledge – knowledge of the customer's needs particular to his or her industry and country – becomes important with high-end software services, similar to management capability.

The level of advancement of technology used to compete in software is low for programming and medium for other software services. This implies that little R&D spending is necessary for the former but some is helpful for the latter. Foreign technology is of medium importance for most software services, but becomes critical for software consulting.

In the view of Indian software managers, financial, legal, and physical infrastructures are of low importance to software services competitiveness. Government policies, both targeted incentives and general trade and investment liberalization, are seen to be important to software business success, but less so for systems integration and consulting businesses. As far as market competitiveness is concerned, ease of its entry into low-level software services has contributed to its success, but this feature of the industry is less important for higher-level software services and products. The presence of foreign competitors exhibits the opposite trend: not important for entry-level software services but critical to competitiveness of the marketplace for higher-end software services and products.

The critical competitive success factors for software products are similar to those for high-level software services except for the additional importance of advanced technology and IPR protection.

Whether or not Indian software companies will succeed in their transition from entry-level on-site software services providers to high value-added end-to-end business solutions providers and consultants is by no means assured. Their new competitors include strong foreign multinational firms that are the world's leaders. In the development of packaged software products, success has been elusive, as the data on revenue from software products shows and as individual company experiences illustrate.

Table 11.4 Competitive factors for low- and high-level software services and products

Low-level software services	High-level software services	Software products
Labor cost	Labor qualifications Management capabilities Domain knowledge	Labor qualifications Management capabilities Domain knowledge Advanced technology
	Foreign technology	
		IP protection
Government incentives Liberalized trade policy Easy entry into the market	Government incentives	Government incentives Liberalized trade policy
	Foreign competitors Non-resident Indians	Foreign competitors Non-resident Indians
English language Time zone differences	English language	

Effects of Offshoring on IP Creation and Protection in India

The movement of jobs from the USA to India in search of lower costs has been a central feature of the growth of the Indian software industry throughout the 1990s. It is only recently that job shifts to the Indian IT sector have reached the headlines of the popular press – and that is due to the apparent shift of good jobs, white-collar jobs, and professional jobs. Economists and politicians debate whether the new breed of offshoring causes net job loss or gain (Drezner, 2004). The question to be addressed here is whether this offshoring trend will affect IP creation and protection in Indian software.

Our speculation is in two parts. First, the very rapid growth in business process outsourcing (BPO) in India (up 45 percent in 2004, nearly double the growth rate of the entire IT industry) has little impact on intellectual property. Most of the jobs in BPO are entry level, while those BPO segments that are higher-skill are not engaged in IP creation. To the extent that offshoring trends refer to software-related BPO business, there is little impact on IP.

Second, to the extent that the new offshoring trend consists of higher value-addition software services that employ more sophisticated and complex skills, it reinforces the desired evolution of Indian software firms. If foreign firms purchase more advanced technology services from Indian companies or invest in their own advanced technology operations abroad, then new IP creation in India is stimulated, and in turn the motivation to protect it increases.

SUMMARY AND CONCLUSION

Intellectual property was not important to the growth and development of the Indian software industry in the past. It did not figure in company strategy or managers' decisions. Indian software companies did not create very much new and valuable IP. Technology inputs that might create intellectual property were small. Indian software firms spent very little on research and development in-house, and much of that was adaptive rather than innovative R&D. They purchased very little technology from foreign sources, and only a few firms had international non-equity strategic alliances for technology.

IP Creation and Protection

IP outputs were small in the past, but software patenting activity is increasing dramatically. Copyrights are a more frequent though less effective method than patents for protecting IP in software. As with patents, US software copyright registrations are increasing dramatically. The small amount of new and valuable IP creation credited to the Indian software industry is due in part to the fact that most of the software services work that Indian firms did was at the entry level of the software services value-addition hierarchy. This work required technically educated labor, but not advanced skills.

India has had a bad reputation for the protection of IP, but this did not discourage the growth and development of the Indian software services industry – instead it may have hastened it. It was not important to protect IP in software in India because there was not much to protect. However, this will not be true in the future.

India, like many countries, does not award patents for pure software because it is a business method, depends on algorithms, and results from a pure mental act. However, software that has a technical effect and is part of a physical system is patentable. A change in Indian software patent policy may occur in the future, but not immediately.

Whatever the status of patent protection for software in India, it has not been important to the software industry. In the first place, patents were sought in the USA where the market was, not in India. Second, most Indian software services were customized for the client. It was the client's property, not the Indian software company's property. Even if it were, it would have limited general use because it was customized to the client's needs. Third, the benefit/cost ratio for patenting in the USA was unfavorable. Secrecy was an option to patenting, and the oligopoly/oligopsony nature of the industry facilitated IT-sharing agreements.

Indian protection of software copyrights meets international standards in some respects but not others. In particular, Indian law does not prevent a properly registered software package from being copied for use on multiple computers, and does allow multiple copies of software to be made for non-commercial uses. High-level discussions now taking place may reverse these two differences from international standards and bring India into full TRIPs and WIPO compliance. A more serious weakness in software copyright protection is its enforcement. Deterrence for copyright infringement is weak because proof is difficult and penalties are small. Conviction rates are low because the judiciary is understaffed and underqualified, and delays are too frequent and too long. Here also improvement might occur in the future in the form of proposals for the creation of special IP courts.

Indian Software and Intellectual Property in the Future

The business model for the Indian software industry in the past will change in the future. To be the low-cost vendor of entry-level customized software services need not be the main basis for competing by Indian software companies. The historical Indian advantage of labor that is abundant, low-wage, low-cost, technically educated, and English-speaking is being eroded. Indian wages are rising as demand catches up with supply, and other countries, especially Ireland and Israel in Europe, and China and the Philippines in Asia, are developing their own competitive labor pools.

The Indian software industry is seeking to move downstream along the value chain toward more complex tasks of design, systems integration, and consulting that require more customer contact, more domain knowledge, more innovation, and more project management. There is also an attempt on the part of some companies to develop mass-marketed packaged software products, although so far these efforts have met with only modest success. The basis for competing in these segments is advanced technology, highly skilled labor, technical labor, and managerial and marketing skill.

These new competitive requirements mean, among other things, that the Indian software industry must create new and valuable IP in the future. IP is more valuable if it is more innovative, which yields bigger margins, and if it is reusable or has a wide range of uses, which yields more licensing revenue without increasing cost proportionately. The implications for IP are clear: Indian software firms must create new, advanced IP, and they must protect it.

NOTES

* This research was supported by the International Intellectual Property Institute, Washington, DC, and the US Patent and Trademark Office, and it is based on a report commissioned by IIPI (see www.iipi.org). An earlier version of this paper was presented at a workshop on

March 2–5 2003 in Bangalore, India, 'Learning from the Indian Development Experience,' organized by George Mason University and the Indian Institute of Science, supported by the US National Science Foundation.

   I wish to acknowledge with gratitude the contributions of Professor N.S. Siddharthan, K. Lal, Niranjan Rao, Michael Ryan, Paul Almeida, Stetson Sanders, Eric Garduno, Charles Eloshway, Mark Hedley, Deepak Balakrishnan, Ashish Arora, Qi Lei, Dennis Butler, and the managers of Indian software firms and Indian lawyers from whom I obtained primary information.

1. Other measures of the value of patents, especially their commercial value, can also be used, such as patent renewal rates and license fee or royalty earnings derived from patents.
2. This section on patents and the one on copyrights that follows it are based on the views of two Indian IP lawyers, Mr Pravin Anand and Mr Saikrishna Rajagopal, and selected journal articles.

REFERENCES

Business Software Alliance (2003), *Piracy Study: Trends in Software Piracy 1994– 2000* (June).

Cornell Research Foundation (2001), 'Bayh-Dole Act', www.crf.cornell.edu/bayh-dole.html.

Dataquest (India). (2002), 'The Year of Survival', **XX** (1) (July 15).

Dataquest (India) (2003), 'Revival,' **XXI** (13) (July 15).

Dataquest (India) (2004), 'Growth!', **XXII** (13) (July 15).

Drezner, Daniel W. (2004), 'The Outsourcing Bogeyman,' *Foreign Affairs*, **83** (3) (May/June), pp. 22–34.

International Intellectual Property Alliance (2003), *2003 Special 301 Report for India*, www.iipa.com (14 October), pp. 109–124, from www.iipa.com.

Jaffe, Adam B. and Manuel Trajtenberg (2002), *Patents, Citations, and Innovations*, Cambridge, MA: The MIT Press.

Jayakar, Krishna P. (2003), 'Cross-sectoral differences in intellectual property enforcement in developing countries: the role of state–industry linkages', *The Information Society*, **19**, pp. 155–69.

Mansfield, Edwin (1994), 'Intellectual property protection, foreign direct investment, and technology transfer', IFC discussion paper no 19, Washington, DC: World Bank.

NASSCOM (2003), *The IT Industry in India: Strategic Review (2003)*, New Delhi: NASSCOM.

NASSCOM–McKinsey Report (2002), *Strategies to Achieve the Indian IT Industry's Aspiration*, New Delhi: NASSCOM.

Siddharthan, N.S. and Y.S. Rajan (2002), *Global Business Technology and Knowledge Sharing: Lessons for Developing County Enterprises*, New Delhi: Macmillan.

US Federal Court Cases

AT&T Corp. v. *Excel Communications, Inc.*, 72 F.3d 1352 (Fed. Cir.1999).

Diamond v. *Diehr*, 450 U.S. 175 (1981).

State Street Bank & Trust Co. v. *Signature Financial Group, Inc.*, 149 F.3d 1368 (Fed. Cir. 1998).

12. Does India's information technology industry need labor mobility in an age of offshore outsourcing?

Ron Hira

INTRODUCTION

For the past few decades, researchers have demonstrated a strong link between investment in information technology (IT) capital and economic growth in developed countries (Dedrick et al., 2003, pp. 1–28). The belief is that investment in IT capital has spurred rapid productivity gains in the US economy and sectors that invested heavily in IT were the leading productivity gainers (Mann 2003, pp. 1–11). More recently, developing countries have been able to leverage their investments in domestic IT infrastructure – an educated workforce and capable IT companies – to drive export-led development even though they have little or no domestic market. The Indian IT services industry is the exemplar leading the wave, exporting the vast majority of its work. NASSCOM, the Indian software services industry association, estimates that the Indian IT industry has grown nearly tenfold from 1994 to 2002. It estimates IT revenues of approximately US$ 16.5 billion in 2002, which accounts for 3.15 percent share of India's GDP (NASSCOM, 2004). In another sign of India's growing IT prowess, the largest Indian IT services firm, Tata Consultancy Services (TCS), recently raised more than US$1 billion in an initial public offering of its stock at a time when the market for initial public offerings in the USA is dismal. In addition to its emergence as the offshore IT supplier of choice, India has been able to derive advantage in the business process outsourcing (BPO) markets. In fact, the Indian BPO market is growing three times as fast as IT services (NASSCOM, 2004). These sectors such as call center operations or tax return preparations are only possible because of the advancement of ITs.

The major factors that have been identified as enablers of India's success in IT and BPO include economic liberalization in the 1990s, a large pool of technically trained workers willing to work for low wages, English language capabilities, a culture oriented towards intellectual abstraction, and low capital requirements for entry into software services (Arora et al., 2000; Das, 2001). These factors help to explain what contributed to the rapid IT expansion in the past six years, but most of them are not unique to India. For instance, many other countries, such as those in Central and Eastern Europe have similar pools of talent and liberalized economies. Why has India gained a first-mover advantage over other countries?

This chapter examines a factor overlooked in explaining why Indian IT firms have an advantage in the US marketplace: Indian IT firms' ability to move low-wage technical workers to US customers on site. Firms were able to leverage loose US labor mobility policies for competitive advantage by placing high-quality technical employees at the site of customers in the USA much earlier and at a greater scale than their competitors. A large portion of revenues and earnings for Indian IT firms depend on labor mobility to the USA, and they use temporary work visa programs such as the H-1B and L-1 to place workers on site. The firms learned this practice from US-based companies, such as Syntel, Mastech (now known as IGate), Intelligroup and others, headed by people of Indian origin. While Arora et al. (2000) and Heeks (1998) have discussed the importance of on-site labor for the Indian IT industry, they have not measured its impact on the development of the industry.

How will the emerging phenomena of offshoring and offshore outsourcing affect the competitive position of Indian IT firms and their need for labor mobility? Offshore outsourcing dominated the headlines in the USA in late 2003 and early 2004, as companies operating in the USA began the process of moving tasks from the USA to overseas locations, most prominently to India, to take advantage of low cost labor. At first glance, one may speculate that as more work is offshored to India and elsewhere this will reduce the need to bring foreign workers into the USA. However, many projects require significant face-to-face interaction with customers and in spite of the rapid acceleration of offshore outsourcing and record unemployment for US IT workers, the appetite for temporary work visas continues to increase. The H-1B quota was exhausted just five months into fiscal year (FY) 2004, and on the first day of FY 2005. The Indian government has been particularly pressing the USA for more liberal labor mobility policies through platforms such as the World Trade Organization (WTO) and the Indo–US free trade agreement.

The chapter explores how offshore outsourcing may affect Indian IT firms' labor mobility needs and the politics of liberalizing US labor mobility policies. The next section presents a brief background on US labor mobility policies and aggregate level data of temporary workers by country of origin.

It shows that the vast majority of high-skilled temporary workers in the USA come from India and most of them work in IT firms. The third section quantifies the leading Indian IT firms dependence on temporary visas for their business. Firm level financial data show that temporary workers generate substantial revenue and earnings for leading Indian-based IT firms. The fourth section discusses how demand for labor mobility may change due to offshoring and offshore outsourcing. The concluding section describes the US mobility policy environment and its potential impact on the Indian IT industry.

US LABOR MOBILITY POLICIES AND DATA

A large number of foreigners enter the USA every year for business, pleasure, study, work, or immigration on visas. In order to enter the USA to work, foreigners must apply to the US Citizenship and Immigration Services (USCIS), formerly the Immigration and Naturalization Services, for a work visa. Depending on an individual foreigner's work purposes and his qualifications, the USCIS issues a particular visa. The IT industry extensively uses two non-immigrant work visas, the H-1B and L-1, to bring in foreign workers. The TN visa, created under the North American Free Trade Agreement (NAFTA), may become more important in the future as some of the limits on workers from Mexico are relaxed and Canada becomes a nearshore destination for IT imports. However, this discussion is limited to the H-1B and L-1 because they are the most frequently used.

The H-1B is a temporary work visa issued to employers to hire specialty occupation workers. By definition, a specialty occupation is a position that requires the theoretical and practical application of highly specialized knowledge and skills at least at a BA degree or its equivalent level. The H-1B covers a wide array of positions including accounting, architecture and healthcare. However, in recent years it has become an important staffing tool for the IT industry and in particular for the Indian IT industry. IT firms would like looser regulations to increase the numbers of H-1Bs and L-1s. The regulations are enforced during the visa issuance process.

The H-1B process starts with employers submitting a Labor Condition Application (LCA) to the US Department of Labor (DoL). The application requires detailed attestations by the employer, including that it pays the 'prevailing wage' for the position. The prevailing wage requirement is weak, as is illustrated later in the chapter, and the DoL denies very few applications based on it. After LCA approval, the employer is able to petition the USCIS to admit a foreign worker to fill the position. The worker then files for an H-1B visa at the nearest US consulate abroad or for a change of status if he is already in the USA under another visa. H-1Bs are good for a maximum of three years but are extendable for another three years. Employers, not workers, hold the visa, so if a worker loses his or her job, he or she is considered out of status and may be forced to leave the USA. This provides an additional source of bargaining power in the hands of the employer.

The primary restriction for employers is that the H-1B is subject to an annual quota. Beginning in 1991, Congress imposed a maximum annual quota of 65 000 for the H-1B visa program to control its use. The cap applies only to new visas and there are multiple groups of exemptions such as extensions and university employees. The cap remained at 65 000 until FY 1999 when the IT industry lobbied Congress to increase the cap because it was being exhausted before the end of the year. The cap was raised to 115 000 for FY 1999 and FY 2000, and after more IT industry lobbying to 195 000 for FY 2001–03 it was raised to 195 000. The cap reverted to 65 000 for FY 2004 and was consumed within just five months into the fiscal year in spite of the rise of offshore outsourcing and high unemployment for US IT workers. The cap was hit on the first day of FY 2005.

Multinational corporations wishing to move foreign personnel into the USA for temporary assignments use another visa, the L-1, which is an intra-company transfer visa. There are two classes of L-1 visas. L-1As are for executives and managers and L-1Bs are for positions that require specialized knowledge. Executives and managers can stay up to seven years while specialist knowledge workers up to five. There is no annual cap for L-1s and no prevailing wage requirement, which make the L-1 more attractive to employers than the H-1B. However, widespread reports of L-1 abuse by Indian IT firms led the State Department to warn its consulate offices to scrutinize applications more carefully. This may have made it more difficult to obtain.

Visa Data

The USCIS does not collect and publish precise data on the number of foreigners working in the USA at any particular time, but we can gain some insight into labor mobility trends from the data available. Figure 12.1 shows that visa admissions, a measure of labor mobility, have increased rapidly over the past decade. H-1B and L-1 admissions increased steeply from 1996 to 2000, and then leveled off with the US economic slowdown in late 2000. Even with the slowdown, it appears that non-immigrant work visas are much more important to businesses operating in the US in the early 2000s than it was in the early 1990s. As we shall see a large source of the H-1B increase were IT employees from India.

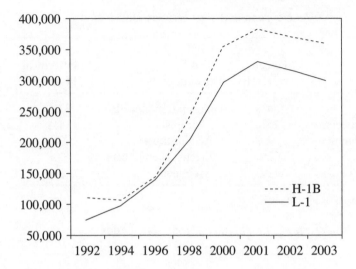

Source: USCIS (1992–2003).

Figure 12.1 Visa admissions by category, 1992–2003

Table 12.1 shows that during the 1990s the occupation mix for the H-1B shifted from primarily healthcare in 1995 to IT in 1998. Not surprisingly, as Table 12.2 shows, the predominant employers requesting LCAs also shifted from healthcare to IT. The 1998 list includes large IT employers such as Oracle, Lucent, and Motorola, which were ramping up their businesses during the technology bubble of the late 1990s. Interestingly number two in the 1998 list was TCS, the largest Indian-based IT company, which was also the first to penetrate the US market in a significant way by using the H-1B. The Indian diaspora also seems to have played a role in developing the H-1B business model. Two firms listed in 1995, Complete Business Solutions (now known as Covansys) and Mastech, were founded by entrepreneurs of Indian origin. By 1998, three Indian-American companies, Mastech, Syntel, and Intelligroup, were amongst the top 10. As more IT firms began to rely on the H-1B, the composition of H-1B workers also began to shift.

Figure 12.2 shows the number of H-1B admissions by worker's country of origin from 1992 to 2002. The UK was the largest source of H-1B workers in 1992 but India overtook it by 1996. As we saw earlier, IT employers were the primary source for H-1B demand between 1995 and 1998. India became the primary source of these workers. While there are no reliable statistics for the stock of engineers and computer scientists in different countries, India did not have a monopoly on worldwide IT labor stock in the late

Table 12.1   Top 5 H-1B occupations shift between 1995 and 1998

1995 Top 5 occupations	Percent of H-1Bs	1998 Top 5 occupations	Percent of H-1Bs
Therapists	54%	Computer specialists	57%
Computer specialists	25%	Therapists	14%
University faculty	2%	Accountants	7%
Physicians	2%	Electrical engineers	3%
Accountants	2%	Architects	2%

Source: US Department of Labor.

Table 12.2   Top H-1B LCA requestors in 1995 versus 1998

Rank	1995 Top H-1B LCA requestors	1998 Top H-1B LCA requestors
	Premier Health Staff	Mastech Corporation
2	Tata Consultancy Services	Tata Consultancy Services
3	Professional Therapy Staffing	Computer People
4	University of California	Oracle Corporation
5	Complete Business Solutions	Price Waterhouse Coopers LLP
6	Mastech Corporation	Lucent Technologies
7	Harvard University	Motorola, Inc.
8	Sunbelt Physical Therapy	Syntel, Inc.
9	Allied Rehabilitation Management	Intelligroup
10	University of Texas	Comsys Technical Services

Source: US Department of Labor.

1990s. Russia produced more than 82 000 and China more than 195 000 engineering graduates in 1999, but neither are high on the list of H-1Bs (NSF 2002, Table 2–18). Thus, it is not clear why India was the primary source for H-1B labor

By 2001, India was by far the largest source of H-1B petitions. The USCIS approved 331 206 H-1B petitions in 2001, and 161 561 or 49 percent went to Indian nationals.[1] The next closest country was China with 27 331 or 8 percent. Almost all, 92 percent, of the petitions for Indian workers were for computer-related or engineering occupations. It is clear that employers of Indian nationals with IT skills were the heaviest users of the H-1B

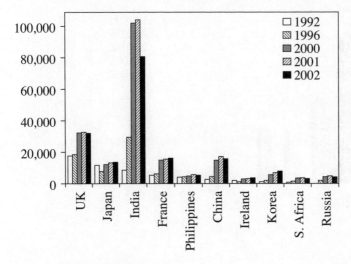

Source: USCIS (1992–2000).

Figure 12.2   H-1B admissions by country from 1992 to 2002

(USCIS, 2000). In 2002, there was a steep drop in the percentage of first-time recipients of an H-1B who came from India. This coincided with the technology slump, high unemployment for US IT workers, and stories of H-1Bs returning to India. A common quip at this time in the IT industry was that the acronym B2B, which had meant 'business-to-business', now meant 'back to Bombay.'

The H-1B has become an important business tool for the IT sector and Indian IT workers have been the primary beneficiaries of the visa program. Is the same true of the L-1 program?

Figure 12.3 shows the number of L-1 intra-corporate transfer visa admissions from 1992 to 2002. The L-1 has been a much smaller source of admissions of workers from India than the H-1B but its importance grew significantly from 1996 to 2000. It is interesting to note that India is the only country with a significant rise in L-1 admissions between 2001 and 2002, a time when overall L-1 admissions actually dropped as shown in Figure 12.1. The UK, Japan, and France are large trading partners with the USA and there is significant cross-ownership of assets and businesses between the countries so it is no surprise that they would have high numbers of L-1 admissions. It is surprising though why India is so much higher than China or Korea.

At the aggregate level India has been an important source of IT workers in the USA, primarily coming on H-1B and L-1 visas. No other country

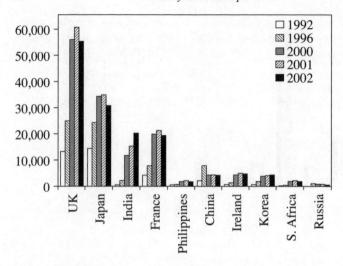

Source: USCIS (1992–2002).

Figure 12.3   L-1 admissions by country from 1992 to 2001

had comparable increases in rates or scale. The data also show that IT firms began to utilize the H-1B visa extensively between 1995 and 1998, and that the primary beneficiaries were Indian IT workers. Next, the importance of the visa programs to the Indian IT industry is quantified.

INDIAN IT COMPANY'S NEED FOR LABOR MOBILITY

The extensive use of H-1Bs by IT firms is a contentious issue in the USA. IT firms claim that acute workforce shortages of the late 1990s forced them to turn to the H-1B (Lewis, 2002, p. C1). However, critics of the visa program have claimed that companies pay H-1B workers below market wages and IT firms' interest is really in cheap labor (Matloff, 2003). IT services is a highly competitive sector where price is often the primary criterion for winning a bid. Since labor is the largest cost for an IT services firm, companies with cheaper labor have a substantial competitive advantage. Zavodny (2003) was unable to find a relationship between H-1B workers and unemployment rates or wage depression among US workers. However, her study is limited because she works at the state level rather than the firm level and her method for determining wage rates paid is unclear.

Notwithstanding the inconclusive findings between US IT wages and H-1B use, we can gain insight into the labor mobility needs of the Indian IT industry by examining them at the firm level. A TCS executive responded to a reporter's question about allegations of H-1B visa abuse by saying that his firm is able to hire cheaper workers and that was perfectly okay;

> Our wage per employee is 20–25% lesser than U.S. wage for a similar employee. Typically, for a TCS employee with five years experience, the annual cost to the company is $60,000–70,000, while a local American employee might cost $80,000–100,000. This (labor arbitrage) is a fact of doing work onsite. It's a fact that Indian IT companies have an advantage here and there's nothing wrong in that (Singh, 2003).

This cost advantage enables TCS to win business from its competitors that use US labor.

As offshore outsourcing rises in importance, some proponents argue that it will diminish the demand for labor mobility because most work will be done remotely. However, the data does not support this theory. Table 12.3 shows the LCA wage distribution data for three major offshore outsourcers: Bermuda-based Accenture, New Jersey-based Cognizant, and India-based TCS. Contrary to the notion that offshore outsourcing reduces the need for labor mobility, they are all also major H-1B users. The data also reveals that on-site TCS workers are paid less than workers of competing firms. Nearly 82 percent of TCS workers earn less than US$ 40 000 but only 15 and 3 percent earn that little at Accenture and Cognizant respectively. One explanation may be that the TCS employees are less capable and less experienced, but this seems implausible because the companies are direct competitors and have to provide similar services.

Table 12.3   Major offshore outsourcer H-1B use and pay

Company	% of jobs < $40k	$40k < % of jobs > $60k	% of jobs < $60k	No. of jobs FY01–03
Accenture, LLC	15.3%	40%	44.7%	12,684
Cognizant Technology	2.5%	74.1%	23.4%	33,148
TCS	81.9%	17.8%	0.3%	13,237

Source: US Department of Labor: Analysis by author using US Department of Labor LCA data.

Why would an Indian H-1B worker accept a lower salary than a comparably skilled American? Salaries for IT workers from India are significantly lower than in the USA and hence salary expectations are lower. Moreover, many Indian H-1B workers prefer to live in the USA, a non-monetary benefit that compensates for a lower salary. Others hope that the H-1B will be a bridge to permanent immigration (Matloff, 2003). While the cost of living in the USA is higher than in India, the H-1B's perception of his or her net pay is influenced by the substantial differences in purchasing power parity (PPP), an international cost of living index, between the USA and India. The World Bank has calculated a PPP of approximately 0.2 between India and the USA, which means that $10,000 in India has the same purchasing power as $50,000 in the USA (World Bank, 2002, Table 5.6). This PPP differential amplifies any savings by the Indian H-1B workers by a factor of five. If an Indian were to save $5,000 on their assignment in the USA, that would be the equivalent to a US saving of $25,000. Table 12.4 shows that an Indian earning $13,580 can live just as comfortably as an American earning $70,000.

Table 12.4   Salaries for equally well-off workers

Country	PPP	Salary
USA	1.0	$70,000
Hungary	0.367	$25,690
China	0.216	$15,120
Russia	0.206	$14,420
India	0.194	$13,580

Source: PPP from the World Bank (2002).

It is impossible with publicly available data to calculate the impact that labor mobility has on the entire Indian IT industry. The USCIS does not collect data on the number of H-1B and L-1 holders currently employed in the USA, nor does it identify the employers. However, it is possible to approximate the impact by analyzing information from leading Indian IT firms who describe their use of H-1B and L-1 in financial statements submitted to the US Securities and Exchange Commission.

Indian IT firms use temporary workers extensively to deliver services to US clients, a critical part of their business strategy. When describing business risks, the largest publicly traded Indian IT firms describe the importance of the H-1B and L-1 visas to their operations. For example, Wipro (2002) has stated in its annual report:

> If U.S. immigration laws change and make it more difficult for us to obtain H-1B and L-1 visas for our employees, our ability to compete for and provide services to clients in the

United States could be impaired. ... This restriction and any other changes in turn could hamper our growth and cause our revenues to decline.

Satyam (2002), another leading Indian IT firm has stated in its annual report, 'U.S. immigration restrictions could limit our ability to expand our U.S. operations.' It is clear from these statements that management believes that US immigration laws will affect the business prospects of their companies.

These firms, unlike most IT services firms, have also identified how many H-1B and L-1 workers they employ. For instance, Infosys (2002) has stated in its annual report, 'As of March 31, 2002, the majority of our personnel in the United States held H-1B visas (1 582 persons) or L-1 visas (445 persons).' H-1B and L-1 workers obviously play a key role in their business models.

Figure 12.4 shows that Infosys' visa use increased from March 2000 to June 2004. Outside the anomalous data point in March 2003, Infosys has steadily increased its usage of H-1B and L-1 visas. The peak of the NASDAQ bubble in March 2000 also marked the peak of the job market for US IT workers. By June 2004, US IT workers faced the worst job market ever recorded. During the same time, Infosys increased its personnel on temporary visas by 460 percent from 963 to 4400. Infosys' use of temporary visas is independent of US IT labor market conditions.

Not only do the Indian IT firms use a large number of H-1B and L-1 visas, but they also are among the leaders in H-1B petitions. The USCIS tracked

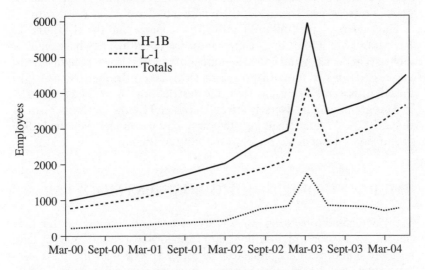

Source: Infosys' 20-F and 6-K filings with US Securities and Exchange Commission.

Figure 12.4   Infosys' use of H-1B and L-1 2000–2004

leading H-1B petitioners for a short window from October 1999 to February 2000 (NASSCOM, 2004). Three of the top Indian IT firms: TCS, Wipro, and Infosys, were in among the top 15 H-1B petitioning employers.

How important is the US market for Indian firms? Between 62 percent and 83 percent of Infosys' revenue and between 70 percent and 80 percent of its earnings comes from the USA. Elsewhere I have estimated that Infosys' H-1B and L-1 visa holders contribute between 62 percent and 83 percent of the US revenues between 2000 and 2002 (Hira, 2004). At the industry level, the US market accounted for 68 per cent of revenue for Indian IT firms (NASSCOM, 2004). In order to service these clients, Indian IT firms need to have a physical presence in the USA and to do so they have to use the H-1B and L-1 visa programs.

Infosys, like the other Indian major IT firms, planned for the lower H-1B cap by requesting more visas than they actually utilize. It is a form of banking the visas. Wall Street analysts who cover the stock are understandably concerned about how the visa cap might affect Infosys' ability to grow. The topic came up during an Infosys earnings conference call in October 2004. In an attempt to assuage a concerned Wall Street analyst, Infosys' chief operating officer told him that the company has more than 10 000 H-1B and L-1 visas, but only utilizes about 55 percent of them at any one time (Infosys, 2004). That means that at any one time, there are about 5 500 Infosys H-1B or L-1 employees in the USA working on site, while the other 4 500 are outside the USA. If business picks up, Infosys would simply tap the 4 500 in reserve, which provides them with a buffer of visas for growth.

The leaders of the Indian IT industry recognize that the H-1B and L-1 programs are important for their industry's health. They have enlisted lobbyists in the USA and issued a number of media releases to fight against any restrictions in the visa programs (Rai, 2003). In fact, NASSCOM President Kiran Karnik has said that restrictions on the H-1B and L-1 visa programs would adversely affect the Indian IT industry (Press Trust of India, 2003). With the emerging offshoring business models, will the Indian IT industry's dependence on labor mobility continue?

EMERGING OFFSHORING BUSINESS MODELS

Many companies operating in the USA have recently discovered that they can effectively source high-skilled labor from low-cost countries. They have begun to shift operations, previously performed by US workers, to overseas locations to tap the lower labor costs. Companies are developing a variety of business models to utilize overseas talent and some require significant cross-border movement of workers. As the offshoring trend accelerates, companies will demand greater flexibility in moving foreign workers into the USA. In this section, I will define terms that describe labor use and in turn examine some business models pursued by different companies to utilize overseas talent.

Many US media reports have erroneously labeled the utilization of foreign labor as *outsourcing*. In fact, different terms are used to describe its many facets. Outsourcing is simply a company deciding to purchase a good or service that it is currently making in-house. This is also known as vertical deintegration. For example, Procter & Gamble (P&G) decided to purchase its IT services from Hewlett-Packard rather than operate its own internal IT department staffed with P&G employees. The magnitude of outsourcing has been increasing as managers of major corporations strategically focus on core competencies and buy generic services from suppliers. IT has traditionally been one of the largest outsourcing sectors, but as companies have been able to modularize their business processes through re-engineering efforts and Enterprise Resource Planning software implementations, the array of services that can be defined as generic is expanding. *Offshore outsourcing* occurs when a company purchases from suppliers who are operating overseas. *Offshoring* occurs when a company moves some of its internal US operations to an overseas in-house location. For instance, IBM has been moving some of its US software development work to its subsidiary in India. *On-site offshore outsourcing*, a term that I have coined, occurs when an overseas supplier delivers services on site by using foreign workers who are in the USA on temporary work visas. This is a common practice of major offshore outsourcing firms such as Accenture, Tata Consultancy Services, and Infosys as well as others. *Insourcing* should mean bringing a purchased good or service in-house – vertical integration. Unfortunately, the media and some politicians use it to represent foreign-based multinational companies with facilities in the USA. The consulting community has coined a variety of other permutations of the-shore and-sourcing terms, for example, *nearshore* means using a supplier operating in Canada or Mexico.

The richness of the sourcing/shore terminology is only an indicator of the actual complexity of the various business models that are being created to utilize overseas labor. Now, I will describe how two idealized business models are implemented and the impact they have on the labor mobility needs of companies.

I will label one end of the spectrum as the *pure offshore* model. In a pure offshore operation, all labor tasks are completed remotely and no direct face-to-face customer interaction is necessary. This means that few, if any, workers need to enter the USA on a temporary basis. A practical example of a pure offshore operation is a call center. They are generally offices with a large numbers of workers who are answering (initiating) phone calls from (to) customers. While this work requires high customer interaction, it does not require face-to-face interaction. Call-center operations are labor-intensive, and since the work can be performed remotely, they have traditionally been located in low-labor cost locations such as rural sections of the USA. In a precursor to the current wave of offshore outsourcing to Asia, many call-center operations moved to Ireland more than a decade ago when cross-Atlantic telecommunications became more affordable. Call-center operations have become one of the fastest growing and most visible positions moving to India and other low-wage countries. Workers complete all their training in India and do not have to travel to the USA. One of the more comical aspects of training is accent coaching where Indian workers learn US accents by watching US television comedy shows. This means that very few, if any, call-center workers would need to enter the USA.

On the other side of the spectrum is the *pure on-site* model. In this case, a firm has to perform all the work on site in the USA and therefore needs to bring in all of its foreign workers on temporary visas. A practical example of this is IT staff augmentation, sometimes referred to as body shopping. In this model, a customer would temporarily augment its staff through an IT contract firm. The IT contract firm's staff work essentially as employees for the customer's company. In this model, which is very common among Indian IT companies, the worker is physically present at the customer's work site. In this case, foreign workers for the contract firm need to enter the USA to complete their tasks.

Many functions combine both offshore and on-site delivery. In fact, many IT services firms are beginning to offer a so-called blended (mix of offshore and on-site) rate when they bid on time and materials contracts. Generally, their profit margins are higher for work done offshore, so they maximize it, but because of the need for face-to-face customer interaction, they keep some work on site. The US and Indian IT firms are driving in opposite directions to adopt a similar blended business model. The US firms are expanding their captive operations in India through acquisitions and organic growth, while Indian firms are expanding their foreign workforce in the USA. The move towards a blended sourcing model may lead to increased demand of work visas in some cases and less in others. Indian IT firms may be able to reduce the number of on-site personnel relative to offshore work as they become more sophisticated at performing higher levels of work offshore. Indian IT firms may also begin to hire US workers to perform the on-site tasks. On the other hand, as US IT firms have a more truly global labor force they may need to bring more workers from offshore locations to service US customers.

The fastest growing segment of India's IT export business is offshore work (NASSCOM, 2004). However, offshore work often depends on on-site personnel. An example helps to illustrate how this works. Mastek, a Mumbai-based IT services firm, provides the following example in one of its marketing White Papers:

> Staff Costs Assumption: U.S. onsite $100 000 per year; offshore cost: $50 000 per year.
> A Fortune 1000 company needs 60 man-year's worth of effort. If they used only U.S. labor, then the cost would be $60 \times \$100\ 000 = \$6$ million. If the company used 60 people that consisted of 20 onsite and 40 offshore, then the costs would be $20 \times \$100\ 000 + 40 \times \$50\ 000 = \$4$ million. Thus if the client used the offshore model, it could realize a 33 per cent cost savings or $2 million.

This example illustrates something that I define as the *offshore to on-site leveraging ratio.* In this example, the *employee leveraging ratio* is 40:20, or 2:1; the *revenue leveraging* ratio is $2 million:$2 million, or 1:1. The leveraging ratio varies greatly from project to project because of the nature of the work and the IT firms' capabilities. Some projects require extensive face-to-face interaction with the client on site, whereas, others can be completed almost entirely offshore.

The relationship between on-site and offshore personnel cannot be easily estimated. However, because of the nature of the software services business, which requires significant customer interaction, on-site personnel are critical to a successful project. If the employee leveraging ratio could be increased significantly through the use of technology or better management, then the need for on-site personnel will be reduced along with the demand for and importance of temporary visas.

It is difficult to estimate an average leveraging ratio, but the ratio is likely to increase for all Indian IT firms because it is in the interests of both the customer and the Indian IT service provider to increase the proportion of offshore work. The customer benefits from lower costs because of lower wages and the Indian IT firms have higher gross margins for work completed offshore (Infosys, 2002). The average leveraging ratio will also increase as more customers gain confidence in shifting a greater portion of a project offshore and as Indian IT firms improve their project management skills and information infrastructure. Information and communications technologies, such as video conferencing and web conferencing, will facilitate more remote work. The beginnings of this is evident from the data in Table 12.5, which shows that Infosys slightly increased both its *employee leveraging ratio* and its *revenue leveraging ratio* from 2001 to 2002. Table 12.6 shows, according to NASSCOM data, that Indian IT industry offshore:onsite leveraging ratios are improving dramatically.

Table 12.5   Infosys' offshore: leveraging ratios

Fiscal year	Revenue leveraging ratio	Employee leveraging ratio
2001	0.94	1.94
2002	0.97	2.26

Table 12.6   Indian IT industry-wide offshore:on-site revenue leveraging ratio

Fiscal year	Revenue leveraging ratio
1999–00	0.60
2000–01	0.69
2001–02	1.12
2002–03	1.49

Source: NASSCOM (2004).

While there will be increases in average leveraging ratios for most Indian IT firms over time, it is likely that they will reach an upper bound because some work will still require on-site presence.

POLICY ENVIRONMENT

India's software services are still primarily exported to US customers and, therefore, the industry's current and future prospects are heavily dependent on US IT demands. According to NASSCOM (2004), the US accounted for 68 percent of Indian IT exports in 2002. In addition to current sales, the USA is critical for India's IT future development because it has the largest market with the most sophisticated customers. The exposure to the technological and business environment in the USA has also been a boon to Indian firms enabling them to pursue new business lines outside of software services, including call-center operations and business process outsourcing.

The IT business and labor market conditions in the USA during the late 1990s provided a golden opportunity to develop India's IT industry. The US IT demand exploded over the past decade because of technological, business, and labor market changes. Major technology paradigm shifts in computer hardware, software, and network technologies created disruptions in the normal evolution of IT systems and sparked demand for IT services and temporary workers (Hira, 2003). However, conditions have drastically changed and US IT demand has stagnated, which has made the market more competitive. Supplier growth will only be generated by increasing market share.

Stagnant demand has led to record unemployment rates for US IT workers, causing a number of groups to call on the US Congress to place greater restrictions on the H-1B and L-1 visas (Steadman, 2003). Figure 12.5 shows that unemployment rates for US technology workers is at an all-time high, and Figure 12.6 shows that US job creation has been sluggish between 2000 to 2004. This has fueled a backlash against offshore outsourcing and increased labor mobility. It makes it much more difficult to sell more liberal labor mobility policies to the US public.

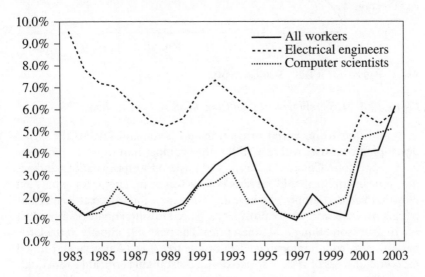

Source: IEEE–USA (2004).

Figure 12.5   Unemployment rates for technology workers and all workers from 1983 to 2003

The political landscape for temporary visas changed markedly in 2003 and 2004. Five bills were introduced in the US Congress to restrict or even eliminate the H-1B and L-1 visas. At least one of the bills, H.R 2154, was introduced as a direct result of L-1 business practices by TCS (Grow, 2003). In addition, the Senate Judiciary Committee held two full committee hearings on H-1B and L-1 visa use and misuse.

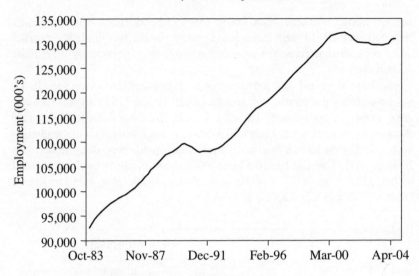

Source: US Bureau of Labor Statistics (2004).

Figure 12.6   US employment level from January 1984 to June 2004

In addition to potential restrictions on labor mobility to the USA, developing countries will face stiffer price competition from the increases in IT supply from China and Central and Eastern European nations. India is not alone in hoping that IT services exports will be the engine for export-led growth. Increased supply with little demand expansion will create significant pricing pressure, and service providers will need to differentiate their product offerings by something other than price. The post 9/11 climate in the USA has also created a dampening effect on the free flow of people and raised the consciousness of risks associated with outsourcing critical IT functions, especially overseas. In addition, as more IT services suppliers from other developing countries enter the US market, there will be more competition for the limited number of H-1B slots.

On the international trade treaty front, developing countries had hoped that the current round of negotiations on the General Agreement on Trade in Services could be used to argue for the elimination of quota and wage parity provisions on visas like the H-1B in the USA (Chanda, 1999). Recent Indo–US free trade agreement (FTA) bi-lateral talks have centered on labor mobility. A preview of how inserting immigrations' provisions into trade agreements might be perceived by the US Congress occurred in July 2003. The US's bilateral free trade agreements with both Chile and Singapore included provisions that significantly loosened H-1B and L-1 restrictions (Magnusson, 2003). The reaction by the US Senate Judiciary Committee was negative, and it is unlikely that such provisions will appear in future trade treaties without prior approval by Congress.

Many factors have spurred India's IT industry development. This chapter has described how US labor mobility policies facilitated India's IT growth. Its importance was presented at the macro and firm levels. Market conditions have changed drastically, and the immigration regulations that were once a competitive advantage for Indian IT firms have already been constrained. The new wave of offshore outsourcing seems to indicate that a global presence is required. As US-based firms expand their operations in low-cost countries like India, they will chip away at Indian IT firms' cost advantages.

NOTE

1. The number of H-1B petitions approved and the number of H-1B temporary workers' admissions are not comparable because they measure different populations. The petitions approved pertain to H-1B petitions authorizing temporary employment for specialty workers, either in the USA or overseas, while admissions represent H-1B workers arriving from abroad. H-1B petitions can be approved for aliens changing non-immigrant status without leaving the USA. Most significantly, H-1B workers can be admitted multiple times using a single petition, and admitted with a petition approved in a prior FY [5].

REFERENCES

Arora, A., V.S. Arunachalam, J. Asundi and R. Fernandes (2000), 'The Indian software services industry', Heinz School of Public Policy working paper, Carnegie Mellon University, Pittsburgh, PA.

Chanda, R. (1999), 'Movement of natural persons and trade in services: liberalising temporary movement of labour under the GATS', Indian Council for Research on International Economic Relations, working paper no 51, New Delhi.

Das, G. (2001), *India Unbound: A Personal Account of a Social and Economic Revolution from Independence to the Global Information Age*, New York: Alfred A. Knopf.

Dedrick, J., V. Gurbaxani and K. Kraemer (2003), 'Information technology and economic performance: a critical review of the empirical evidence', *ACM Computing Surveys*, **35**(1), 1–28.

Grow, B. (2003), 'A loophole as big as a mainframe', *BusinessWeek*, 10 March, p. 82.

Heeks, R. (1998), 'The uneven profile of Indian software exports', Development Informatics working paper series, 3, Manchester, UK.

Hira, R. (2003), 'Boom–Bust: new paradigm for EE employment', *Research Technology Management*, **46**(2), 2–9.

Hira, R. (2004), 'U.S. immigration regulations and India's information technology industry', *Technological Forecasting and Social Change*, **71**(8), 837–54.

Infosys Technologies Limited (2002), Form 20-F, annual report, 31 March, retrieved from www.edgar.sec.gov.

Infosys Technologies Limited (2004), Q2 FY05 investor earnings call, 12 October, retrieved from www.infosys.com/investor/default.asp.

Institute of Electrical and Electronics Engineers – USA (2004), 'Unemployment rates for various occupations', unpublished report, Washington, DC.

Lewis, D. (2002), 'For IT workers, guarded optimism about jobs', *Boston Globe*, 6 May, C1.

Magnusson, P. (2003), 'Is a stealth immigration policy smart?', *BusinessWeek*, 21 July, p. 54.

Mann, Catherine L. (2003), 'Globalization of IT services and white collar jobs: the next wave of productivity growth', international economic policy brief, PB03–11, Washington, DC: Institute for International Economics.

Matloff, N. (2003), 'Needed reform for the H-1B and L-1 work visas: major points', 17 August, unpublished, retrieved at www://heather.cs.ucdavis.edu/Summary.pdf.

NASSCOM, (2004), 'Indian software and services exports', 8 August, unpublished, www.nasscom.org.

National Science Board, US National Science Foundation (2002), Science and Engineering Indicators 2002, Arlington, VA: US Government Printing Office.

Press Trust of India, (2003), 'H1B visa reduction to affect Indian IT industry', 22 August.

Rai, S. (2003), 'Software success has India worried', *The New York Times*, 3 February, section W, p. 1, col. 3.

Satyam Computer Services Limited (March 31, 2002), Form 20-F, annual report, 31 March, retrieved from www.edgar.sec.gov.

Singh, S. (2003), 'US visas are not a TCS specific issue', *Businessworld*, 30 June, retrieved from www.businessworldindia.com.

Steadman, J. (2003), 'Examining the implications of the H-1 visa for the American economy: testimony to Committee on the Judiciary of the U.S. Senate', 16, September, retrieved from www.ieeeusa.org/forum/POLICY/2003/091603.html.

US Bureau of Labor Statistics (2004), current employment statistics survey, July, retrieved from www.bls.gov/ces.

US Citizenship and Immigration Service (USCIS) (1992, 1996, 2000, 2001, 2002) *Statistical Yearbook of the Immigration and Naturalization Service*, Washington, DC: US Government Printing Office.

Wipro Limited (2002), Form 20-F, annual report, 31 March, retrieved from www.edgar.sec.gov.

World Bank (2002), *World Development Indicators*, Washington, DC: World Bank Group, Table 5.6.

Zavodny, M. (2003), 'The H-1B program and its effects on information technology workers', *Economic Review*, Federal Reserve Bank of Atlanta, **88**(3), 1–11.

Index